Literacy, Power, and the Schooled Body

"Few early childhood studies have embraced theories of space and time in coming to understand the demands of early schooling. This book makes a new contribution to literacy studies by examining the taken-for-granted nature of classroom space and time. It encourages us to think again about what learning literacy practices entails."

Barbara Comber, University of South Australia

What effects do space and time have on classroom management, discipline, and regulation? How do teachers' practices create schooled and literate students? To explore these questions, this book looks at early childhood classrooms, charting the shifts and continuities as 4-year-old children begin preschool, move from preschool into primary school, and come to the end of the first phase of schooling at 9 years. The literacy classroom is used as a specific site in which to examine how children's bodies are disciplined to become literate (for example, holding pencils, reading from left to right, turning pages, and what they understand are the uses of reading and writing).

This is not a book that theorizes space, time, discipline, bodies, and literacy in complex and abstract ways. Rather, working from a Foucaultian premise that discipline is directed onto children's bodies, it moves from theory to practice. Theory is used as an aid to understanding real classroom events. Photographs, lesson transcripts, interviews, and children's work are used to show how teachers' practices are enacted on children's bodies in time and space. In this way, teachers are offered practical examples from which to think about their own classrooms and classroom practice, opening space for them to reflect on what works, why it works, and what can be changed.

Kerryn Dixon is a Lecturer in the Department of English and the Department of Applied English Language Studies, Wits School of Education, University of the Witwatersrand, Johannesburg, South Africa.

Literacy, Power, and the Schooled Body

Learning in Time and Space

Kerryn Dixon
University of the Witwatersrand

Routledge
Taylor & Francis Group

NEW YORK AND LONDON

First published 2011
by Routledge
270 Madison Avenue, New York, NY 10016

Simultaneously published in the UK
by Routledge
2 Park Square, Milton Park, Abingdon, Oxon OX14 4RN

Routledge is an imprint of the Taylor & Francis Group, an informa business

© 2011 Taylor and Francis

Typeset in Minion by Wearset Ltd, Boldon, Tyne and Wear
Printed and bound in the United States of America on acid-free paper by
Walsworth Publishing Company, Marceline, MO

Library of Congress Cataloging in Publication Data
Dixon, Kerryn.
Literacy, power, and the schooled body: learning in time and space/Kerryn Dixon.
p. cm.
Includes bibliographical references and index.
1. Literacy–Social aspects–South Africa. 2. Early childhood education–Social
aspects–South Africa. 3. Classroom management–Social aspects–South Africa. 4.
Critical pedagogy–South Africa. I. Title.
LC158.S6D59 2010
302.2 244–dc22
2010018990

British Library Cataloguing in Publication Data
A catalogue record for this book is available from the British Library

ISBN13: 978-0-415-87962-0 (hbk)
ISBN13: 978-0-415-87963-7 (pbk)
ISBN13: 978-0-203-85148-7 (ebk)

For Hilary,
for so generously sharing your time and space(s).

Contents

Foreword

Kevin M. Leander

In an educational era of a turn to 'the fundamentals', there is something all the more compelling about an analysis of truly fundamental dimensions of schooled practice: space, time, and bodies. If schooled literacy learning is a kind of geography, or earth writing, then what terrestrial bodies are involved and how are they written upon? Dixon provides a two-part answer to the geography question. Look first, she argues, at the writing and reading of the child's body by schooling – the way in which the illiterate, unruly body is developed into the disciplined, docile, student body.

In this first perspective, even before the child picks up a piece of paper or crayon, the body literate is already being read and written upon, is being located and positioned on an institutional map. What is learned in school is to be in school – to become at home in the spatial and temporal relations that are naturalized in school. As Lefebvre (1991) reminds us, space is not a container for social relations, but is rather constitutive of social relations. Furniture, corridors, classroom walls, timetables, routines, lesson pacing, and other material, social, and symbolic resources and relations constitute a spatio-temporal apparatus for the making of bodies. These bodies are written upon by the structures and practices of school buildings and educators, but are also interpreted or *read* through acts of teacher, peer, and self-surveillance.

The other side of Dixon's analysis is then to follow how bodies, made literate within schooled space and time, become writers, readers, and test takers, or literate *producers* of schooled space and time. Look second, she argues, at the micro-geographies of literacy learning and the forms of literacy that emerge from them. Here, the child's hand is shaped by the teacher around the pencil and the child's eyes are fixed on book pages and tests. Textual products – written bodies of work – serve as surrogates for student bodies in assessment. Literacy – as circuits of power and knowledge articulated across texts and bodies – emerges as something that is produced *by* space and is also productive *of* space.

Yet, beyond these relations and in response to expansive educational standardization, surveillance, and accountability regimes, Dixon assumes a radical position for theoretically informed practice: literacy pedagogy can also be *for* space. Literacy pedagogy can also be directed toward the ethical and political project of transforming learning for kids and the lives of teachers. To make this project *for* space means to reconceive of pedagogical transformation as fundamentally spatio-temporal. What is at stake are not the same old abstractions concerning change, mindsets, belief systems, or forms of teacher 'reflection'. Rather, Dixon's advocacy *for* space is about recovering the flesh and bones of literacy learning, about remembering, in a time of massively reductive spreadsheets and charts, that the relations of words, power, and bodies are teeming with transformative potential.

Preface

This is a book about discipline. But it is not an instructional *how to* book. It is a book that seeks to explore *how* things happen by asking a number of questions. This book arises from my living in South Africa, a society in transition from an apartheid world to a post-apartheid world. It is a place of contradiction and complexity where old worlds and new worlds, colonial and postcolonial discourses, local, African, and global forces, jostle with each other. It is a place where a violent history has left an indelible mark shaping how we move forward. In this moment it asks questions like how does order get restored when violence has been the norm for many South Africans? How do institutions like education, that have been at the heart of conflict and inequality, re-establish themselves? How do we get individuals to conform to a set of norms that result in a functional, functioning society that can compete globally? These questions shape this book. They are essentially questions about power which are important for all educators in all contexts. The questions remain the same; what changes from context to context are the answers.

It is, of course, impossible to answer them fully. And this is not the intention. Rather my interest, like Foucault's (1977), is in the small details. It is in trying to see how the 'big' questions play themselves out in the small, daily routines in education. And these lead to another set of questions: How do schools educate and train children to function in society? Part of this training is about behaviour, about doing the 'right' things at appropriate moments. This is where the body is important. Bodies that are in close contact with other bodies for hours need to know what the rules are. How do schools and teachers teach these rules? Compliance and understanding of rules such as 'If everyone talks at the same time no one gets heard', or 'Children get hurt if everyone runs out of the door at the same time', are evident in the ways in which individual children manage their bodies. Schools also transmit academic knowledge. In order for teachers to transmit this content, children need to have enough control over their bodies so that they can receive it. Of course, what they receive in terms of the rules and knowledge has an impact on their ability as individuals to critique, imagine, work, and contribute back to the society in which they live.

For me, literacy is at the heart of this teaching. So much depends on children's ability to read and write. They are foundational skills. If children are not trained to read and write, then understanding disciplines like science, history, mathematics, and philosophy will be severely impeded. So too is an ability to fill out a tax form, or receive welfare from the government. This book goes to the beginning of schooling, to the beginnings of children's literacy training, so that it can ask questions about schooled and literate people. It looks at children in two preschool classrooms of 4- and 5-year-olds and three early primary school classrooms of 7- and then 9-year-olds. In doing so, what emerges is a picture of what happens not in one lesson, or one year of lessons, but across five years of schooling in one educational system.

Literacy works in two ways in this book. Schooling is the focus of the first half of the book. The literacy classroom is used to provide examples of the ways in which children are schooled. In the second half of the book the way in which literacy is taught is examined to provide insights into the kinds of literate human subjects that are produced. Such examples invite readers from other disciplines and contexts, as well as teachers, teacher trainers, and academics within education, to consider points of congruence and divergence. A knowledge of early literacy or literacy is not essential for the reader, rather the examination of literacy learning and teaching provides a way to think about the child who emerges from schooling with particular beliefs and abilities.

In order to explain the connections between schooling, literacy, and the body, the work of Foucault is of paramount importance. Foucault is sometimes dismissed as too complex. But this is not the case as I show. His work, particularly on discipline, provides a rich resource for thinking about schooling, regulation, power relations, and subjectivity. Foucault (1977: 170) argues that 'discipline "makes" individuals; it is the specific technique of a power that regards individuals both as objects and as instruments of its exercise'.

How then are literate individuals made in South African classrooms? Children are the objects of discipline that are taken and moulded in particular ways. In this process they also become subjects who take on ways of knowing and behaving. Once they do this, both teachers and children become the instruments of discipline.

Foucault's quotation underpins each of the chapters in the book in a different way. In trying to understand how discipline 'makes individuals', or how they become *subjects*, the word I use in the book, several disciplinary techniques are identified through classroom events. They are then analysed for the effects they have on constructing children as schooled and literate subjects. The point is not to theorize: Foucault has already done that. It is to use real, practical classroom examples to show how the theory works, in this case the workings of disciplinary power. In working from practice to theory, space and time are central themes that run through the book, presenting powerful ways in which to understand classroom management and regulation.

Chapter 1 sets up some of the key concepts that run though the book and locates this work in a social practice paradigm. Chapter 2 asks the question, how does space work to produce a schooled subject? It tracks the use of space across the preschool and into the primary school. It then considers how a knowledge of space is important in managing children. Chapter 3 asks how the organization of time 'makes' subjects. It then brings space and time together, arguing for their interrelatedness by showing what they reveal about literacy teaching across the years. Consciously thinking about space and time in this way can have a major impact on pedagogy. Discipline is also about 'small' techniques, taken up in Chapter 4. It asks questions about how teachers, who are themselves 'instruments' in the exercise of power, regulate children. In order to do this, it locates the five classrooms in the broader South African context. How did the management and regulation of population groups during apartheid affect subject construction? Resistance runs alongside complicity. People can resist subject constructions, or they can take them on, or they can do both. Schooling young children often engenders several types of resistance and complicity. People are not without agency.

Chapters 5 and 6 ask how children are trained to be literate. They also ask how our understandings of literacy affects such training. This is followed by a consideration of assessment practices in Chapter 7. The ways in which children are assessed, and the records left in documents like school reports, are revealing of the skills and knowledge that are valued in a schooled and literate subject. This chapter pulls together key Foucauldian concepts discussed in previous chapters to draw a fuller picture of the ways in which the literate subject is constructed. Chapter 8 concludes by moving beyond the classroom to consider the implications for literacy education.

Although this detailed case study from South Africa cannot be generalized to other contexts, it creates an understanding of how to think about any context using the tools that Foucault provides. It also demonstrates ways of considering the operation of time and space that have become naturalized for teachers and thus remain unquestioned and invisible. By linking content knowledge (literacy) with the body in time and space, this book offers educators a different way of thinking about pedagogy and its effects.

Acknowledgements

Books are not written by themselves. They require a huge amount of support from a range of people. I would like to acknowledge the debt I owe to the people who enabled me to present this work. The first group of people I have to thank are from 'Acacia Preschool' and 'Southside Primary'. The principals, teachers, and children of these schools welcomed me into their educational spaces with an astounding warmth, making me feel at home and part of their community.

I am extremely grateful to the Carnegie Foundation for the grant I received to take three months off to work on this book which is based on my PhD entitled *Literacy, Power and the Embodied Subject* that was awarded by the University of the Witwatersrand. I am also grateful to the university for allowing me time off. It was a wonderful experience to have this time to write. I also need to thank my colleagues in the departments of Applied English Language Studies and English for their overall support, corridor conversations, questions, and theoretical challenges to push me further. A special thank you to Yvonne Reed who understands the final push but is still gracious in dealing with day-to-day university life! And, to Hilary Janks who got me in to this in the first place and who has been an unspeakably generous mentor, friend, and fellow whale-watcher. A particular mention to my colleagues and friends Jacqui Dornbrack, Belinda Mendelowitz, Lynne Slonimsky, and Lisa Hosking, who provided a never-ending source of academic and moral support. My friend Renfrew Christie who manfully ploughed through the manuscript making careful, provocative, and sometimes hilarious suggestions – I'm using a dash and not a comma here – you know you always have a standing supper-and-single-malt invitation. And to Daniel Janks who performed several artwork miracles – I am in awe.

To Naomi Silverman my amazing editor, who undertook this project and was always available to me in cyberspace, thank you for allowing me to write this and for the care and patience with which you dealt with all aspects of putting this book together. Phillippa Nichol, Emilie Littlehales and Annie Jackson need a special mention for the work they have done and support they have provided to complete this manuscript.

Throughout the writing of this book I have become more aware than ever before of how important family support is, and how work and deadlines whittle away time spent with our greatest supporters. David, Mom, Dad, Braydon (and Shandy) I appreciate the long-term concern, care, and love more than you know.

Versions of the work presented in Chapter 3 and Chapter 6 have appeared in the following journals and we are grateful to the publishers for their permission for this work to appear here:

Dixon, K. (2009) Producing literate subjects? Using the spatial and temporal as lenses in early literacy classrooms. *Journal of Education*, 47, 31–54.
Dixon, K. (2009) A space to write: the construction of the writing subject in early schooling. *English Academy Review Special Edition on Language and Identity*, 24(2), 85–101.

Chapter 1

Schooling the body

How do we know when someone is a good listener? A large part of this answer lies in what their body tells us. A good listener keeps quiet so that we can talk. They are attentive and watch us for our body's signals and respond appropriately. They might laugh, smile, or grimace. They might incline their head to hear us better. In focusing their complete attention on us, not another task or person, they might lean forward, or sit closer. When we listen well our mouth, eyes, ears, hands, and posture all work together to produce a 'picture' of listening which gives the impression that the person being listened to is heard. We are also generally not aware of what our bodies are doing to show we are 'good' listeners. The act of listening well is embodied.

But we did not start out like this, unconsciously enacting the role of a good listener. Good listening is something we learn to do. It is modelled by those around us, our parents, our communities, our teachers. There may be variations in what we do with our bodies to show we are listening attentively, depending on cultural mores and values in our communities. We learn implicitly and explicitly what our bodies need to do to listen well when we are young.

If a discussion about listening seems a strange way to begin, I would like to draw attention to A poster, entitled 'Rules for Good Listening' (Carson-Dellosa Publishing), that was stuck on the walls in the Grade 1 classrooms at Southside Primary School. Southside Primary and Acacia Preschool (both pseudonyms) are the research sites discussed in this book. The poster also hangs in many other classrooms in South Africa. The poster set on a bright yellow background depicts a picture of a smiling child sitting at a desk with a pencil and sheets of paper on it. The child's fingers are interlocked with arms resting on the top of the desk; the feet are placed next to each other underneath the desk. The child's body parts are labelled with the following phrases with the body parts in capital letters: 'EYES are watching', 'EARS are listening', 'LIPS are closed', 'HANDS are still', and 'FEET are quiet'. These labels run along the left hand side of the poster. This is a useful starting point with which to illustrate the key concepts which inform the thinking of this book. It is also the first example of how this book works with theory. Theory and practice are not separate. Rather, each time a new concept is introduced it is explained, using practical examples that arise from data collected at Southside and Acacia. Each term is **bolded** so that it can be easily identified. When smaller terms are crucial to understanding how a major term functions, they are *italicized*.

Chapters 2, 3, and 4 each have a particular focus (space, time, and regulation) where specific terms are introduced and applied to the data. The use of these terms is also cumulative: where relevant they are used again in the analysis of later data. This works to extend the examples used originally, so as to create a fuller picture of the ways in which we can understand the application of the theory. Their application in the later chapters on reading, writing, and assessment presents a richer picture of classroom life.

For example, **surveillance** is a frequently used term. Knowing that we are being eyeballed, supervised, or watched, often helps us to regulate behaviour. Foucault uses the example of the panopticon. Constructed as a central tower in a prison, it presents the guards with full visual access to all prisoners' cells. The prisoners cannot see into the tower. They never know when they are being watched. What it does is 'induce in the inmate a state of consciousness and permanent visibility that assures the automatic functioning of power' (Foucault, 1977: 201). A teacher who watches her class carefully would know which children are good listeners and which are not by identifying compliant and non-compliant body postures and behaviour. Children would know that their behaviour is monitored. But **surveillance** is not a one-way process, because as later chapters show, children watch each other (Chapter 4), the state watches teachers (Chapters 4 and 7), and records of **surveillance** are captured in writing (Chapter 7).

In order to illustrate the overarching concepts that inform the thinking of this book, this chapter is divided into two categories.

The first category sets out several Foucauldian concepts that are useful in thinking about schooling, the body, and power. It is the work of Foucault that allows for a sustained examination of practices across five classrooms that make up the research sites. One of the benefits of using this theoretical lens to analyse these classrooms is that it focuses on transitions. What are the shifts and continuities in learning, as children move from preschool into primary school? What remains constant and what changes, emerges, or disappears when children reach the end of the first phase of schooling in South Africa, at the end of Grade 3?

The second category deals with literacy. It describes the ways in which literacy can be understood and foregrounds the way in which I work with literacy.

The schooled body

What is the connection between schooling and the body? Managing children's undisciplined bodies that wriggle and chat and laugh and play is one of the big challenges in early primary education, to say nothing of the management of adolescent bodies in secondary schools, and the bodies plugged into their MP3 players currently presenting themselves in first-year university lectures. The Rules for Good Listening poster effectively illustrates an idealized version of a schooled subject, compared to the wriggling mass of bodies that arrive on their first day of school. Schools have an important role to play. Schools are one of the central institutions that work to regulate society (Foucault, 1977). This is not a bad thing. This is part of the social contract. A functioning society efficiently provides services to people. This of course requires a competent workforce made up of members of that society to render them efficiently. Obedience to rule thus becomes a mutually beneficial practice. As part of the society, children must learn obedience.

It is in schools where many of these rules are inculcated and reinforced. What is valued in some schools in South Africa, and in classrooms around the world, is the child who listens well. Listening is necessary for navigating one's way through school because schools are places where a great deal of information is disseminated every day. Children need to know what to do with such information. Learning to listen is also important in the socialization process. Children who can listen are able to work with others. When they move into the workplace they will need to listen to instructions to do their job.

Schools are training grounds. Children undergo training to function in the school environment itself, and are trained to function in the broader world. Much of this training is directed at the body. It is through teachers' pedagogy, which targets the body, that a schooled subject emerges (Luke, 1996). If we think about our own schooling and teachers' exhortations to stand straight, sit still, pay attention, write neatly, tuck in escaped shirts, pull up socks, stop talking, running, hitting, screaming, sniffing, swearing, spitting, chewing, and so on, these are all directed at the body. They work to produce a particular person who does not, for example, sniff, because it is not polite to do so. Polite, respectful, neatly attired children conform to a set of norms valued by society. Some of these rules are reinforced in other spaces, like homes and religious institutions.

Taking on the behaviour that marks one as 'schooled' does not happen overnight. Bourdieu's (1992) notion of **habitus** is useful in thinking about the way in which bodies are transformed into schooled bodies. **Habitus** is a set of dispositions that affects the ways in which people act and react to situations. Many of these dispositions are inculcated during early childhood through mundane processes of training and learning. If the child in the poster were indeed real, and responded each time the teacher asked for watchful eyes, listening ears, closed lips, still hands, and quiet feet, and heard these exhortations from other teachers, this would become part of the child's schooled **habitus**. Our thoughts, tastes, and dispositions are formed through our membership of particular communities and are part of our early socialization. Language is also a part of our **habitus**. The **linguistic habitus** of the children and the teachers at Southside and Acacia is revealing of class and race – in terms of accent, pronunciation, semantic choice, and syntactic organization. Once a particular **habitus** is taken on, it is almost impossible to erase it. We know this if we think about our own accents. Although we may be able to mimic other accents, when we stop trying, we revert back to our original ways of speaking. Although accents may shift for people who have spent a long time living in a different speech community, traces of the original accent remain. Thus, in the process of becoming schooled and socialized, our bodies take on particular patterns of behaviour until they become part of who we are.

Foucault gives some indication of the process of inculcating a set of dispositions that make up one's **habitus**. He talks about disciplinary power, which one could argue, in the case of schools, is channelled most often through the pedagogical power teachers wield. Foucault (1977: 24) argues that 'power relations have an immediate hold upon it [the body]; they invest it, mark it, train it, torture it, force it to carry out tasks, to perform ceremonies, to emit signs'. This brings me to the next part of the discussion: the issue of power, which in the school system one hopes is less about torture and more about training.

Power: discipline and subjectivity

For Foucault, power embraces an 'analytics' in which context and history are taken into account (Dreyfuss & Rabinow, 1982: 184). He illustrates this when he shows how power relations changed. In medieval times power was located in the hand of the sovereign. Sovereign power operated though the absolute control a sovereign had over his people, which was often wielded through violence. This violence was enacted on people's bodies in spectacular displays of public torture. A change occurred in the seventeenth and eighteenth centuries when a modern form of power emerged. This modern form of power relies on a set of 'procedural techniques'. It is also 'dependent upon bodies and what they do' so that time and labour can be extracted from them. **Surveillance** is constantly exercised. And it presents a 'new economy of power that one must be able simultaneously both to increase the subjected forces and to improve the force and efficacy of that which subjects them' (Foucault, 1980: 104).

In his writings, Foucault (1977, 1978) presents several propositions about power. Gore (1995: 99) summarizes these features of Foucauldian power:

- power is productive and not solely repressive,
- power circulates rather than being possessed,
- power exists in action,
- power functions at the level of the body, and often
- power operates through technologies of the self.

The fact that power is productive is fundamental in thinking about modern power. It is genera-tive because Foucault argues that it 'produces reality; it produces domains of objects and rituals of truth. The individual and the knowledge that may be gained of him belong to this produc-tion' (Foucault, 1977: 194). The productive nature of power links back to the connection between schooling and the body. Hunter (1994: 9) argues that pedagogical power, which is often directed at the body, 'appears to be productive of human abilities; equipping students with dis-tinctive capacities for ethical self-concern and self-cultivation'. It is desirable to have schooled subjects who are able to reflect on who they are as ethical human beings. In addition, the fact that power circulates means that it can be held by different people at different moments. Teach-ers do not hold power all the time, neither does the state which can lose control to various groups. This circulation of power may come in the form of action like riots by citizens, foot-dragging by children, or children who negotiate to change a test date. The technologies of the self, which Hutton (1988: 132) describes as the ways in which 'the individual participates in the policing process by monitoring his own behaviour', could be said to operate when a child looking at the listening poster in the classroom is reminded how she should behave and then regulates her own behaviour.

Power also needs to be thought about in relation to knowledge and discourse. Power and knowledge are joined through discourse. Discourses, for Foucault, are bodies of knowledge, like academic disciplines. They are historically contingent, subject to change, and they also limit the ways things can be talked about and by whom. Modern power operates through institutions like the school. In these institutions, people become the objects of knowledge ('the knowledge that may be gained from him') as they are observed, judged, and recorded. Power then becomes associated with producing and using specific forms of knowledge. Foucault (1977: 27) argues that 'there is no power relation without the correlative constitution of a field of knowledge, nor any knowledge that does not presuppose and constitute at the same time power relations'.

Foucault's notion of discourse also shows the relation between bodies of knowledge (or dis-ciplines) and disciplinary practices (the means of social control). Discipline is a technique of power that 'provides procedures for training or coercing bodies' (Smart, 2002: 85). So the way in which bodies are trained (disciplined) is directly related to the way in which the disciplinary knowledge allows us to see the world. The bodily training a scientist receives is not the same as that of a chef. The way in which both may use a bowl of vegetables is affected by their discipli-nary knowledge. One may use them to prepare a new dish, the other may be genetically modify-ing them. Although both may cut the vegetables, the chef chops while the scientist dissects. The fact that discipline is about both knowledge and social control is fundamental in thinking about how subjects are constructed.

This distinction drives my exploration to discover what constitutes the schooled subject and the literate subject in these schools. So, literacy instruction (in schools and communities) is not just about teaching children to decode and encode texts; rather it works to constitute children in relation to social and cultural beliefs about what it means to be literate (Maynak, 2004). As children take on these beliefs and practices, a particular literate subject is produced. We need greater insight into the ways in which literacy practices are affected by teachers' understanding of literacy; and how the literacy training children undergo conforms to these understandings.

If we return to the Rules for Good Listening poster again, a particular version of the school subject is represented in it. It presents a picture of a child sitting at a school desk. Part of the process of schooling is learning to sit at a desk. There is a close association with the desk and schooling in our cultural schemata. Sitting at a desk also requires a level of passivity because actions and movements are constrained by the physical presence of a desk placed in front of a body. This picture speaks of compliance. The good listener is compliant and needs to be docile. Foucault talks about the techniques that create relations of 'docility-utility' (1977: 137). This power allows, in this case, a teacher to have a hold over bodies so that they operate quickly and efficiently. This creates docile, practised bodies. Children need a level of docility to learn to write so that eventually the task of writing is useful in recording other disciplinary knowledge. Schooling is about creating docile bodies. The way in which this is achieved is through techniques which affect how space, time, and movement are regulated.

Thus the way in which children are disciplined to become school subjects and literate subjects (and learn to take on other subject positions) is affected by how space is organized. It is also affected by how they are distributed in space, how time is ordered and controlled, the movement of children and resources in space and across time. Spatial and temporal workings are interrelated and affect the ways in which classroom practices are enacted.

Literacy

Placed on the desk of the child in the poster is a pencil and sheets of paper – the tools required for literacy. At the beginning of schooling, pencils and paper are vital resources used in teaching children to read and write. Mastery of these tools also opens up access to literacies required from other bodies of knowledge: in later years the child may use the paper and pencil to solve a calculus problem, record the results of a chemistry experiment, work with contours on a map, or experiment with perspective to create a piece of art.

This work is informed by a social practices perspective of literacy and the work of the New Literacy Studies. This perspective is underpinned by Brian Street's distinction between literacy as an autonomous model and as an ideological model. When literacy is viewed as autonomous, children acquire a set of technical skills which affect social and cognitive processes. Literacy is then seen as a neutral set of skills. This is challenged by Street when he sets out the ideological model. He argues that the focus of the ideological model 'signals quite explicitly that literacy practices are aspects not only of "culture" but also of power structures' (Street, 2001b: 434). Acknowledging the ideological nature of literacy reveals the variety of cultural practices associated with reading and writing in different contexts: meanings and practices are contested – we may perform the same reading task but it may be valued differently in our communities or homes (Barton & Hamilton, 2000). The technical and cognitive aspects of reading and writing are encapsulated in cultural wholes and structures of power. There are many types of literacy: as the communication landscape develops and new technological innovations come on-line, the ways in which people use literacy will change. The significant point is that engaging with literacy is always a social act.

This work uses a social practices perspective to identify how literacy is conceptualized and enacted at Southside and Acacia. Because it acknowledges the social nature of literacy, this perspective provides insight into the power relations that ensue from the way in which literacy is conceptualized in these classrooms. It thus provides a picture of how the literate subject is constructed. It takes up Street's point when he notes that, from an educational perspective,

> [t]he ways in which teachers or facilitators and their students interact is already a social practice that affects the nature of the literacy being learned and the ideas about literacy held by the participants, especially the new learners and their position in relations of power.
>
> (Street, 2001a: 8)

This research is an attempt to document the nature of the literacy these 'new learners' are subjected to.

Although the analytical framework here is a social practices one, the reason for applying it is that it allows one to identify the ways in which children are taught literacy and how this is informed by particular understandings of literacy. This means that the cognitive aspects of literacy are not discounted as unimportant in the process of learning to become literate. But they are encapsulated in cultural wholes and structures of power. Janks (2010) quite rightly points out that the binary thinking that sees literacy as either a set of cognitive skills or a set of social practices is not helpful. She neatly describes the cognitive processing required to read and points out that the meanings assigned to the ways in which we read are not valued in the same ways.

> Reading depends on the ability to recognize the visual shapes of letters and words, to understand letter–sound relationships and the structure of words and sentences, as well as the ability to synthesize all of these processes in order to make meaning from print. Readers have to recognize words, memorize patterns, synthesize information, comprehend meaning, evaluate content, all cognitive abilities … The social practices of reading a book for pleasure, of using writing to work out thoughts, of reading newspapers, of writing poetry, of reading non-fiction, of surfing the net, of making notes, of researching information are not part of everyone's daily lives.
>
> (Janks, 2010: xiii)

In order to work out how literacy is conceptualized and enacted in classrooms, I use concepts of literacy events and literacy practices. Heath (1983: 93) describes a literacy event as 'any occasion in which a piece of writing is integral to the nature of participants' interactions and their interpretative processes'. Literacy events are observable and often repeated, and routine. These criteria are used as a way of identifying literacy events that are representative of classroom activities. From literacy events, literacy practices can be inferred. Street (1993: 12) uses literacy practices to refer to 'both behaviour and conceptualizations related to the use of reading and/or writing' – but it is the patterned regularity with which events happen that turns them into literacy practices. Underpinning literacy events are values, attitudes, feelings, and social relationships that shape the event itself.

The following chapters take up the issues raised here by examining data from the classrooms. They show how various techniques of disciplinary power work to construct both schooled subjects and literate subjects with a particular focus on how these techniques are targeted at the body. They consider how literacy as a form of disciplinary knowledge is conceptualized and enacted in classrooms which results in a particular kind of reading subject and a writing subject. They also consider the way in which a discourse of literacy is recorded through assessments to provide additional insights into these constructions. Each chapter describes the shifts and continuities in classroom pedagogies and literacy teaching, as children move from preschool into primary school. In line with the thinking of both Foucault and Street, in order not to present this research in a decontextualized, ahistorical way, Chapter 2 locates the schools and the research in space and time.

Chapter 2

Schooling and space

The geographical location of the schools children attend is not neutral. These locations are shaped and coloured by histories of class and race and culture. These histories are dynamic and shift as people move into and out of areas. New groups bring change. These are sometimes seen to revitalize an area or to 'bring it down'. Demographic changes also affect people's perceptions of schools as 'good' or 'bad'. Often the values of schools are in line with the local communities in which they are located, but at other times demographic shifts have meant that there are tensions between what a school represents and the values of a local community. The relationships between schools, the children who attend them, and local communities can be complex when there are broader social changes taking place in a society. This is very much the case in post-apartheid South Africa. The desegregation of schooling in the early 1990s has led to the movement of many Black children from outlying townships to what are perceived to be well-resourced 'White' schools located in 'White' suburbs. In some cases this has resulted in diverse, multicultural school populations where schools work hard to deal positively with difference. In other schools, there has been 'White flight' where White parents who have the economic resources move their children from local schools perceived to be 'too Black'. In all cases, desegregation has brought with it the challenges of learning to work with multicultural school populations.

The demise of apartheid and its resulting political and social reconstruction have impacted on the movement of people. The racial and socio-economic profiles of many urban areas have begun to shift. In order to have an understanding of the two research schools and the influences and issues at play within them, their historical, geographic, and socio-economic contexts need to be foregrounded. This exploration is by its nature broad. It serves as a means of mapping some of the complexities that are present in the suburb Acacia and Southside are located in, painting a broad picture of the area's shapes and colours. In locating the schools in a particular space it is also necessary to locate the workings of this research study in its place because the nature of the research is such that an omnipresent gaze is impossible. Rather the research findings presented here are the result of a localized, subjective gaze; a painting on a smaller canvas.

One of the key aspects of this gaze is the spatial. The presence of the spatial in itself is a major finding of this research. Using the spatial as a lens to analyse what was happening in schools and classrooms became more and more important as the research progressed. It seemed impossible to talk about discipline, regulation, and the construction of subjects without considering the spaces within which these happen, and the ways in which these spaces are used. There are a number of spatial theories which could have been applied to this research but Foucault's understanding of space and its interconnectedness with discipline was the most apt. Thus the discussion in this chapter is read from a Foucauldian perspective. It begins broadly by examining the schools in relation to the suburb in which they are located to provide a social, historical, and spatial context. The focus narrows to thinking about the spatial organization of the schools themselves and then to the utilization of space within individual classrooms. This results in a final discussion that considers some of the possibilities and challenges of classroom spatial organizations in teachers' management and regulation of children.

The socio-spatial location of Acacia and Southside: a contextual background to Johannesburg's southern suburbs

The 'place' that Acacia and Southside are located in influences the type of schools they are and more importantly how they are perceived by parents and communities. These perceptions are shaped by the history of Johannesburg as a mining town that, from the beginning, was fractured by social and racial stratification. Acacia and Southside are located in the southern suburbs of Johannesburg. Like all Johannesburg suburbs they owe their existence to the development of gold mining in the late nineteenth century. Johannesburg developed as a city in the triangular tract of land surrounded by three farms: Doornfontein, Braamfontein, and Turffontein (van Zyl, 1986). Doornfontein and Braamfontein are now areas in the inner city. Turffontein lies to the south of the city, and although the farm no longer exists, one of the suburbs adjacent to the schools and the local racecourse still bear its name. From the beginnings of residential development class stratification was evident through spatial location. Affluent inhabitants settled to the north of the city to avoid the dust of the gold mines (Grant & Flinn, 1992: 99) and the greater exposure to winter winds. In contrast, poorer White workers settled south in areas like Jeppe, Fordsburg, Mayfair, and Turffontein.

Local residents in 'the south', as it is generally referred to, are used to the joke made by people living in the northern suburbs about requiring a passport to enter on the occasions when they have to. The erroneous perception exists that the south is a place where all residents are poor and rough, and fights are common. It is a place unknown and thus feared by many living in the leafy, affluent northern suburbs. Although there is no 'border control', it is the gold reef that creates a physical boundary between north and south. Main Reef Road follows the main gold reef across the Witwatersrand[1] from east to west, separating north and south. Although the south of Johannesburg has the oldest working-class suburbs, it also has well-established middle-class suburbs and growing areas housing the nouveau riche. But the stereotype of the working-class south and upper- and middle-class north persists.

After the 1994 elections, administration of the city was decentralized and Johannesburg was divided into 11 regions. Johannesburg South was Region 9. It has since been joined with Region 8 which includes the inner city (see the shaded area in Figure 2.1). Johannesburg South's northern border abuts the mining belt and the inner city. To the south and the east it forms one of Johannesburg's boundaries. To the west it meets the traditionally Black townships Soweto, Ennerdale, and Orange Farm.

At the time of the study (2002–2003), approximately 130,000 people lived in the old Region 9 with Whites still in the majority. This is unsurprising when the region was predominantly constituted by White suburbs during apartheid. The suburb Acacia and Southside are located in what used to be a working-class Whites-only suburb. In the decade after 1994 the racial demographics of the population within the suburb has begun to shift. Parnell and Webber foreground the reasons for this:

> The attractions of a centrally located home increased as the liberalisation of South Africa's racial laws gradually created a more hospitable environment in which public amenities such as libraries, cinemas, parks, restaurants, hospitals and public transport were desegregated.
>
> (Parnell & Webber cited in Parnell & Phiri, 1991: 140)

Figure 2.1 Map of the regions of Johannesburg. (Image Daniel Janks. Used with permission.)

This is true of the south of Johannesburg. Its location and road and rail links provide better access to places of work. The location of the southern suburbs means that Black people who have moved here from Soweto have access to better facilities but can maintain social and family ties in Soweto (City of Johannesburg, 2009). Property prices of these older 'White' working-class suburbs are attractive compared to middle-class suburbs for those who want to make the move from the township.

This movement from townships into suburbs added another stress to South Africa's housing crisis. As a predominantly working-class suburb, large areas consist of council flats that have housed lower-income White families for decades. At the time of the study, residents earning less than R3,500 a month[2] could qualify for a council flat in the area. Because there is such a need, the council has compiled waiting lists. The slowness of the council has been counteracted by incidents of illegal occupation and evictions from the council flats and houses. In some instances self-appointed housing committees have evicted residents and moved other people in. Some of these tensions have flared up in the form of racial incidents.

Education levels in Johannesburg South reveal a working-class bias: 28% of the population has a Matric (12 years of schooling), and only 11% a post-Matric qualification. But there are a fair number of schools (30 primary schools and 99 secondary schools) which are located in the older suburbs, as is the case for Acacia and Southside. In terms of intake, schools are required to accept applications from children in the surrounding suburb first, and then, if they have additional places, accept children from other areas. Schools submit their numbers to the Education Department showing that they have reached their capacity. If the government decides the school has additional capacity other children are sent to the school from outlying areas. Although the government-decided teacher : pupil ratio is 1 : 35 per class in the early years of schooling, this number is often exceeded.

Many of the children at Acacia and Southside live in the surrounding suburbs. Others come from outlying townships: Black students are drawn from Soweto, Coloured[3] children from Eldorado Park. Indian and White children appear to live mainly in the area. A small proportion of Indian children attend the school – another local primary school has a larger proportion of Indian students and a growing Indian community in its surrounding suburb.

To conclude, I want to reflect on the connection between demographic shift and school admission policies implied at the beginning of this section. Collins and Coleman (2008) make a distinction between spatial organization inside schools, which the second half of this chapter takes up, and the spatial boundaries beyond schools particularly in relation to neighbourhoods and community. This relationship has become increasingly complex. While desegregation has opened up educational opportunities, inequalities still exist. The fact that admission to South African government schools is controlled by zoning means that strong ties between schools and communities can be developed, but at the same time can reinforce racial and class segregation (Collins & Coleman, 2008). If there are enough children living in a zone to populate schools and the community has remained mostly racially heterogeneous, the school is likely to remain so. This is the case for many township schools that have remained Black.

But, for many children in South Africa, and across the world, the school they attend is often not in close proximity to where they live. This most often has to do with the quality of education provided in poorer, working-class areas. Thus access to better education in South Africa is perceived by an aspirant and growing Black middle class as a way through which their children will have greater social and cultural capital. This capital resides in ex-White and Indian areas. If parents cannot afford to move to these areas they can send their children to the schools there. Class inequalities are further reinforced because while schools are not obliged to take children 'outside their community', they often select children whose parents can pay the school fees. Such movements cross the spatial boundaries set up by apartheid. But they do not necessarily overcome racial and class boundaries across the board.

In moving from township schools to suburban schools the tie of the local community can be eroded and the new expectations of (White) middle-class spaces begin to prefigure. Attending schools that are often strongly assimilationist has had an impact on students' identities. Several South African studies are beginning to show many of these students dealing with the tensions of not fitting in with the assimilationist norms and expectations of schools and feeling increasingly marginalized by their own communities who no longer see them as the same (McKinney, 2007; Morrow, 2007). Distance is an important factor in schooling. Unreliable public transport means that many children are required to leave school as soon as it ends to get home. They are unable to attend after-school activities that have an important role to play in socialization. This also has an impact on parents and their relationship with the school. Parents who live close by can have a greater say in the management of the school. Parents who live further away rely on public transport, and are constrained by working hours, have less power to support or challenge school practices and attend meetings and events. This is exacerbated by the low level of education many parents received under apartheid.

It is important to think about the spatial scales which influence schooling. Thinking about the distance required for students to get to school gives insight into the challenges many children face merely to attend school. The spatial location of areas also provides us with insight into issues of race, class, gender, and culture and the tensions of what are often 'marginal' 'other' spaces moving into a 'dominant' centre.

Acacia Preschool and Southside Primary

There are several reasons for choosing to locate this research at Acacia and Southside. The first is personal. Having grown up in the south of Johannesburg, I chose to study schools in the southern suburbs as an attempt to understand and extend the knowledge I have of the practices of my own community, and to share it so that it is of benefit to those working there. As these Johannesburg suburbs are on the 'wrong side of the tracks', it often seems as if what occurs here is marginalized. This feeling was validated when I searched for information on the southern suburbs – while there are specific references to development in the north, there are vague references to the south or none at all. One of the advantages of my own schooling was that children from middle- and working-class homes were sent to the same local schools. What I did not experience was a racially or linguistically desegregated schooling system. English- and Afrikaans-speaking children generally did not go to school together. Today Acacia and Southside are fully multiracial, multicultural, and multilingual.

The location of the schools was an important consideration. Acacia is located a block away from Southside and is Southside's feeder preschool. The spatial proximity has led to a close working relationship between the schools and occasionally Acacia uses Southside's facilities. This proximity was useful for me in terms of continuity: if I was to look at schooling in a community without following a specific group for five years, then the composition of children in the preschool needed to reflect the composition of children I would find at the primary school.

Acacia Preschool used to be a government school. Several years ago the government threatened to close preschools. To keep Acacia operational it was privatized. Although it is now private, it is not elite and exclusive. Acacia is fully equipped with five large classrooms, an administration area with space for a secretary, a principal's office, a large kitchen, storerooms, and a playground with sandpits and equipment for the children to play on.

Southside Primary caters to the first eight years of school. Traditionally primary schools catered to the first seven years of schooling (Grade 1 to Grade 7). Since the government has included the reception year (Grade 0) as part of the first 10 years of compulsory schooling, Southside added a reception class. The 2002 Grade 0 class was run for the first time with the sanction of the Education Department. The primary school is divided into a junior and senior section. The junior section of the school contains all the Foundation Phase classrooms (Grade 0 to Grade 3) as well as two special education classes. During the study, there were 11 teachers in the Foundation Phase – three per grade, and two special education teachers. The senior part of the school contains the Grade 4 to Grade 7 classes, the computer laboratory and the library. Children move on to high school in Grade 8. Southside is well resourced and has sporting facilities such as a swimming pool and sports fields.

There are many children at the primary school whose parents are unemployed or whose financial circumstances are precarious. Southside has a government-funded feeding scheme in place so that children have access to at least one meal a day.

Multiple case studies and data collection in five early-years classrooms

This research used a multiple case study approach to investigate the management, regulation, and construction of the schooled body. Five classrooms constituted individual cases in which practices could be analysed within individual classrooms and across the classrooms. The choice of classrooms can be further broken down in terms of the type of schooling children receive. Grade 00 and Grade 0 are considered to be informal schooling and Grades 1 to 3 are the first phase of formal schooling. At present, it is compulsory for children to attend school from Grade

1, which is viewed as the beginning of formal schooling. This is supposedly when learning takes place in a formalized setting and in a formalized way. The South African curriculum has a strong emphasis on the type of subject it desires schooling to construct. By locating my research at the beginning of children's schooling I was able to study them at the start of their subjection to the school environment. (This is explored further in Chapter 4.)

This study takes the form of 'quasi-longitudinal' research. The focus is not on individuals but on overall trends – thus the children were not followed over a period of five years. Rather, five classrooms were central in investigating practices in and across early schooling: Grade 00 (4- to 5-year-olds), Grade 0 (5- to 6-year-olds), Grade 1 (two classes of 6- to 7-year-olds) and Grade 3 (8- to 9-year-olds). The Grade 00 classroom constituted the first case study. Located in the pre-primary phase, and the year before children are assessed to see if they are ready for school, Grade 00 can be understood to be part of informal schooling where the emphasis is still on play. It presents a means of comparing 'informal' and 'formal' schooling and the impact this has on the construction of the schooled subject, as well as general patterns of transition. Observations of this class took place once a week over the first six months of 2002.

The Grade 0 class provided a more specific focus on transition and thus observations took place at the end of the 2002 school year. This class enabled me to see what the particular emphasis was in terms of constructing a partially schooled subject, but also one in the process of being prepared for formal school socialization. I followed some children in the Grade 0 class into Grade 1 in 2003. Grade 1 marks the beginning of formal schooling. Observations focused on the broad requirements of formal schooling, and the kinds of literacy practices children are required to master. Classes were observed once a week for the first five months of the school year across two Grade 1 classes. In order to gain a sense of the kind of disciplined and self-regulating subjects that emerged, I looked at children in Grade 3, the end of the Foundation Phase, for the last two months of their school year in 2002. Table 2.1 provides a summary of the classrooms constituting the case studies and time spent observing in them.

A variety of techniques was used to record classroom observations. Fieldnotes were used predominantly. They contained spatial maps of the classroom layouts as well as movement flows to show children's interactions with each other. Fieldnotes were supplemented by photographs and videotaping. This was crucial not just in providing an exact record of classroom interactions; the nature of the visual allows a focus on the body and is a reminder of mundane routines, practices, and norms. Filming was impacted on by my movements with a handheld camera. Because I chose to sit with the children where there were spaces at desks, not all the children could be filmed. Audiotaping was limited because video was far more effective in capturing sound and movement. Teacher interviews and the collection of chil-

Table 2.1 Classrooms that constituted the case studies

Grade	School	Age of children	Period of observation	No. of observation sessions
Grade 00	Acacia Preschool	4–5 years	21 January–20 June 2002	15
Grade 0	Southside Primary	5–6 years	1 October–3 December 2002	22
Grade 1	Southside Primary	6–7 years	15 January–21 May 2003	28 (includes both classes)
Grade 3	Southside Primary	8–9 years	8 October–3 December 2002	21

Table 2.2 Time spent observing classes

Grade	No. of times class observed	Hours of observation	Hours of filming	Hours of audiotape
Grade 00	15	28	8	0
Grade 0	22	35.5	5	2
Grade 1	14	50	8.25	0
Grade 1	14	53	9.25	0
Grade 3	21	38	5	1
Total	86	204.5	35.5	3

dren's artifacts and administrative records supplemented the data. Table 2.2 is a record of time spent in each class.

Teachers and their classes

The five teachers were integral to my observation: Dawn, Lisa, Catherine, Helen, and Thulisile (all names are pseudonyms). I also engaged in several discussions and informal classroom observations and interviewed Gail, the Foundation Phase Head of Department at Southside. Although Gail was not a focus of the study, her knowledge of the phase provided necessary contextual information.

Dawn is the principal of Acacia and the Grade 00 teacher. She was willing to allow her school to be one of the research sites and have her classroom observed. After initial contact and confirmation with the principal of Southside Primary, my liaisons there were via Gail. She suggested which teachers to approach in the Foundation Phase. There was only one Grade 0 class and Lisa granted permission to be observed. Helen and Catherine, two of the Grade 1 teachers agreed to be observed. Of the three Grade 3 class teachers, Thulisile was the only one who had been with her class for the full school year and Gail felt that this continuity was important. Thulisile graciously allowed access to her classroom.

The teachers came from a variety of backgrounds and their teaching experience ranged from two years to 15 years. They had also spent time teaching other grades. Table 2.3 is a summary of their backgrounds and experience. Where participants' names reflect membership of a particular racial or ethnic group I have used pseudonyms to mark this. Several participants' names do

Table 2.3 Teachers in the study

Name	Grade	Racial/ethnic group	Home language	Teaching experience	Previous experience	Time employed at school
Dawn	00	White	Afrikaans	10 years	high school	1.5 years
Lisa	0	White (Portuguese)	English	4 years	3–4 year olds	First year
Catherine	1	Indian	English	15 years	special education	4 years
Helen	1	Coloured	English	10 years	high school	2.5 years
Thulisile	3	Black (Zulu)	Zulu	2.5 years	primary school	First full year

not reflect their racial, ethnic, cultural, or linguistic backgrounds and the pseudonyms reflect this. Where relevant, these identity markers are explicitly noted in discussions.

Negotiating access to teachers' classrooms is not without problems and often teachers feel pressurized to comply with their superiors. I was extremely lucky that this on the whole was a smooth process. The observation period bore out teachers' perceived willingness to have me in their classes. I found the time spent in these classes fascinating. I had many informal discussions with the teachers and was interested to hear what they had to say about the children, their class, various lessons, teaching and their lives.

The children

Although each of the classes constitutes a group in itself, several children are used to illustrate events that reflected key moments or regular patterns that emerged from the data. Each child's parents received letters outlining the study and the fact that their children would be videotaped and that samples of their work would be collected and possibly discussed as part of the findings. The parents of the children discussed here have given permission for their children to participate in this study.

In all the classes, the children's backgrounds varied as did their academic abilities. Within these five classrooms there were boys and girls who were confident and those who were shy, those whose proficiency in English was an impediment to learning, and those who were fluent. Several came from stressful homes. The composition of children in each class included compliant subjects as well as resistant ones.

The preschool classes were smaller than the primary school classes. Table 2.4 provides a summary of class size, and the racial demographic within each. The point of the table is to give an indication of what desegregation looks like in these schools – which is not necessarily the same profile for all desegregated schools in South Africa. But producing a table such as this essentializes race. The South African reality is far more complex. For example, using apartheid racial markers are inadequate to 'classify' a child where one parent is Indian and the other Coloured. Such classification draws on individual cultural identities that are beyond this study. The table also does not show which children come from other African countries. Nor does it reflect ethnicity within and across race groups (e.g. Whites who have Portuguese or Afrikaans backgrounds).

There were originally 32 children in the Grade 00 class and when Dawn hired an additional teacher early in the year the number was reduced to 23. There were 12 girls and 11 boys in the class. Different levels of language proficiency were marked. Several Black children were beginning their schooling with little or no English while others were communicatively competent.

Table 2.4 Racial profile of children observed across the grades

Class	Black	Coloured	Indian	White	Total
Grade 00	12	5	0	6	23
Grade 0	8	6	6	6	26
Grade 1 (Helen)	16	10	4	5	35
Grade 1 (Catherine)	16	12	6	2	36
Grade 3	17	7	0	10	34
Total	69	40	16	29	154

Table 2.5 Children who were followed from Grade 0 to Grade 3

Name	Sex	Racial group	English as L1 or L2	Teacher
Amanda	Female	Coloured	L1	Helen
Polosoa	Male	Coloured/Black	L2	Catherine
Jason	Male	White	L1	Helen
Jenny	Female	White	L1	Catherine
Claudia	Female	Coloured	L1	Helen
Boitumelo	Female	Black	L2	Catherine
Zama	Female	Black	L2	Catherine
Tshepo	Male	Black	L2	Helen
Stella	Female	Black	L2	Helen
Vukani	Male	Black	L2	Helen
Faizel	Male	Indian	L1	Helen

One of the key issues of the research was transition. A crucial stage was the move children make from Grade 0 to Grade 1. Thus I observed the Grade 0 class at the end of the year, and the two Grade 1 classes at the beginning of the following year. Eleven of these Grade 0s were allocated to the two Grade 1 classes I observed. While they could not be called focus children (Dyson, 1994) in the sense that all of my attention was directed on them, I had established relationships with them and they were used to my presence. The advantage of following more than one child from Grade 0 to Grade 1 meant that I had a broad perspective on how they were dealing with the shift to more formal schooling. The disadvantage of course is that breadth does not lead to depth. They provided a comparison between children who had been to preschool and those who had not.

Table 2.5 presents a short profile of the children by indicating sex, racial group, the teacher they were allocated to in Grade 1, and whether English was their home or second language.

Spatial layout of the schools

Space for Foucault (2002) is essential in any exercise of power. The school is a nexus of power relations. Before examining the impact of spatial relations in the classrooms it is necessary to examine the school as an institutional space that 'is dedicated to the control and regulation of the child's body and mind through regimes of discipline, learning, development, maturation and skill' (James et al. cited in Holloway & Valentine, 2000: 11). This requires thinking about the school in terms of its architecture, since architecture is a means through which regimes of discipline and training work (Foucault, 2002). This general spatial organization has an impact on what is possible but also reveals how architectural designs work to discipline particular subjects.

The design of Acacia is common to a number of preschools in the area that were built by the apartheid government (see Figure 2.2 and Figure 2.3). Although they are well built and resourced, the sameness of these preschools makes an architectural point about undifferentiated mass schooling. Schooling the masses is an exercise in social control and the ways in which that control is extended are supposedly uniform. Although the outside environment may be different, the sameness of the schools' design potentially works to create the same kinds of schooled, in this case, preschooled subjects. It also means that there are limitations as to how space can be organized and used.

In addition to this, the design of the preschool speaks to understandings of what its role is. The preschool is smaller, thus the ground it is built on is smaller. The preschool is the place one

Figure 2.2 View of Acacia Preschool.

goes before school, the place where children are prepared for 'big' school. Acacia could be said to reflect a microcosm of the ('big') school through its design. Rather unimaginatively, all the classrooms are built in a row along a corridor, rather like the blocks of classrooms in primary and secondary schools. All the classrooms look out onto a playground that also spans the length of the corridor. The corridor divides teaching space from outside play space. But, the power of the teacher is not solely located in the classroom. Positioning herself outside on the corridor allows her unfettered visual access to children on the playground (see Figure 2.2).

This 'block' of teaching space is divided evenly into what can be six large classrooms. At Acacia the third 'room' is administrative and divided into a smaller office for the principal and behind this an open-plan space for the school's secretary. The rest of the space behind the offices is referred to as a small hall. The room is carpeted and a television is mounted on the wall where videos can be shown to the children. Although predominantly empty, chairs can be added to this room for larger meetings with parents. These schools were also designed so that some class-rooms have concertina doors to allow confined classroom spaces to be opened up into large meeting areas. Where such a school is too small for a hall and the routines of a preschool do not demand such gatherings of children (and adults), this is a clever use of space. It also shows that schools may also be used as community spaces for other activities.[4]

There is also far greater access to the classrooms because of a set of interconnecting doors between some of the classrooms. This suggests a more intimate teaching environment where teachers can move into another class without accessing the more formal 'front' door. This movement can challenge the notion that a classroom is a teacher's private space and instead establish collaborative relationships. On the other hand, their use may be more negative if they are used as instruments of **surveillance**.

There are two other spaces whose functions point to the regulation of school life. The first is the large institutional-looking kitchen behind the offices/hall. The kitchen is operational and children get fed from it every day. The presence of an institutional kitchen is an indication that access to food is regulated. It is also an adult space. The other space set up to regulate bodies is the toilets. At the back of each classroom are child-size toilets with open lockers to store school bags. Two aspects of the construction of the young child are revealed here: the first is about fear and proximity – young children are considered to be less in control of excretory processes and the proximity of toilets potentially allows for fewer 'accidents'. Second, food and excretion can be controlled. The presence and operation of these spaces is linked to time (see Chapter 3).

Southside Primary reflects traditional South African school architecture (see Figure 2.4). There is a distinctive division between teaching and recreational space. This space has been expanded to become a sports area with a swimming pool, tennis courts and fields for cricket, soccer, and athletics. Teaching space is divided by the hall and office block. Teaching of the younger children takes place on one side of the hall. Along with the hall the classrooms form a square with a quadrangle in the middle that functions as a meeting-place for the morning announcements for the younger children. At the back of the Grade 3 classrooms is a smaller playground with wooden jungle gyms. Its location is significant because it is hidden from the rest of the school. This space is the domain of the Foundation Phase and speaks of conceptions of childhood and play. It is utilized by all the grades during teaching time. On the other side of the hall, Grades 4 to 7 are taught in a three-storey block of classrooms. The increase in numbers has meant that their morning announcements take place in the open space between the teachers' parking and the teaching block. There is no longer sufficient space for the entire school to meet in the hall for regular assemblies.

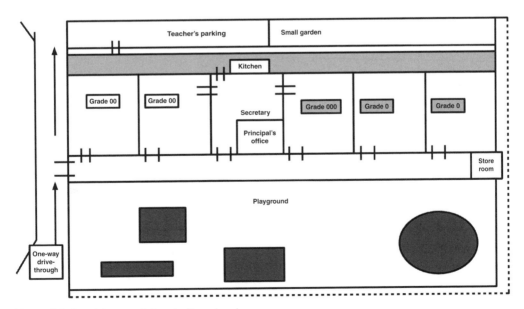

Figure 2.3 Spatial map of Acacia Preschool.

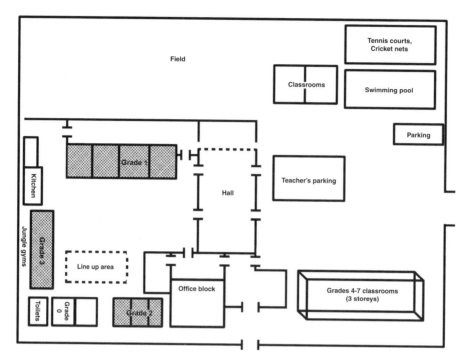

Figure 2.4 Spatial map of Southside Primary.

Enclosure

If space is essential in the exercise of power it is because 'discipline proceeds from the distribution of individuals in space' (Foucault, 1977: 141). How this happens Foucault ascribes to four techniques that can be seen to operate in both schools. The first technique is **enclosure**. As the name suggests it is a place closed in on itself. Confining an area limits inconveniences and unwelcome disturbances. Both schools are literally closed in on themselves. They are surrounded with barbed-wire fencing and monitored by closed-circuit television cameras.

Foucault (1977) also argues that space can be thought about as real and ideal. On the level of the real, the fencing and surveillance cameras indicate that the physical space is protected and confined. On the level of the ideal, spaces can be symbolic. Schools can be a protective space. It is important that schools be safe spaces and children feel safe within their confines. Recent international work addresses a growing concern about the vulnerability of children within public spaces (Holloway & Valentine, 2000; Percy-Smith & Matthews, 2001; Molnar, Gortmaker, Bull, & Buka, 2004; Veitch, Salmon, & Ball, 2007). The work of Walkerdine (2001), Jones & Cunningham (1999), and Veitch et al. (2007) makes the point that play spaces and children's safety are regulated by adults who overly constrain children's independence because of their fear. This fear is exacerbated by reports of abuse. In South Africa, with child abuse and community violence major concerns, this fear is justifiable. Thus a frequently expressed concern of the teachers and principals in the study was that their school environment be a safe one, particularly when incidents have shown them that the everyday spaces many children frequent, particularly their home environments, are not.

Access to both schools during the school day is restricted. Visitors access the schools via one gate where they have to ring a bell and are captured by the surveillance cameras. It is adults who vet visitors and control access to children. Another level of protective **enclosure** at Acacia is a narrow one-way drive-through where parents drop their children off. A brick wall facing the road has been built along the drive-through, and while it functions as a way to move traffic in one direction it has the added benefit of hiding the school. Although the perimeter of the school is fenced off, bushes have been allowed to grow so that it is extremely difficult to watch the children from outside the school when they are in the playground. This is not the case at Southside because the grounds are much larger.

Foucault (1977) points out that **enclosure** is not constant enough as a technique. This was illustrated by the encroachment of a violent society into the space: during the time I was present at Southside, bullets were found on the playground, a Grade 3 boy had threatened his classmates with a knife, and at the end-of-year school concert, in an altercation over seating, parents threatened each other with guns. These incidents are not isolated to this school, and are perhaps minor in comparison to a growing number of incidents of school violence by children in primary and secondary schools. There have been several incidents of peer-on-peer violence that have resulted in children's death over the last few years (News24.com, 2008; *Mail and Guardian Online*, 2006, 2007; South African Institute of Race Relations, 2008).

This also raises the question of bullying and victimization. Children are enclosed within schools to protect them from outside adult spaces. Within this space they are trained to take part in an adult world. They are also enclosed with groups of children whose own behaviour defies school and general social norms reflecting the microcosm of a violent society. It is beyond the scope of this chapter to explore children's use of spaces beyond the classroom in relation to this. But there is a body of work that looks at this. For example Andrews and Chen (2006) look at the spatial tactics used by children who are bullied, and Newman, Woodcock, and Dunham (2006) consider the strategies boys who play football use to territorialize the playground.

Partitioning and ranking

Enclosure works to concentrate individuals so that progress can be monitored. Schools collect groups of children together so that they can be monitored in their education. This monitoring takes place in far more intense ways through two other techniques: **partitioning** and **ranking**. **Partitioning** is more detailed and flexible than enclosure. It allocates individuals to their own space and space to individuals; in this way it creates an analytic space. It aims to eliminate unsanctioned groups; it makes distribution precise and it regulates movement. It establishes

> presences and absences, to know where and how to locate individuals to set up useful communications, to interrupt others, to be able at each moment to supervise the conduct of each individual, to assess it, to judge it, to calculate its qualities and merits.
>
> (Foucault, 1977: 143)

If one of the features of **partitioning** is the allocation of individuals to space then it is worth thinking about the location of partitions and what these signify. At the centre of both schools is the administrative space. Acacia's office and 'hall' are in the same room. At Southside the principal and senior management's offices are located in the office block; from here the administration of the staff, children, and the school is overseen, and here staff congregate in the staff room. Leading off this space is the hall. These spaces effectively divide the Foundation Phase from the Intermediate Phase. This central location of the administration space is indicative of the place as a powerful hub. It is here that the overall management and discipline of the children is decided upon, managed, and maintained. These are the repositories where children and their parents become objects of knowledge through the housing of documents such as school reports, personal information, and records of meetings. This is an adult space.

Space is also allocated to individuals on the basis of whether they are teachers or children in the Foundation Phase or Intermediate Phase (Grades 4–7). Such a separation works to regulate movement so groups are in particular spaces (i.e. the quadrangle, Grade 1 classrooms). This separation is practical: younger children are not disturbed when the older ones change class at the end of a period. In addition there is less chance of the younger children being victimized by older children. Within the Foundation Phase there are further partitions because each grade is allocated a particular space. All the Grade 1 classes are grouped together along a corridor, as at Acacia. This corridor has gates on either side that can be locked which limits access through the school property. But partitioning is also flexible and allows for movement. Children attend computer classes and the library on the other side of the school. This movement is regulated by the timetable and the conduct of children moving from one space to the other is supervised by the teacher.

Disciplinary space is cellular and the clearest example of this is the classroom. Groups of classrooms make up partitions, or cells, where individuals are assigned a particular class and places within it. The allocation of space allows for movement to be monitored and regulated. This is where the technique of **ranking** operates. **Ranking** places bodies in a system of classification that is not fixed but influenced by a number of factors. Children are ranked by grade – as they pass one grade they move on to the next. This ranking is based on age and performance. Ranking can also be in terms of behaviour. The Grade 0 and Grade 3 classes had desks for naughty children and individuals allocated to this particular space are marked as deviant. Within the classes children were variously ranked according to gender, height, age, performance, language proficiency, and behaviour. As things change, for example a child begins to perform better, then the space that they occupy shifts. Ranking has a regulatory impact, by assigning individual places to children individuals can be supervised while the whole class is occupied with other tasks.

The rule of functional sites

Classrooms are multipurpose rooms and Foucault's last technique comes into operation here: **the rule of functional sites**. This rule allows a space to have several uses. For example, a carpet area can be used to supervise small groups of children; children can be moved to the carpet away from others if they are naughty, and the carpet can be used as a storage space. From data gathered across the five classrooms I have identified four key sites where literacy practices take place: carpet space, desk space, teacher's desk, and a Reading Corner (Dixon, 2004). These areas can be read as functional sites because each space can be utilized for a number of purposes. The following section focuses on the utilization of these spaces in relation to literacy events. It also shows the continuities and shifts in how spaces are used across schooling. First, with the use of spatial maps, a comparison will be made of the classroom configurations themselves.

Spatial organization of classrooms

Each of the five classrooms observed in this study has similarities and differences in terms of their spatial organization. The most marked contrast is between the Grade 00 classroom and the others. The most obvious reason is the fact that it is situated at another site. The basic layout for the other classrooms is the same across the Foundation Phase. However, differences between these classrooms result from individual teachers' choices.

The Grade 00 classroom is the biggest classroom space (see Figure 2.5). At the back of the classroom is a door leading to the toilets and lockers. There is also a walk-in storeroom. Dawn's desk is situated at the back of the classroom in front of the storeroom. There are five hexagonal tables and one rectangular table that are placed between the wall and the carpet. In the centre of each desk is a picture representing a group of children allocated to that table. The third space is the carpet space; it is the only space that is literally **partitioned** into three sections. The top of the carpet nearest the teacher's desk is a play space that, through the use of furniture and equipment, creates fictional places: a shop, a hospital. These change regularly. **Partitioning** divides this area from the Reading Corner and the Interest Table. Partial **partitioning** separates the Reading Corner from the desk space. The rest of the carpet is open space. The Reading Corner is a cleverly designed space that uses the classroom wall and a partition to create a corner. The bookshelves are designed to display the front covers of books, and there are cushions placed underneath the shelves.

All of the Foundation Phase classrooms have a storeroom, sink, and a fixed low wooden ledge of pigeonholes running along one of the walls. The carpet is fixed to the floor underneath the blackboard. Like the Grade 00 classroom, the two Grade 1 classrooms also have toilets. The fact that these are absent from the Grade 0 classroom is because of the recent introduction of Grade 0 into the primary school. However, the school's toilets are immediately adjacent.

The organization of the Grade 0 classroom indicates some similarities to the Grade 00 class (see Figure 2.6). There is an Interest Table, displaying various artifacts for the weekly theme. Lisa's desk is at the back of the classroom facing the blackboard. At the back of the class is the wooden ledge that functions as the Reading Corner. Books are displayed upright or flat on the ledge, with additional books being stored in the pigeonholes.

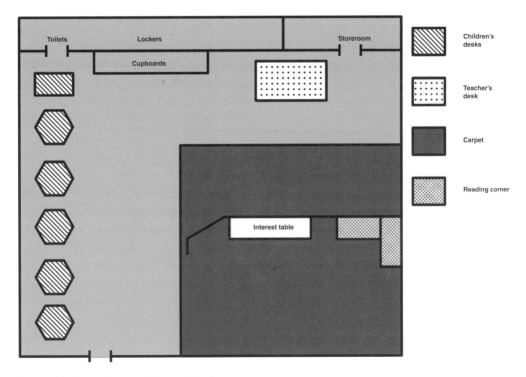

Figure 2.5 Spatial map of Grade 00 classroom.

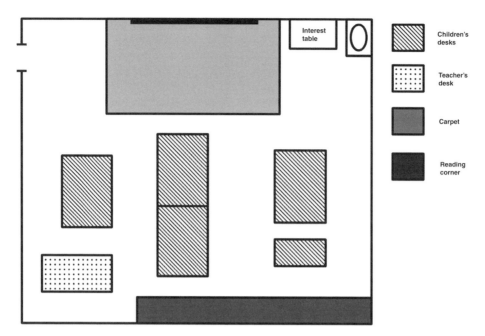

Figure 2.6 Spatial map of Grade 0 classroom.

The children's desks are between the carpet and Lisa's desk. Each desk seats two. The arrangement of desks creates three groups of children, with the desks organized into a rectangular shape. The group in front of Lisa's table seats eight. The next group seats 12 as the tables form a long row, and the last group seats eight, although there are only six children at it. There is an additional desk behind this group. It provides an example of a **functional site**. Sometimes extra children were sent to this class if their teacher was absent and they were allocated this space. It also has a disciplinary function as an incarceratory space. Children who were disruptive and unable to work with other children sat here by themselves in the classroom version of solitary confinement – marking the subject as non-compliant.

In both the Grade 1 classes and the Grade 3 class (see Figure 2.7) the Reading Corner no longer exists. In its place is a bookshelf, which resides either at the front or back of the classroom. The teachers' desks were either at the back of the class or in the front. In Grade 1, the children's desks at the beginning of the year were arranged in rows facing the board in both classes, and were later arranged into groups similar to the Grade 0 configuration. This grouping of desks continued in Grade 3.

The utilization of four classroom spaces

The teacher's desk

A clear shift in how teachers' desks are utilized is evident. In Grade 00 the desk is barely utilized at all. It is out of bounds for the children. During class time Dawn herself is rarely there. It is a place to put things, like letters, worksheets, or children's texts, rather than a work space during teaching time. This lack of utilization is not surprising. These children need and seek constant attention – the position of the desk at the back of the class behind the partitions does not allow

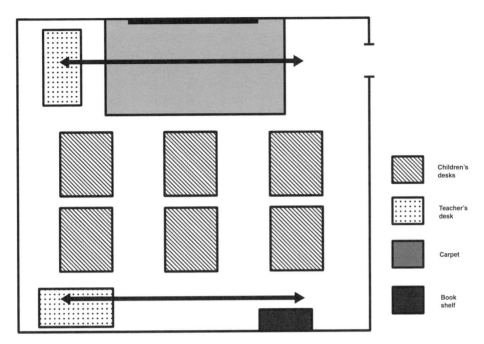

Children's desks

Teacher's desk

Carpet

Book shelf

Figure 2.7 Spatial map of Grade 1 and Grade 3 classrooms.

for the close monitoring that 4-year-olds require and demand. Dawn spends more time in other spaces and her movements are fluid, influenced by the daily routines of the classroom.

This positioning of the teacher's desk in Grade 0, on the other hand, where there are no partitions impairing vision, allows for unhindered **surveillance** of the classroom. It is here that the first shift occurs – the teacher's desk as a space is now utilized. Lisa spends time at her desk in the morning when administration takes place and when the children are seated at their desks doing their creative activities. The rest of the time she is usually in the same space as the children. Unlike in Grade 00 where this space is restricted, the children enter this space when they have to produce something – to return a form, to hand in money, or to have their work marked. Children are expected to line up to do this and not crowd the space. They are in the space of the teacher, the power relations are clear and behaviour prescribed. The act of lining up speaks to a particular kind of subject, one who needs to cultivate patience, whose needs are not primary, who is part of a collective, who displays work that will be judged, assessed, calculated, and ultimately **ranked**.

By Grade 1 the teachers spend more time at their desks. While the class is busy with a task the teacher is often working at her desk, marking or preparing books for the next part of the lesson. At the beginning of the year much time was spent cutting and pasting worksheets into books because of the children's limited skills. The desk remains a site of **surveillance**. Children have to line up and produce what they have done. The space also operates as a place where individual attention is given. Children who struggle may be closely supervised by the teacher and receive individual attention. In addition, reading also takes place here – children either line up or are called to read aloud to their teacher.

By Grade 3 the teacher spends the most time at her desk compared to the other teachers. There appears to be a correlation between the increased time the children are confined to their desks and the time the teacher spends at hers. One reason is that these children are more independent and do not need her constant presence, so children who want clarification approach her. (This is not to say that she spends all her time here – she moves through the class frequently supervising work.) The desk remains a site of **surveillance** and its placement at the back of the classroom means that the entire class can be surveyed while children get individual assistance and **rankings** can be constantly evaluated and reformulated. This is the first example of a shift in the use of space where teachers' fluid movement in and through classroom space slowly diminishes across the grades as they spend more time at their desks.

The Reading Corner

While access to the teacher's desk increases and provides a source of individual attention through reading aloud or assistance, the Reading Corner as a space is systematically shut down in the higher grades. As a **functional site** in Grade 00, it is a space designed for children. It is minimally supervised and individuals enter it during their free time. Thus time is the only real factor that restricts access. The cushions on the carpet are bright and an appropriate size for children. The fact that the shelves display the book covers rather than the spines means that children can respond to the visual messages of front covers because they cannot read titles. The books change regularly depending on the theme the class is doing. There is a variety of books – some are children's storybooks with a predominance of print, while others are more accessible for the children to read themselves, e.g. short books with colours, shapes, and numbers. In this space children begin training their own bodies to become readers through handling the books, learning to hold them, reading the images and telling stories, as well as being aware that they must not, as Dawn tells them, 'hurt the books'. This space invites an exploratory reader who may read with a friend or by themselves. Although the least amount of time was spent here by the children comparative to the other spaces, it was used. The entry of one child in this space often encouraged others to move into it (see Chapter 5).

The design of the Reading Corner in Grade 0, in contrast, does not encourage reading. Although several of the books are displayed upright on the back ledge where the 'corner' is situated, there is no place to sit and read the books. There is no space for an exploratory reader, and during my period of observation no children approached this space to take a book. Reading in Grade 0 is a teacher-controlled group activity. But there is space to have a Reading Corner in this classroom – and homely cushions are not necessary. This is where the **rule of functional sites** can come into play. The under-used desk at the back of the classroom could be reorganized as a Reading Corner (and used as desk to work at, or a disciplinary space when needed). By Grade 1 the Reading Corner can no longer be classified as a **functional site** – it is merely a functional bookcase with prescribed readers. The Grade 3 bookcase had battered books and some children's annuals that were occasionally taken out and read or paged through by the children, but this was infrequent. Constructing a Reading Corner in these grades is hampered by the fact that a significant portion of space is taken up with additional desks and children as the class sizes increased. Added to this is additional space taken up by the larger bodies of 9-year-olds compared to 4-year-old bodies. Despite access to some books, the spatial configurations work against them being properly utilized.

The carpet

The carpet is one of the more interesting sites and, like the Reading Corner above, is also a site where access is systematically shut down to the children in the higher grades. Of all the sites it potentially has the most **functions**: both open and restricted, it is a space for play and performance, teaching and learning, a space to gather together as a class or in small groups, or it can be used for **surveillance** and discipline. It is in Grade 00 that is it most utilized.

Sibley (cited in Walkerdine, 2001) has argued with regards to playgrounds that children prefer waste ground and open space to play in rather than formalized playgrounds. This argument can be transferred into the classroom carpet space. The partitioning of the Grade 00 classroom illustrates this point – the carpet is divided into a fictional space, the Reading Corner, and an open space. Of these three spaces the open space is most frequented by the children. In times that belong to the children, like before the school day begins or when they have completed assigned tasks, the majority of the children play on the carpet.

After the bell rings the use of the site shifts, it becomes a site of both **surveillance** and whole-class teaching. The distribution of children in allocated rows facing Dawn, who sits on a chair, means that she has an unimpeded view of all the children. In this space Dawn's position of authority as the teacher is demonstrated by her control of the class both verbally and physically. The rules for what constitutes appropriate behaviour are most often targeted directly at children's bodies. One of the first things children need to learn is where they situate themselves in this space. It is not enough to know which group one belongs to. Each group has to create a straight line where there is enough space for everyone. This was a hard-learned practical lesson for several of the children who squashed into a space and found resistant bodies, or who were wedged into a space because other bodies moved. What was fascinating was how often the children tolerated their uncomfortable position before they were 'rescued' by Dawn, or literally took matters into their own hands. Verbal commands like 'Move your legs, don't sit on Chris', 'Sit away from those boys' were a frequent part of the lesson. Opposite to the encroachment of personal space was bodily dispersal, and children were told 'You are not in line', 'Come to your line', which was often accompanied by Dawn physically repositioning whole lines of children as well as individuals. Next, children had to learn how to sit – they were told to sit straight, with their legs crossed, flat on their backsides, and once again personal space was an issue with children told not to touch and hurt each other. Sitting still was another challenge, particularly since attention spans are limited – Dawn spent lots of time telling the children to turn around, so she could see their eyes and not the back of their heads. Even if negotiating space with peers had been mastered, sometimes children's own bodies did not respond to accepted social mores – with fingers needing to be extracted from noses.

At the end of their time on the carpet children are sent to the toilet and then to their desks. What is interesting about this routine is how the organization of bodies in these spaces allows for disciplinary control. One of the elements of a **functional site** is that it allows for supervision. Groups are sent one by one to the toilet, thus limiting disturbances in a confined area. For that moment groups are unsupervised by the teacher, but are subject to peer-regulation. The children who remain on the carpet are subject to supervision by the teacher as well as those returning from the toilet. The control of access to spaces by Dawn creates minimal disturbances.

The Grade 0 day also begins on the carpet. Children wait there until all the administration has been completed – the functioning of the carpet as a 'waiting area' then means that the space around Lisa's desk can be better utilized. This routine also indicates a decrease in the proximity of the teacher to the children. Dawn spends the majority of her time in the same place as the children. Lisa is not always with them. This indicates something about the level of control that is operating – the younger children require assistance that is often physical. The discipline is often instant and directed to the body. I do not mean this in the sense of corporal punishment. Rather, the children are told, shown, or moved to where they should be by the teacher. The Grade 0s on the other hand, have a little more space without direct teacher presence. The invisibility of disciplinary power becomes more evident because, although Lisa many not be occupying the same space, they are still under **surveillance**.

Children's distribution on the carpet is influenced by the first activity, Language Ring, with the children sitting on the edge of the carpet to make a circle (although the shape of the carpet creates a slightly 'rectangular' circle). Each child is allocated a particular space within the ring. By the end of the year this routine is habitual – children move to sit in their allocated spaces. What was striking was that they had internalized what was spatially appropriate for the body. On a day near the end of the year, when several children were absent, the remaining children sat in their space leaving the absent children's places open – these were not encroached on for both ring times that day.

The circle as a means of spatial distribution is an effective way of targeting the body in the exercise of power. The children *are* the circle. In this configuration they are all part of the disciplinary gaze as they watch each other, and are subject to the eyes watching them. It also means that children are not obscured by others as they might be when sitting randomly or in rows. Although a complete comparison cannot be made because the Grade 00s were at the beginning of the school year and the Grade 0s at the end of theirs, I suspect that there may have been less wriggling and touching of each other had the Grade 00s been in a circle. The closed nature of the circle also works to create a sense of unity. The teacher is a part of this and above it: her chair indicates a higher level of authority. The circle is also about inclusivity, it is easy to involve all the children and listen to individual voices. Lisa often went around the circle asking each child to read a word, identify a number, sing a song, or discuss their weekend, without the problems of direction encountered with other spatial formations. The literate subject who is constructed here is one that forms part of a group that learns to work together with the others.

The carpet is a **multifunctional site** in this class – it confines and limits disturbances, it allows for surveillance, the circle creates an intimate atmosphere, and it is big enough to play games on. But its openness is also a dangerous space because it invites expansive movement. It invites performance. For example when Lisa was called to the office one day some of the boys stood in the middle of the carpet and began to dance. The rest of the children began to clap in rhythm with the dancers (see Chapter 4 for a detailed discussion of this incident).

By Grade 1 the carpet space begins to be more highly regulated. It is no longer a space to play. If playing does happen it is not sanctioned. The activities that take place on the carpet are, on the whole, related to literacy: whole-class reading, group reading, individual reading, and story time. Alongside this, discussions take place, like Weekend News, as well as the introduction of new letters of the alphabet often accompanied by stories and pictures.

There was a marked difference in the time the two Grade 1 classes spent on the carpet. In the one class it was minimal, with children on the carpet for individual reading. This was done either by the teacher herself or a teaching assistant who moved between classes. On one occasion the class sat on the carpet to discuss their Weekend News. They sat randomly. Story time usually takes place on the carpet with the whole class, but in this class the children sat at their desks while the teacher read a book to them from the carpet.

In contrast, the other class spent more time on the carpet. The Monday Weekend News discussion often, but not always, was on the carpet, before the children drew their news. The end of the day story time took place on the carpet. The children were also taught to read on the carpet as a whole class, or in small groups. This latter organization reveals a **ranking**: the groups were organized in relation to ability, while the spatial positioning of the teacher facing towards the desks allowed for whole-class **surveillance**. To be on the carpet involves training bodies to behave appropriately. Not all children had the benefit of preschool training. The first aspect is getting there quietly – the children are told to go 'on tips of toes' and not to scrape their chairs when they move from their desks. In order to lessen the chaos, girls or boys are sent to the carpet first. The children are also allocated a place to sit. They are **ranked** according to height and are seated next to the opposite gender in a particular row so that they can all see. This procedure took a while to orchestrate. They were told where to sit on the second day of school; a week later they had forgotten where they were placed, and a month and a half later still had to be told. If the children sit on the carpet in a smaller group then they are often arranged in a circle. Once again the shape of the circle enables the systematic orchestration of tasks so that each child participates with the group and contributes as an individual.

By Grade 3, the carpet is predominantly a restricted space. The only time children sit there is to eat lunch. At other times it is empty or occupied by the teacher. It functions primarily as a teaching site. Only on one observed occasion did children enter the space to report back on definitions of spelling words. The groups they sat in were given spelling words to look up in the dictionary. Once the definitions were written down, one or two children were chosen from the groups to read these out to the class (see Chapter 6 for a discussion of this task). At other times it functioned as a disciplinary site of **peer surveillance**. Children stand at the blackboard and write down the names of 'talkers' (see Chapter 4 for a more detailed discussion).

Children's desks

The organization of children's desks plays a role in disciplining and constructing subjects. What emerges is how spatial distribution is a means through which children are classified. The clearest example of this was in the Grade 00 class. At the beginning of the year five groups were randomly created and identified by colours: pink, blue, purple, white, yellow. But Dawn had expressed a desire for a smaller class, and on the employment of another teacher she reduced her class size and reorganized the groups. This reorganization illustrates the operation of **rank**, where bodies are individualized and placed in a system of classification that is not fixed. Knowledge of the children resulted in a new system of classification. Four groups existed and were renamed: bees, butterflies, snails, and grasshoppers. Children were grouped according to their perceived learning abilities:

> I've got the … butterfly table, I've grouped them as the more advanced group, that's the girls who are quick … and then I've got the little grasshopper group and they are slower … and the snail group is my slowest group.
>
> (Interview 7 June 2002)

It is interesting that the group names reflect the children's ability with the butterflies being the 'high fliers', and the snails the traditional representation of 'slow movers'. It is probably not coincidental either that the perceived levels of academic achievement mirror the levels of flight and speed these animals can or cannot achieve. The names of the groups hold within them constructions of the quick/intelligent, average, and slow learner. This was unconscious on Dawn's part and when her attention was drawn to it she commented on the need to alter this naming practice.

This **ranking** is also practical. In a classroom constituted by children who do not speak English as their mother tongue, as well as children who do, the groups are classified in terms of their ability to comprehend instructions. Each group is seen as a singular entity, so there are four sets of instructions to deliver as opposed to 24. With particular groups located in specific areas, Dawn has more time to give attention to specific children or activities (e.g. baking, painting) that require her intervention. She says:

> When you give out your instructions you give them to one group, you try to group your children in a homogeneous fashion on a table so the instructions going to those children are on one level and when you get your next table for the same activity you give it in another fashion.
>
> (Interview 27 June 2002)

She communicates these instructions verbally and with her body, demonstrating what the children are required to do. While this may imply a connection between language acquisition and academic ability, the distinction is not as clear-cut. Gender also comes into play in categorizing and classifying the groups. The butterfly table was made up of girls who had been constructed as 'quick'. Only one of the girls in this group speaks English as her mother tongue. The teacher's observations and experience with children have led her to believe that girls are better regulated subjects than boys. While she was hesitant to make any generalizations about gendered behaviour, the subject that is constructed as 'quick' displays a range of behaviour that conforms to notions of a disciplined subject, a subject who has begun to internalize the practices necessary for operating in a school environment. Such subjects 'regard their work as more important', 'fall into routine faster', are quieter (than boys who are 'lively'), and 'are better listeners and can concentrate better' (Interview 27 June 2002).

While language acquisition and gender affect how subjects are constructed and classified, power relations are not unidirectional. Power exists in action, and children are complicit in their subjectification. It is through the actions of the children that space is made in this classroom for reclassification. As they are subjects under constant **surveillance**, assessments of them alter. The groups are not rigid and children are moved depending on their performance. The classification of these children is influenced by understandings of child development and by the subjective opinions of the teacher. An example of the problems of communicative competence, teacher subjectivity, and developmental norms is illustrated by a girl whose abilities came as a surprise, and were then duly acknowledged:

> And if you ask me where, what level is that child, or that, at first you make your own opinion of what you think they can do and then they surprise you. Like Thandeka – she hasn't got the language, she didn't have the language at all and I thought her skills were behind and eventually when she got the self-image and confidence and everything to talk to me, her skills went up like this. And, she won the prize for the best colouring-in in my class and the best cutting.
>
> (Interview 27 June 2002)

In Grade 0 the grouping of children at desks remains (Figure 2.6). This layout of desks echoes the significance of the open carpet in this classroom; it is a place for groups rather than the individual. Effective classroom organization has been linked to achievement. Teachers who organize their classrooms effectively make decisions about grouping children according to their needs and the tasks set (Wray, Medwell, Poulson, & Fox, 2002). Although the classification of children via seating arrangements is not as explicit as in Grade 00, a level of ranking still operates. In this class of 26, the girls outnumber the boys by six. Twenty of the children were seated next to a child of the opposite gender, the six 'extra' girls sat in an all-girl group. Placing boys next to girls in a co-educational setting is not unusual, and the accepted wisdom is that girls exert a calming influence over the boys. The choice of the girls in the girls' group was not random. Their placement on the opposite side of the class to Lisa's desk implies a measure of independence. They are still under **surveillance**, but members of this group were all competent and confident students. This is in contrast to the weakest students who were placed in the group in front of Lisa's desk – she is close to them in order to monitor them and provide assistance.

One of the disadvantages of arranging children in groups is the prevalence of copying. This is pervasive across all the grades. The children have not internalized what is an important aspect of the schooled subject – the need to work independently. Lisa says:

> But I find what's incredible, is um they, their pictures are, like if I told them to draw a spider web with the spider inside, they can all draw it and that's not because they can all draw it, that's all because they copy each other and that's OBE [Outcomes Based Education]?... But I wonder how many of them actually knew how to draw it in the first place?... When they bring me their work, their work's done, but how many of them can actually do it by themselves the first time?
>
> (Interview 26 November 2002)

The greatest change spatially for the children moving from Grade 0 into Grade 1 is the increased amount of time they are required to spend at their desks. It should also be remembered that for some this is their first experience of schooling. Although a fair amount of teaching, listening, and discussion takes place at their desks, all of this leads to tasks requiring children to draw and/or write. This presents its own challenge because children have to position themselves correctly in a desk space:

> Sitting at a desk involves a complicated break up of patterns, i.e. flexed ankles, knees and hips with an extended spine and controlled flexion (to look down at your book) and extension (to look up at the board) of the neck. This needs to take place against a background of unconscious postural stability. In addition to this you need to be able to free your arms from your body in order to perform fine motor tasks such as writing, move your eyes independently of your head and to organize your desk. As if that is not enough, the child is also expected to listen to information, process it and remember it.
>
> (Parker, 2003: no page number)

Thus not only do children spend more time in this space, but the bodily training required to function here is far more complex than needed for sitting on a carpet. A further complication is that at the beginning of the year the Grade 1s were required to share desks that were organized in rows. Sitting two to a table involves the children negotiating and organizing their space. This proved to be quite tricky for many of them. For the first time they worked in books as opposed to loose sheets of paper. Their books overlapped each other, or they were positioned at incorrect angles, children wrote across and over each other, and pencil boxes were imbued with kinesthetic qualities. Overall classroom organization plays a role in how children negotiate this space. At the beginning of the year both classes' rows of desks faced the board – this arrangement is beneficial in terms of spatial perception as many children appear to have difficulty transferring information written on the board to their books if they are not facing it. But while the hexagonal tables of Grade 00 and the groups of desks in Grade 0 provide some bulk and stability to limit movement, one table with two children does not. Tables, chairs, and children regularly gravitated in different directions, and Grade 1 teachers spent a large amount of time repositioning bodies and furniture.

Unlike the other classrooms in the study whose organization did not vary, both Grade 1 classroom layouts, and particularly children's desk space, altered frequently. Fieldnotes and spatial diagrams reveal that although the children in Catherine's Grade 1 class sat in rows until the end of the second term when they were reorganized into groups, the children were reseated on eight occasions during the term. Some of this reorganization took place during periods when I was present observing in the class; if the class had been reseated when I was not present the new arrangement was noted during the next observation session. Thus it is possible that more incidents of reseating may have occurred. Over the course of two terms this seems to be quite a substantial reorganization. On the first day of school the children in this class chose their own place to sit. Two weeks later they were moved. The most obvious **ranking** was according to gender, with girls being placed next to boys. This was the one constant in the **ranking** that continued throughout the reshuffling. Reorganization appeared to arise as a result of breakdown in classroom discipline – when the children were very noisy or disruptive changes came about. There was no set time at which it occurred. The reasons for which these children sat next to each other at various stages does not indicate the type of classification present in the Grade 00 or Grade 0 classes, or indeed in the other Grade 1 class. In these reorganizations, the teacher was aware of children whose English was limited. Placing children together was a means of providing peer support:

> Like children with language barriers ... they don't understand what is expected of them, they'll probably just copy from somebody next to them. So then they probably need to talk to somebody.... You know to relate to the topic. Even we, adults, if we're in a new place with a new uh things to be done, like assignments and things like that, we need to liaise with other people, you know, to help us.
>
> (Interview 14 May 2003)

In contrast, observations revealed that Helen's Grade 1 class was reorganized three times. The reasoning for this reveals the disciplinary practice of classification operating in a far more systematic way. The teacher describes the way the class is organized:

> At the beginning of the year I put them alphabetically, usually, but I put them like in rows of four where they're all just facing the front and then after about two weeks in which I have watched them do different things then what I try to do is to put the weak ones close to my table, or those that aren't finished their work close to my table ... in the beginning of the year I group them according to how they work, like if they work quickly and they know their work they go to one group ... and then at least you don't have to waste time ... and then you can spend a bit more time with the others. Then, the second term what I do is mix them, but I still try to keep those that don't finish their work closer to where I am.
>
> (Interview 21 May 2003)

The classroom organization reflects this. In the beginning the children were arranged alphabetically in rows, with a girl and a boy allocated to each desk. In the fourth week of schooling the desks were rearranged into five groups seating eight children. At that stage children were not ranked according to ability, but rather were grouped from the original alphabetical classification. Moving the desks together created groups. At the end of the month, academic ability was the classificatory factor, and the arrangement of children revealed that the weakest group was situated next to the teacher's desk with the weakest child closest to her. The final recorded organization took place on the first day of the second term. The teacher's desk was placed at the back of the class in the centre, flanked by two groups. This placement allowed her access to the two weakest groups.

Classroom control is also affected by the distribution of girls and boys. To be able to maintain some order, groups are mixed. The teacher commented how seating can affect children's equilibrium, and her own:

> I won't put eight girls together, even if they work the best, I will never do that to myself … it's just too much yakkety, yakkety, yakkety, yakkety – come what may. Even the boys, can't put them all together 'cos they all fight. Sometimes the girls are also nasty to each other: 'I don't want to be your friend' and blah blah and then they start crying. But … they do form friendships, I sometimes just put the one on this side of the classroom and the other on that side and then maybe for two weeks I'll decide okay maybe I'll put all the friends together and see how it goes, like give them a chance, even if it's just for a week. Sometimes even just for a few days and then I can't handle it anymore, then I just split them up.
>
> (Interview 21 May 2003)

By Grade 3 the children are expected to have sufficient discipline to work properly for an extended period. Incorrect posture was more often a sign of resistance to the expected norms than ignorance. For the first time in a classroom in this study, the desk set aside for disruptive children was utilized. It was placed in the front of the classroom next to the door. This placement, being slightly away from the other groups of desks, signalled its marginal position and isolation from the group. This desk was regularly occupied by two boys during the term (see Chapter 7 for a discussion of Manny's incarceration).

The constraints and possibilities of spatial distribution in classrooms

The detailed discussion across all five classrooms presented here aims to provide evidence for Foucault's claim that the use of space and the distribution of individuals within space play an essential role in the production and construction of subjects. But these five classrooms cannot represent different classrooms locally, or globally; nor the sole means through which children are regulated and managed in spaces. What the practices in these classrooms do reveal in their similarities and differences are practical issues around managing children and their impact on pedagogy.

One of the areas that struck me most in considering these findings was the connection between the use of space and classroom order. Many of the disciplinary problems encountered by these teachers were exacerbated by a limited understanding and control of the classroom space. Efficient use of the space often limited problems. An important point can then be made: controlling space to maintain discipline is not necessarily about keeping children confined to a particular space. Keeping children confined to a space may in fact be an act of incarceration. Overall it seemed that there was little understanding and reflection from the teachers about the decisions they made with regards to how they utilized space and distributed children within it. Understanding the connection between the constraints and possibilities that classroom space affords, and the impact it has on constructing subjects, is an issue that needs careful consideration.

The constraints teachers face in relation to space can be broadly categorized as those that are practical and those that are affected by teachers' knowledge and beliefs. Space cannot be utilized in uniform ways. It needs to be analysed in relation to what it offers and the needs of individual teachers. Classroom size is a constraining factor. How space is used in Grade 0 cannot be the same for Grade 3, because although the size of the classroom remains the same, the number of children increased by 15. Nine-year-olds are also physically bigger than 6-year-olds. So it is not surprising that a greater fluidity of movement was present in the largest classroom (Grade 00), or where numbers were smaller (Grade 0). Large numbers of students mean that available space is taken up by children's desks to seat children. This is the reality in many South African classrooms. Resources are another issue. Spaces are clearly demarcated in the resource-rich preschool classrooms. Such demarcations show when and how spaces are used. But spaces do not need overt boundaries. Setting up an activity in one space, or labelling a desk as a space for transgressive children, and designating a Reading Corner, are just as powerful.

The use of space also reflects a certain mindset which points to teachers' knowledge and beliefs. The pre-primary subject is expected to play, and in the process learns to spend more time on tasks. Formal schooling requires a far more sedentary subject who, for the most part, learns alone without the closeness that is established by the morning rings of the preschool. The question to ask is whether it is essential that children become more sedentary as they move through school, especially with growing concerns about childhood obesity. To answer this it is useful to think about how movement flows through the pre-primary classroom can be effectively implemented with older classes. The key difference between the preschool and primary classes is the degree of movement through space – the younger children worked in one space and played in others. They were not confined to one area for most of the day. In the older grades where play is restricted, movement does not have to be. The clearest example of this is the one Grade 1 class – the children no longer have a space to play, but movement from the carpet to their desks can take place throughout the day for various activities. The children are allowed to move. As a class they displayed more discipline when at their desks than the other two primary classes. This movement from one place to another is highly regulated by ritual. So these children are subjected to a higher level of disciplinary control as their movements from one space to another are controlled. The positive effects of disciplinary power can be seen – access to space is controlled and orderly, there is no unknown, children know where they should be and how to get there, no child is forced out of a space. The level of disciplinary control is constant because the subject is under close scrutiny by the teacher. Yet, within a more controlled environment these subjects have greater access to space and movement (see Chapter 4).

Probably the most important aspect of spatial distribution is the **rule of functional sites**. Thinking about space as multifunctional rather than fixed is very powerful and perhaps also requires a change in mindset. The carpet is the clearest example of a multifunctional site but across time it is under-utilized. It does not make sense to confine children to their desks and intensify disruptions when groups can be split and sent to complete tasks on the carpet, thus shifting the classroom dynamic. There is no rule stating that a classroom, or part of it, cannot be rearranged during the day to do this, or that, in large classes, older children cannot be productively engaged just outside the classroom. Part of this 'fixedness' about classrooms comes from government 'wisdom'. There is pressure on teachers to arrange their desks so that children sit in groups, to 'reflect' the Outcomes Based (OBE), learner-centred teaching system that South Africa has adopted. Conversations with teachers revealed that education officials visiting the school required that the children be arranged in groups. These kinds of demand have led to the perception that OBE can be equated to group work and a misconception that learner-centred lessons cannot be focused on individuals instead of groups.

There are some serious disadvantages to arranging classrooms in this way. From an early literacy point of view, when children are learning to write and the majority of work is written on the blackboard for them to copy, facing away from the board increases the probability of making perceptual mistakes. From a disciplinary point of view, this configuration can also create a number of problems. The first has to deal with inter-group confrontation. While fighting among each other is prevalent in all classes, the proximity of sitting in groups can exacerbate tensions which teachers have to deal with. Alongside this is copying, itself a source of contention among children. While there are merits to peer teaching, merely placing children next to each other does not guarantee that instruction will take place. The Grade 3 group I spent most of my time with is a case in point. There was no real peer teaching. Travis, who was academically the strongest child, was annoyed by the demands for help made by the others. It may also have been a reason why he worked exceptionally fast, and often untidily (see Chapter 6). Sitting in groups increased the noise levels to the point where some teachers at Southside resorted to whistles to regain control.

The impact of arranging children in groups needs to be carefully thought through. Arranging desks in rows, or another configuration that creates some distance between individuals, may be more helpful for inexperienced teachers in maintaining initial control of a class. Moreover, children need to be trained to sit together in groups for the positive elements of this configuration to work. This brings me back to the point about seeing spaces as fluid or fixed. In my interview with Gail, she discussed how, in her Grade 3 classroom, desks are arranged in rows for the majority of lessons; however, when group tasks are required, desks are turned to face each other to create groups. A classroom can become a Reading Corner for a short time and children can be trained to reorganize their space effectively. In classrooms that are fixed, space can still be reconfigured. Many children in Africa are taught in spaces that were not originally built as schools. For example, at a preschool in rural Malawi children are taught in a church. The children sit on fixed concrete pews. Although the pews are immovable the children are not, they are also small. If the pews are not seen solely as seats but also as desks they could be used far more profitably. Children would not just be required to listen and repeat but could draw, and touch and feel and work with items placed on the 'desks' (Dixon, Place, & Kholowa, 2008).

My observation of pre-service teachers' lessons during the practical component of their degree brings this home to me. I am often struck by how ineffectively they, as the 'teacher', use the space/s in the classroom: how they manage and control access to spaces; how the classroom itself is organized; how they distribute students within classrooms. Some minor adjustments can often provide answers as to why seemingly well-thought-out lessons go awry for no apparent reason. As with the limited reflection on the part of the teachers in this research, student teachers' lack of understanding points to a failure on the part of teacher trainers to take the workings of space into account. When discipline and classroom management become more and more of an issue and teachers struggle to maintain discipline, it makes sense to provide explicit information about techniques that teachers, especially inexperienced ones, can use in their classrooms.

Thus, understanding the relationship between classroom order and spatial organization is important. Such an understanding foregrounds what is often implicit or intuitive knowledge gained though trial, error, and experience. Such knowledge is a way of enabling teachers to reflect on decisions made in classrooms that have an impact on the way children learn and the type of learning they are exposed to. Since much of this knowledge is implicit and disparate there is work to be done. The questions that end this chapter are preliminary questions that can be used by pre-service teachers to research the use of space in classrooms, or for teachers to reflect on practice and consider the possibility of transforming practice. They could also be rephrased to consider other educational settings:

- Which spaces are used in the classroom?
- What are they used for? (How are they used?)
- How often are they used (daily, weekly, monthly)?
- Who has access to these spaces?
- What are the rules for being in these spaces?
- How are these rules taught?

- What does this reveal about classroom power relations and the kind of subjects that are being produced?
- Are there any under-utilized spaces? Why?
- Can any spaces be used more or reconfigured?
- What would be required to do this? (Is this possible?)
- What other spaces are available (e.g. outside for some activities)?

Chapter 3

Space and time

The previous chapter concluded with a discussion of some of the challenges teachers may face in thinking about classroom spaces. But, the discussion of the relationship between space and classroom order is limited. This is because, as May and Thrift (2001: 3) put it, 'time is irrevocably bound up with the spatial constitution of society (and vice versa)'. Social theory has a tendency to make distinctions between space and time, treating them separately or privileging space over time when in fact they are interlocked (Foucault, 2000a; May & Thrift, 2001; Soja, 1980, 2000). This argument can be illustrated quite simply. Schools are microcosms of societies that work to train and produce particular kinds of citizens. As established in the previous chapter, an essential part of this training focuses on the ways individuals are distributed in space. But the distribution and redistribution of individuals in space take place at specific times. Regular distribution also points to the establishment of routines. The existence of a routine is dependent on an act being reinforced and internalized over time. Conforming to regular routines reflects submission to disciplinary power. Classroom management and the construction and disciplining of subjects are dependent on routine as well as a number of other disciplinary techniques that are temporal in nature.

Before considering the connections between space and time it is necessary to explore the organization and operation of time in and across these classrooms. This picture of daily routines is then mapped in the form of movement flow diagrams across classroom spaces. The space–time relationship is further explored through the use of photographs of bodies in classrooms. These set up a space to reflect upon what an understanding of space–time can add to our knowledge of classroom practice.

The temporal control of activity

Foucault (1977) refers to the disciplinary nature of time as the **control of activity**. The overarching means through which time is used to control activity is the **timetable**. There are four specific means of control: **the temporal elaboration of the act, the correlation of body and gesture, body–object articulation**, and **exhaustive use**. These terms will be explained in greater detail using practical examples.

Timetables establish a general framework of activity in three ways. They *establish rhythms, impose particular occupations, and regulate cycles of repetition* (Foucault, 1977). In order to establish what this general framework looks like at Acacia and Southside, daily class routines were examined across the data. From this, timelines for each grade were constructed. Figures 3.1 to 3.4 outline the school day with its starting and finishing times and what Jenks (2001) calls 'curriculum time', which is controlled by teachers, and 'play time', which is time perceived by children as under their control. I find the use of the term 'play time' problematic as there are a number of instances in the early years where 'play time' is scheduled into the curriculum and is thus teacher controlled. An example of this is when the Southside teachers would take the children to play on the jungle gyms behind the Grade 3 classes during the day, or before the end of the school day (see Figure 2.3). The children were observed by the teacher, but their play was not for the purposes of formal assessment. The issue of who controls time is useful in making this distinction more nuanced. I prefer to use the term 'free play' to indicate when play is child-directed. This takes place most often in the playground during breaks. The term free play does not mean that it is unaccompanied by teacher **surveillance** though.

The timelines show a recurring daily sequence of events that indicates the *establishment of rhythm*. This rhythm and daily *cycle of repetition* are regulated by the bell (which is indicated by the horizontal black lines in each figure) and marks a major shift in activity from curriculum time to free play or vice versa. The bell is a marker of time and a signal of authority to which the children need to submit.

The signal of the bell to start each school day at 8:00 a.m. also illustrates the second aspect of the control of activity: the **temporal elaboration of the act**. This requires that bodies perform particular acts where they are positioned, or given directions. Acts may also be of a certain duration and performed in a specific sequence. These scheduled movements of bodies are referred to as the 'anatomo-chronological schema of behaviour' (Foucault, 1977: 152). At Acacia many children play in the classroom before the school day begins. The bell signals that they are to stop

08:00	BELL: DAY STARTS
	CURRICULUM TIME
10:30	FREE PLAY
11:30	CURRICULUM TIME
12:30	END OF SCHOOL DAY

Figure 3.1 Grade 00 timeline.

08:00	BELL: DAY STARTS
	CURRICULUM TIME
10:00	FREE PLAY
10:15	CURRICULUM TIME
11:50	FREE PLAY
12:10	CURRICULUM TIME
13:00	END OF SCHOOL DAY

Figure 3.2 Grade 0 timeline.

08:00	BELL: DAY STARTS
	CURRICULUM TIME
10:00	FREE PLAY
10:15	CURRICULUM TIME
11:50	FREE PLAY
12:10	CURRICULUM TIME
13:00	END OF SCHOOL DAY

Figure 3.3 Grade I timeline.

08:00	BELL: DAY STARTS
	CURRICULUM TIME
10:00	FREE PLAY
10:15	CURRICULUM TIME
11:50	FREE PLAY
12:10	CURRICULUM TIME
13:30	END OF SCHOOL DAY

Figure 3.4 Grade 3 timeline.

playing. They are given directions to perform the task of tidying up any toys or equipment they have been using. They then are positioned, because they have to arrange themselves on the carpet in rows according to the group they have been allocated to. The duration of this procedure is relatively fluid and is dependent on how much the children have to put away. This is in contrast to Southside where the **temporal elaboration of the act** is more tightly orchestrated. The entire Foundation Phase is required to perform the act of lining up in the quadrangle that is flanked by the Foundation Phase classrooms (Figure 2.3). Each class is allocated a space with a row for boys and one for girls. This procedure is to be carried out as quickly as possible and in silence. Important messages and instructions for the day are relayed. Each class is then led off in rows, class by class, by their teacher to their classrooms.

The most obvious change across the grades is the lengthening of the school day and the insertion of additional curriculum time. In Grade 00, of a four-and-a-half-hour school day, three and a half hours are spent on teacher-controlled activities, with an hour allocated to free play. Not all this curriculum time is given over to formal learning. By Grade 0 the school day has been extended to five hours. The organization of the Grade 0 day mirrors the Grade 1 day. Although the day has been extended, free play has been reduced to 35 minutes and is divided into two 'breaks', one of 15 minutes and the other 20 minutes. Curriculum time is now divided into three segments. However, it should be noted that because the Grade 0 class was located at Southside Primary, their timetable is directly affected by the rest of the school; had this class been at Acacia Preschool, the school day would have the same duration as the Grade 00 class. In addition, the length of the school day indicated here reflects the standard school day, but the school day is shorter for the first month of schooling for the entire Foundation Phase. The Grade 0s and Grade 1s end at midday for the first month of school, and the Grade 3s at 1:00 p.m. By the end of the Foundation Phase, although time allocated for free play remains the same, an additional half hour of curriculum time has been added, with the Grade 3s ending at 1:30 p.m. Thus in terms of the school day, an hour has been added from preschool (four and a half hours) to the end of the Foundation Phase (five and a half hours), but curriculum time increases by an hour and a half. The next time the school day will be lengthened is upon entrance into high school (in Grade 8).

Timetables as imposers of occupation and repetition

The general timelines of Figures 3.1–3.4 give an impression of overall continuity in the move from preschool to primary school. This is in fact not the case. By adding the specific daily routines into the timelines and examining them in relation to the additional functions of the timetable, that of the *imposition of occupation* and *regulation of cycles of repetition*, shifts emerge between the two phases of schooling (Figures 3.5–3.8). This section also considers how literacy is 'timetabled' into the curriculum across the grades as a way of beginning to think about the construction of the literate subject.

Grade 00

Jenks (2001: 73) sums up the connection between disciplinary regularity and time when he argues that:

> Discipline it would seem involves a control of a body, or more specifically an activity, and does so, most effectively through a timetable, children are required to eat, sleep, wash and excrete mostly at specific and regular times. For the child then even the most elementary functions are scheduled and play which we superficially regard as free and perhaps creative occurs in designated spaces in the curriculum.

This is very much the case in the Grade 00 classroom. As Figure 3.5 illustrates it is not just learning that is timetabled but the regulation of children's behaviour. The day-to-day routine is divided into seven clear sections: tidy-up time, morning activities, toilet time, perceptual activities, lunch time, play time, and story time. It is interesting that five of these routines use the word time; indicating the importance of time as an organizing factor. Each day follows the same pattern in Grade 00. After tidy-up time the children sit on the carpet. Requiring children to tidy up is a means of constructing subjects who have internalized norms about their environment as well as working with others. This task also functions as an immediate disciplinary technique by focusing the children's attention and thus quietening them down, since the play they have been engaged in is often at odds with the docile posture they are required to assume for more formal schooling. On average, children spend an hour and a half on the carpet, where the majority of the activities are done orally.

08:00	BELL: DAY STARTS
	Tidy-up time **Morning activities:** **Prayer, register, Lunch Book,** **weather and days of the week,** **weekly theme / Interest Table /** **Show and Tell, singing, story** **Toilet time** **Perceptual activities**
09.45	**Lunchtime**
10.30	**FREE PLAY**
11.30	**Story time** **(Sleep)**
12.30	**End of school day**

Figure 3.5 Grade 00 routines.

In terms of the literacy practices that take place for Morning Ring, the regulation of repetition is evident in the pattern of events. Dawn does all the reading and writing required, while the children listen and speak. The first literacy event is the taking of the register where administrative **surveillance** comes into play. A question–answer format is followed: Dawn asks '[Name of child], are you here?' The required response from the children is 'Yes, Teacher, I am here'. This response was enforced by Dawn. The children's answers were reinforced with compliments like 'That's nice answering'.

Once the register is completed, numeracy becomes both a disciplinary and learning tool. The class count aloud together from one to twenty while Dawn counts the number of children she has marked down on the register and then writes this number in the Lunch Book. Counting each morning is a way to learn numbers, but in this exercise the children do not assign a value to the number of bodies present in the class, as Dawn is constrained by the fact that she should only teach the numbers up to 20. There are more than 20 children in the class. Counting has a greater disciplinary function than an educational one because the children are not told that they are counting to see who is present. The counting occupies their attention. This was clearly evident on days when children were restless; once the counting began and they all joined in, disruption ceased.

The Lunch Book is then taken to the kitchen; the child who takes it returns to do the weather. She or he stands in the front of the class and is asked 'What's the weather like today?' A weather chart is stuck up on the wall at the appropriate height for the children to read and use. When the children have reached agreement on that day's weather, the appropriate picture on the chart is identified and a marker placed on it. Next come days of the week; the class is asked what day it is and then they all repeat the days of the week. The influence of Christianity is felt through the morning prayer.[1] A child is chosen to lead the class in praying for help in order to become what is an essentially compliant subject. The class is trained to assume the correct bodily position: 'hands together, eyes closed'. The prayer is the same each morning:[2]

> Thank you dear Lord Jesus for watching over me all night long
> Now in this new day help me to be good and kind
> And bless everyone that I love. Amen.

After this the children sing a variety of songs. Some days the choice of songs is determined by Dawn, at other times children suggest songs or Dawn begins the songs and then lets the children choose their own. There are a number of activity songs requiring movement to correspond with the lyrics. Once again, such songs are disciplinary in nature; the class is controlled via the movements of individual bodies engaged in the task.

The individual bodies are controlled via the activity. The **control of activity** is evident through the **temporal elaboration of the act** – children are given directions to move particular body parts, and a **correlation between the body and gesture** needs to exist.

The better the children know the songs the greater their speed and efficiency in moving particular body parts in time with the words of the songs. These techniques are powerful and evident throughout all the classes. The moment these children's bodies are engaged in directed movements they become engaged. Disruptions and inattentiveness halt. Children are unable to be inattentive when they focus on the words of the song and move their bodies in time with the words.

Each week there are discussions about the weekly theme when various objects related to the theme are placed on the Interest Table. Every Friday is Show and Tell, when what the children bring may, or may not, be related to the theme. Sometimes the children are also told Bible stories. If a child brings a story book to class Dawn makes a point of reading it aloud.

When the activities on the carpet are completed the children are sent to the toilet. The children are being trained so that their excretory processes are brought into line with curriculum time. This is not strictly enforced as there is no rule in this class that children cannot go to the toilet any time they need to. However, access to this space is controlled by the teacher because children ask for permission at other times during the day.

Children spend the next hour of the day at their group table. Each group is given a particular task to do that is set out at their table. Some tasks deal with fine motor co-ordination like threading beads, playing with dough, building puzzles; others are more clearly related to emergent literacy practices like drawing, painting, colouring in, cutting and pasting. Performing each task requires the **temporal elaboration of the act** (of threading, colouring in, etc.) as well as the **correlation of the body and gesture**. The fourth element of the control of activity is significant and comes into play with these tasks: the **body–object articulation**. This is where the children learn 'the relations the body must have with the object that it manipulates' (Foucault, 1977: 153). For example if a child is going to cut out a picture, the object that they need to manipulate is a pair of scissors. A series of gestures must be mastered in order to make the blades of the scissors move up and down to cut a piece of paper. The child needs to put their thumb through the top handle of the scissors and two or three fingers through the bottom handle (depending on the size of the scissors), bending them around the handle to hold the scissors. They then need to move their thumb and fingers, opening the hand slightly to open the blades. The other hand holds the piece of paper being cut and inserts it between the blades, and the fingers in the scissors contract, closing the blades and cutting the paper. The more complex the cutting, the more small movements need to be made simultaneously with the hand holding the scissors and the hand holding the paper. The **body–object articulation** is crucial for early literacy; in this class children learn to handle pencils, felt-tipped pens, paintbrushes, magazines, paper, glue, and scissors to create their own texts.

Sometimes the distinction between work and play is blurred as a group's designated activity may be to play. Children are sent to the fictional play area, or may play with building blocks on the carpet. Although there is a set time in which activities are done, the time it takes to complete each activity is not highly regulated. When children have finished their task they move to another table – Dawn often tells them where to go, sometimes they move of their own accord. Some children work faster than others. Sometimes children work for a bit, have a 'play-break' and then return. It takes some children a while to settle into this routine. Ideally, once all tasks are completed the children are free to play by themselves. Dawn believes that the classroom is a space that allows 'free movement' so that the children

> experiment on their own.... Our school is a play school and what we do here is not formal, if they want to walk around and if they want to play you leave them ... life is very formalized, let them play as long as they want to.
>
> (Interview 27 June 2002)

While this comment may be true to a degree and indicates that time is not so tightly regulated because there can be a blurring between teacher-controlled play and free play, time as an element of disciplinary power still operates, as is evident from the comment Dawn made when reflecting on the children's development in six months:

> I can see there're children who wouldn't sit to work, that I had to prompt to come to table that are now sitting properly and using the apparatus and they can sit and do a picture. I mean, for instance, Thumi, Thumi if you leave [him] he'll play in a corner and he would never come to the table, but you call them and keep pulling them to the table and he'll actually sit and do a picture.
>
> (Interview 27 June 2002)

Children are required to conform to the daily routines; it is through these routines that they learn to be both schooled and literate subjects. It is through the daily inculcation of the routine that behaviour is internalized – thus the emphasis is on the aspects of the **control of activity,** i.e. the **temporal elaboration of the act,** the **correlation of body and gesture,** and the **body–object articulation**. At this stage of schooling discipline is central; bodies need to master activities first before they can be performed within tasks that have a specific duration. There is no preoccupation with allocating precise units of time to prescribed activities; rather, the repetitive nature of daily routines is central. This has implications in the on-going construction of the schooled subject. As children move into more formalized schooling, a greater number of occupations will be imposed with regularity that they will be expected to complete. These children are internalizing these routines. If their development in six months suggests a greater acquiescence to completing tasks and limiting play in curriculum time, then they are on the way to entering primary school as well-regulated subjects.

Grade 0

The pattern of regulation of repetition that the timetable provides emerges again in the Grade 0 class. When asked to describe the daily routine of the Grade 0s, Lisa replied (see also Figure 3.6):

08:00	BELL: DAY STARTS
	Administration First ring (language)
09:30	Toilet Lunch
10:00	FREE PLAY
10:15	Creative activity Second ring
11:50	FREE PLAY
12:10	Story time
13:00	END OF SCHOOL DAY

Figure 3.6 Grade 0 routines.

Right we come in, uh, what we do is we do register, we do tuckshop, we do all the admin first. At half past eight we do our language ring and with language I bring in numbers, uh, because they are saying the numbers, they're counting from one to whatever they talk about and discuss, we talk about the uh, the theme for the week um we sing songs, so anything they can vocalize we do in the morning, then what they do is straight after that um at about quarter past nine, we go to toilet, half past nine, we eat lunch, that, until ten past ten, first break, they come back at about half past ten, we start our creative activity, after creative act, creative activity we um we have our second ring which is usually at about eleven, half past eleven, um no I'd say about quarter past eleven, half past eleven we start our second ring, which is music or movements or perception or drama, like we did um what's it called Christmas play today. Or whatever the second ring is, or maths ring, that kind of thing then um after that is second break after second break, uh second break's twelve, after second break we go and play on the perceptual playground,[3] so they can use their gross motor muscles until half past twelve, half past twelve we come in, we read a story and then they go home.

(Interview 26 November 2002)

What is striking about this answer is the increasing temporal organization. There are eleven references to time as well as specific references to sequencing activities. What happens in this class is similar to the Grade 00s. Both days begin with the register and organizing food (tuck) for those who require it. But in Grade 0 administration is no longer a part of the lesson, it precedes it. The morning activity, Language Ring, contains similar elements to the Grade 00s. As in Grade 00 it is predominantly teacher directed and operates in the oral mode. A weekly theme remains, as well as an Interest Table. The level of discussion varies depending on the day of the week. Each morning the previous day's work is recapped and new information is added. Lisa starts from what the children know and moves on to give additional information:

Well I start off with the common, like on a Monday we'll talk about common sense like we'll have a general conversation on the theme. Towards the end of the week we'll talk about the more detailed stuff, so yeah, beginning of the week they basically know every-thing, everything we're learning about, by the end of the week … they've learned new stuff.

(Interview 26 November 2002)

This explanation can be seen as an example of an '**analytical pedagogy**' (Foucault, 1977: 159) where each stage of development is hierarchized into small steps. The themes are given a week's duration. They grow in complexity as Lisa begins with the 'common sense' and then teaches new things. Children are examined daily on the previous day's work and assessed at the end of the year in a report. The themes become more complex as weekly themes at the end of the year were divided into sub-themes of a larger theme. For example, an overarching theme was animals; this was divided into weekly themes that dealt with habitats, insects and spiders, wild animals, and birds. Discussions also became more complex over the course of the year. Through constant **ranking** Lisa knows the level at which each child is expected to contribute. The chil-dren also sing – action songs are popular and hold attention. The children are required to make connections between the content of the songs sung and the weekly themes. For example, the insects and spiders theme elicited a number of songs: 'Incy Wincy Spider', 'If I Were a Butter-fly', 'There Was a Bee', 'Here Is a Bee', 'Little Peter Rabbit'.

The training of bodies through songs is also evident in the numeracy aspect of Language Ring. In a pattern that manifests itself in various ways across all the grades in this study, numer-acy is often dealt with in conjunction with literacy. The children are required to count in unison and maintain a rhythm. Maintaining a rhythm requires efficient control of speed in **correlating the body and gesture**. A typical example of the exercises required in this part of the lesson calls on children to count to 20 then to count backwards from 10, first clapping their hands on their thighs, then clapping their hands, and finally counting with a thigh clap, a hand clap and a finger click. There is another element to time. Teaching children to maintain a rhythm requires them to measure time in order to maintain their rhythm.

Reading is also part of the Grade 0 morning activity. As with Grade 00 classes, Grade 0 teach-ers do not teach reading formally. But 'pre-reading' or indirect reading is acceptable. Lisa had taught the children to recognize the letters of the alphabet by using Letterland Letters. She had also taught them a number of Dolch[4] words on flashcards.

Like the Grade 00s, the Grade 0s also spent time completing an activity at their desks. There are two differences now, one related to time, the other to how the activity is organized. In the first block of curriculum time the Grade 0s have only Language Ring, then free play is sched-uled, after which another hour and a half is scheduled for the creative activity (usually a literacy task), which is followed by another Ring time. This is in contrast to Grade 00 where the bulk of work is done in the first block of curriculum time which is usually two hours if lunch and toilet time are eliminated. This is the first indication that the period of time allocated to work relating to the curriculum begins to be extended.

The whole class is required to complete the same activity and no time is allocated (or taken) in which they can stop and return to it. Children are again required to draw, cut out, colour in, stick things on paper, paint. But the children complete one task rather than a number of them as the Grade 00s do. There is no specific time allocated to this activity each day but the tasks are relatively simple so that all children should complete them. Children work at their own pace, and on completion of the activity take the work to Lisa to be marked and sit on the carpet waiting for the others to finish. In the time that it takes the rest of the children to finish, chil-dren sitting on the carpet should wait quietly. But in this classroom, space is opened for the children to engage in a limited form of free play as long as they do not become too boisterous. Girls often start hand-clapping games and the boys 'play fight' with each other. A small gap opens up in curriculum time when children can engage in some free play.

Play is often the defining characteristic of the second ring as many of the activities take the form of games. The most popular games are ones that involve music. The class plays Musical Chairs, Musical Statues, and Musical Bumps. They also play various memory games like Pick and Mix, where they have to identify matching cards, or remember which item has been removed from a tray.

Similarly to the Grade 00s, the final part of the day is story time. This is popular with both groups. Another difference occurs here, but one where time is affected by the site rather than practices across the grades. While the Grade 00s have story time and then wait to be collected by their parents, the Grade 0s have another half hour at the end of the day. Sometimes, along with the story, Lisa schedules an additional period of free play. The children are taken to the jungle gyms outside, which are set aside for the Foundation Phase.

Grade I and Grade 3

The move to Grade 1 heralds a break in the rhythm established via the timetabling of *regular cycles of activity* in the preschool. The blocks of curriculum time and free play in the **timetable** remain the same from Grade 0 to Grade 3 but there is no longer a predictable regularity of tasks, although a greater number of occupations are imposed.

The first month of school is a time of transition for Grade 1s and to a lesser extent Grade 3s. The first element of this is the shorter school day which allows for a period of adjustment, particularly for those children who have never attended school before. The organization of the day in the first month also reflects this transition from the preschool timetable. Disciplinary time is clearly present in the scheduling of lunch times and toilet times. This routine then falls away. This reflects an assumption that at this age the school subject, after being introduced to such routines, will internalize them and then manage their bodily needs in a much shorter period of time. Similarly story time at the end of the day is infrequent. During my period of

08:00	BELL: DAY STARTS
	Administration during first class task (literacy or numeracy) Second Task (literacy or numeracy) (Toilet time) Lunch
10:00	FREE PLAY
10:15	Class task (literacy, numeracy or life skills) Second class task (individual reading)
11:50	FREE PLAY
12:10	Story time / play / task
13:00	END OF SCHOOL DAY

Figure 3.7 Grade I routines.

08:00	BELL: DAY STARTS
	Administration during first class task (literacy or numeracy)
	Additional task (literacy or numeracy)
	Lunch
10:00	FREE PLAY
10:15	Class task (literacy, numeracy or lift skills)
	Additional tasks
11:50	FREE PLAY
12:10	Task / (play)
13:00	END OF SCHOOL DAY

Figure 3.8 Grade 3 routines.

observation in Grade 3 I observed no story time. This does not mean this time does not exist because Gail, the Head of Department, mentioned it did:

> The story reading between half past twelve and half past one, in the day, you know, it doesn't matter which day, um, it kind of winds them down, and it's a good creative, you know they're … in a mood, they're in a mellow mood, they've had lunch, they've had breaks, they're actually more receptive to it.
>
> (Interview 6 March 2002)

Of interest is the fact that story time takes place at the end of the day across all the grades, as well as the reasons given for this. By the end of the day the children are tired and have used up much of their energy. The bodily disposition required for story time is a docile one; children are expected to sit still and listen. But it does diminish story time's importance if children are too tired to listen attentively.

There are several other changes that occur in the way time operates. Elements of the pre-school timetable such as the morning register and general administration are still present but are dealt with in a way that illustrates another conception of time. This goes beyond the administrative only and begins to be employed across occupations and the Foundation Phase. Events no longer operate linearly in time, but several events can take place simultaneously. For example, administration will be done at the same time as the class is engaged in a task. Managing time to complete two activities simultaneously requires a different school subject capable of moving from one to the next – subjects have to be able to engage themselves in a set task, for example, a handwriting exercise, then break the rhythm of the task to attend to another task like reading aloud to the teacher, and then return to complete the original task.

Another shift occurs in terms of the activities that are prescribed – the morning activity or Language Ring that involves the whole class in discussion is now superseded by individual tasks.

This does not imply that there is no whole-class engagement, since the teacher is required to teach or explain what is required to complete the work, but this work is to be completed individually. More time is spent doing set activities rather than together with the class. This means that the time taken to complete activities is highly variable across the class, and as such the situation arises where children can be doing different tasks at the same time. No longer is there time set aside to wait for all individuals to finish a task, as in Grade 0.

This leads to the next point – the number of tasks and activities increases in the primary school. But the total number of activities completed in a day varied depending on the day in all three Southside sites. What also varied was the order of daily activities. Although no uniform pattern emerged, it seemed that various forms of writing, especially handwriting, were done at the start of the day, with numeracy taking place at a similar time or after the first free play session. Individual reading would take place between the two free play sessions or at the end of the day. It seems that writing and numeracy are tasks that need to be done earlier in the day when the children's levels of concentration are higher.[5]

In order to identify where literacy is timetabled into curriculum time in Grades 1 and 3, tasks associated with the two other learning areas in the Foundation Phase needed to be identified. Learning areas are fields of study in the OBE system. In the Foundation Phase, children's learning is divided into three learning areas: literacy, numeracy, and life skills.[6] I had assumed that since the three learning areas would have been timetabled by teachers when they planned their teaching, these would have been easy to identify. This was not the case. Attempting to code every task done daily as literacy, numeracy, or life skills in the data proved to be difficult, as many evaded easy classification and involved all three learning areas. At the beginning of the Grade 1 year, many of the exercises the children do are perceptual exercises involving all three learning areas. One exercise that extended over a period of weeks involved all the learning areas. Children had the name of a colour written on a page that they had to trace over in the appropriate colour. They then had to find five pictures containing that colour from a magazine to cut out and stick into their book. The tracing (letter formation) and attempt to instil word recognition are literacy skills, so is finding pictures in magazines while finding the number of pictures requires a level of numeracy. But it could be argued that the acquisition of these literacy and numeracy skills are in fact life skills.

This timetabling is further complicated by the fact that Southside works on a seven-day timetable with certain lessons allocated to a specific duration, with changes signalled by the bell. This in itself is interesting and points to the arbitrary partitioning of time. Convention dictates that there are five workdays and two weekend days, but the seven-day timetable shifts this to seven workdays that are interrupted by the two weekend days. The justification of a seven-day timetable is to limit disruptions and could be read as the broad implementation of **exhaustive use**, the final aspect of the **control of activity**. **Exhaustive use** is a way of accumulating time. In order to accumulate time it is broken in to fragments. The more these units or fragments are divided the more tasks can be inserted into these units, increasing the amount of work done daily or weekly. Often holidays and school activities (like sports days) are scheduled on the same weekday across the year. This means that teachers teaching subjects on those days lose teaching time. The implementation of the seven-day timetable negates this problem and the loss of time is more equally shared across teachers, evening out teaching time allocated.

But the Grade 1s and 3s have a limited number of periods in this timetable when they attend a class given by another teacher – computers, music, and library. These periods are in fact disruptive to the rhythm of the class. When the bell rings to signal changing periods for the Intermediate Phase these are largely ignored by the Foundation Phase and they continue with whatever task is at hand. The seven-day cycle increases the disruption because there is no weekly routine. Thus what frequently happens is that the classes were interrupted in the middle of a task and sent off to another lesson. Or time is wasted as teachers cannot start another task before the class leaves. In some cases the teachers forgot to send their class and had to be reminded by the teacher waiting for them, thus reducing her teaching time.

In light of this point, the principle of **exhaustive use** does not operate fully. I would argue, however, that this principle might be in the process of being instilled. These children are beginning their schooling, and the primary objective of preschool is school socialization rather than formal learning. Children are required to get used to the rhythm of the school day, and have to learn to follow teacher-controlled activities. What the pre-primary timetable with its regular routine allows for is a sense of security – the children know exactly what will happen every day. When the routine is disrupted the children are confused. Commenting on this Lisa said:

> Oh yes, and they know the routine very well, and what's funny is if you break the routine,… for instance … we went on an outing we came back and it was twelve o'clock, they wanted to go out to break, they said, 'When are we going to toilet, to go out for, for first break?' and because they never had their first break.
>
> (Interview 26 November 2002)

An additional factor is the mastery of tasks. The fact that the timetables are constructed as blocks of time allowing for a level of flexibility to complete a task is crucial. The skills the children are acquiring in terms of literacy are essential for later on in their school careers as the timetable becomes more fragmented in order to fit in more learning areas. Enough time needs to be spent mastering reading and writing so that these skills become habitual.

The organization of the primary school timetable into a seven-day cycle with a number of units or periods is geared towards the education of older children. Thus a tension exists in the Foundation Phase where teachers do not follow official timetable slots. Younger children need greater blocks of time to master tasks. They also have less content to cover. Regular daily routines are more important in the temporal organization of days than the completion of tasks in smaller, allocated units of time. But in being required to fit into the school timetable with its scheduled subject periods is often a disruption for Foundation Phase classes, breaking work flows in their curriculum time.

A final point to be made that is related to time concerns play. In the pre-primary school there are places in curriculum time for free play to occur. Play is also scheduled by teachers at the end of a day. It serves an educational purpose by developing fine and gross motor co-ordination at a time when children's concentration levels are not high. Spontaneous free play is not sanctioned during curriculum time in the primary school, but it has not disappeared. There were occasions when the Grade 1s and Grade 3s spent time on the perceptual playground at the end of the day. For the Grade 3s, reaching the end of the Foundation Phase, this is the last time such play is sanctioned.

Time–space–movement

Reading data in relation to the spatial and the temporal sets up an understanding of what happens in and across classroom environments. There are several ways to do this but this section brings the timelines and spatial maps of the classrooms together. Movement flows were drawn onto the spatial diagrams by considering where children were distributed in space in relation to the daily activities represented on the timelines. This mapping cannot show the nuances of individual movements in classrooms, nor does it intend to. What it does reveal are broad patterns and changes over time in the way spaces are utilized.

As a visual depiction, Figures 3.9 to 3.12 are useful because they provide an overview of the spaces children move to and from and in which they locate themselves during the day. Class

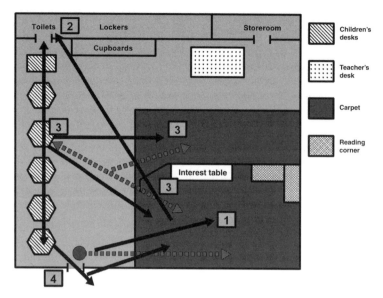

Figure 3.9 Movement flows in space and time: Grade 00.

Notes
The arrow with the circle at the bottom indicates the start of the school day.
The dotted lines indicate spaces where free play takes place during curriculum time.
Numbers in boxes next to arrows indicate the sequence of movements from spaces across the day.

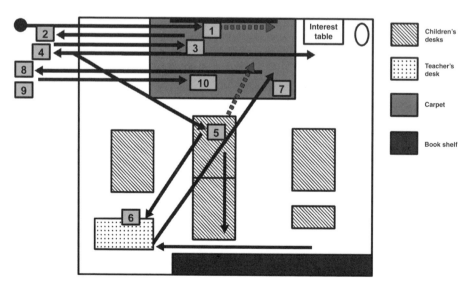

Figure 3.10 Movement flows in space and time: Grade 0.

Notes
The arrow with the circle at the bottom indicates the start of the school day.
The dotted lines indicate spaces where free play takes place during curriculum time.
Numbers in boxes next to arrows indicate the sequence of movements from spaces across the day.

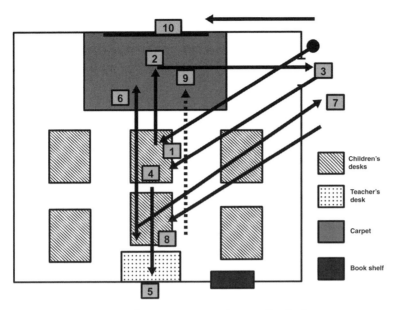

Figure 3.11 Movement flows in space and time: Grade 1.

Notes
The arrow with the circle at the bottom indicates the start of the school day.
The dotted lines indicate spaces where free play takes place during curriculum time.
Numbers in boxes next to arrows indicate the sequence of movements from spaces across the day.

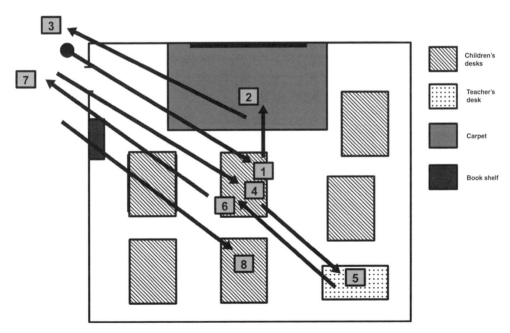

Figure 3.12 Movement flows in space and time: Grade 3.

Notes
The arrow with the circle at the bottom indicates the start of the school day.
Numbers in boxes next to arrows indicate the sequence of movements from spaces across the day.

Table 3.1 Approximate time children spend daily in four classroom spaces

	Grade 00	Grade 0	Grade 1	Grade 3
Children's desks	1.5 hours	1 hour	3 hours	5 hours
Teacher's desk	0	5–10 minutes	5–10 minutes	5–10 minutes
Carpet	2 hours	3.5 hours	1	15 minutes
Reading Corner	0	0	0	0
Total hours in a school day	4.5 hours	5 hours	5 hours	5.5 hours

movements from one space to another are depicted by arrows with numbers next to them to indicate the sequence of movements through the day. Clear patterns emerge from these movement flows which can be compared. Based on the timelines and activities reported in the field-notes, a rough calculation was done to work out how much time children spent in different classroom spaces during the day. These times are represented in Table 3.1 and should be read in conjunction with the movement flow diagrams. They are approximations, intended to gain a general sense of the amount of time children spent in the different classroom spaces. They do not include the time children take to enter their classrooms after break and settle down at their desks, or the time taken for a whole class to move from one place to another, or the child who moves around to sharpen pencils and borrow items from others instead of working, into account.

What is clear is that the Grade 00s are the most mobile, and have the greatest access to spaces. The carpet is a space that could be considered a hub where children begin the day, spend time playing during the day, and end the day for story time and to sleep. Overall two hours of the four-and-a-half-hour day is spent there. The important point to make is that this time is interrupted because there is a great amount of movement by the children coming to and leaving the carpet. Slightly less time is spent at their desks – but only one hour is spent working here. The other half hour the children sit at their desks to eat their lunch. But, as was described in Chapter 2, the children spend this 'work time' completing one task before moving onto another table (or the carpet) to complete all the assigned tasks for the day. Although Table 3.1 shows no time spent in the Reading Corner as part of the daily class routine, individual children did enter this space and read the books when there was time for free play after they finished tasks at their desks. Less time was spent here than in the more open space of the carpet.

What is striking about Figure 3.10 is how central the carpet space is in the Grade 0 class. It is the place where activities start and the school day ends. So it is not surprising that the children spend three and a half hours on the carpet of a five-hour school day. Some of this time is taken up by eating lunch rather than taking part in activities scheduled into curriculum time. As the directionality of the arrows in the movement flow diagrams and Table 3.1 indicate, the three hours of time spent on the carpet is broken up by movements outside of the class and to their desks. Children spend the same amount of time working at their desks as the Grade 00s do – but movement is restricted as are the number of tasks to be completed. Children may spend short periods of time at the teacher's desk to get work marked. The school subject that spends the majority of their day on the carpet is not the same as the child who spends more time at their desks. Hadi-Tabassum (2006), in talking about the use of the carpet in an American Grade 5 class, notes how it functions as an inclusive space that works to produce a community. Many of the practices that are central to literacy lessons point to a conceptualization of learning as a collective activity that will be discussed in later chapters. Being together on the carpet requires an ability to be with, and work together with, other children. Desks can then be arranged individually for individual work because group work happens on the carpet.

The opposite is true in the Grade 1 and 3 classes. The most obvious difference between the Grade 1 diagram (Figure 3.11) and the Grade 0 diagram (Figure 3.10) is how movements originate at and spread out from the children's desks. This increased time is also evident. Table 3.1 indicates a two-hour increase in the time children spend at their desks. This additional hour has been subtracted from the carpet time in Grade 0 where, on the whole, only an hour is spent. (This includes a short time for children to eat their lunch before the first break.) This diagram was based on Helen's class who spent time between breaks on the carpet for literacy activities that included the whole class, or sometimes involved reading with children in groups. She was more likely to do News Time on Mondays and have story time at the end of the day on the carpet than Catherine. The five minutes children may have spent at the teacher's desk was for reading aloud. But children did not read aloud every day.

By Grade 3 children spend on average five hours at their desks. The 15 minutes on the carpet are for eating lunch before first break. The time spent at Thulisile's desk may have been for reading aloud, which also did not happen on a daily basis. Some children may have spent more time here if they needed one-on-one assistance with an assigned activity. Although the five hours spent at their desks is interrupted by break time, the children spent longer chunks of time at their desks. Different tasks are not assigned to different groups of desks as in Grade 00, neither do children frequently read or discuss issues together in groups or as a class on the carpet. For the docile, compliant child the day is predominantly spent behind a desk. For the child who is less compliant there are a number of ways in which to occupy restricted spaces and stretch curriculum time for more pleasurable pursuits.

The movement flows in the spatial diagrams show the increasingly restricted movement of children across early schooling and the timelines indicate the greater amount of time that children are required to sit in one place. If one considers these patterns, a particular conception of the schooled subject emerges. The greater concentration of time spent on the carpet in the pre-school grades works to construct a cohesive collective. Children are required to talk, listen, look, sing, move, and read together. The movement flows of the Grade 1 and 3 classes illustrate an increased emphasis on the individual who is required to complete work on their own. While the shift from the collective to the individual is not a criticism and speaks to a more independent subject, this fostering of the children's independence need not be restricted to one space.

So far this chapter has described the organization of school time and discussed the broad patterns that emerge when time and space are combined in the form of movement flows. It has not considered the children themselves and their acquiescence to or manipulation of school time. The first part of the following section considers several incidents from the data and the questions they raise about docility and resistance. The second section revisits points raised in the final discussion in Chapter 2 and provides some insights for practice that are gained when space and time are seen as interlocked.

Playing for time: docility and resistance in the classroom

Understanding space and time in relation to Foucault's understanding of power reveals several aspects of classroom dynamics. Where there is power there is also resistance and children exploit both time and appropriate space. When teachers see signs of resistance, children's bodies are most often disciplined so that time can be efficiently used in tasks they have been set. Jenks (2001: 81) argues:

> Although children's activities are momentarily punctuated in time – they are made to stop work and sit still – the intention of such commands is to instruct them about the way to proceed more efficiently and to make more efficient use of their time through adapting

more disciplined behaviours. It is thus, through punctualising children's time by imposing a particular bodily order that the connections between continuity and curriculum time are restored and enabled.

These commands become part of the schooled subject's **habitus**. In the photograph (Figure 3.13) of Grade 1s, the children demonstrate a number of postures that are indicative of an attentive and docile child. In this instance the intercom went off in the classroom. Both children and teachers are supposed to listen carefully to these messages. The bodies of several of the children indicate postures that reveal acquiescence – they either have their arms folded, hands on their heads or fingers on their lips. This is not behaviour that is demonstrated by the entire class – several of the children in the background are still cutting out pictures. While they are engaged in the task set by their teacher, and as such could be considered compliant, the moment the intercom comes on power relations shift and the teacher is no longer the highest authority in the class. The voice from the administrative centre of the school is. It may be the principal or a secretary representing him. Disciplined subjects' bodies should reflect their position in this hierarchy. Of course the children still engaged in the task may be listening, but the fact that they are involved in something else indicates that their attention is elsewhere. At the same time, taking on the expected posture does not automatically guarantee attention either.

Figure 3.13 The intercom.

Figure 3.14 Writing a test.

The Grade 1s in the second photograph (Figure 3.14) are on task. The children in this photograph were writing a spelling test. This is revealed by the girl's folded arm over her book to create a protective space against prying eyes. There is also an interesting contrast between the photographs in relation to spatial organization. In the first photograph the children are working in bigger books and have magazines on their desks. This can result in a lack of control over what is a limited space, resulting in regular forays around and under desks to recover objects that have fallen, as is evident in Figure 3.15. A docile and disciplined subject has control not only of her/his body but over the objects in space.

Children challenge teachers' spatial organizations and their accompanying behavioural norms as they recreate the space they are in. Two boys in Grade 1 demonstrated this aptly by revealing how space is a mixture of the real and ideal, and how effortless this transition is (Figures 3.16, 3.17). In this case, space functioning as an ideal supersedes space as real. The two boys move from the real space of the classroom where they are involved in a set task to a new space, an ideal space, where they reconfigure their identities as 'gangsta' rappers and perform with each other. In moving to this space of performance they transgress because they are no longer schooled subjects. Their entire body language changes as they recite the words of a popular song, mimicking the actions of rappers. Their transgression begins with a probable awareness that what they are doing is not appropriate; their hands are in their laps and their gestures are contained. As they begin to get into the performance their hands are lifted above their desk until finally they break free of its restriction and stand to perform. They also mark themselves as different by adjusting their school uniform – the knitted 'beanies' they wear as

Figure 3.15 Falling objects.

Figure 3.16 Rappers under cover.

Figure 3.17 Rappers in the open.

part of a winter uniform are pulled over their faces and become balaclavas. Although the boys are 'playing rappers', the use of the balaclava carries the threat of violence and gangsterism. Walkerdine (1997) has argued that, in the case of girls, explicit lyrics are closely connected to working-class culture and identity. This performance is probably an indication of this, but with gangs both existing and forming in areas these boys live in, the performance and emulation of a genre full of male violence reveals the taking on of an alternative identity.

The Grade 3s are an interesting group. They showed the most signs of subtle resistance. Transgressive bodies emerged in this class. These bodies transgressed spatial boundaries, finding ways to escape from the confines of desks. These bodies talked and whispered about the world outside the classroom; they moved around looking 'purposeful' in sharpening a pencil, fetching a file, borrowing stationery, and in doing so sought attention from the other children nearby. These children also realized they can stretch time – making the task they are participating in longer while actually doing very little work, or they are occupied by non-curricular tasks. Jenks (2001: 80) argues that children's knowledge of appropriate body postures 'may enable them to strategically take control of their own time at school as they pass leisure as work'. While looking studious, and hiding paper in books, several of the Grade 3s produced letters or pictures for me when they were supposed to be completing set tasks.

Time to play: dangerous outside spaces

In Chapter 2 the question of bullying in schools was raised as well as the fact that in an **enclosed** school space there may be certain non-compliant and resistant individuals on the inside rather than on the outside. The following incident is one that highlights some of the potential problems preschool children can encounter when they are scheduled to share space with older primary school children.

Jason was one of the boys I followed from Grade 0 to Grade 1. In Grade 0 he was considered a behavioural problem and was on daily report. This meant that he was under closer **surveillance** than the other children. Jason was 'captured in a network of writing' (Foucault, 1977: 189); his teacher would send a written comment about his behaviour to his parents at the end of each day. The problems continued into Grade 1. This reporting to his parents was problematic for the teachers – there were indications from Jason that reports of bad behaviour resulted in corporal punishment at home. Home could be a dangerous space. Jason is a loud and exuberant child whose behaviour was often considered wild and disruptive – he would shout out, have loud conversations, not sit still, and would often start fights with other children. Despite this, he fully and eagerly participated in lessons, seeming relatively unfazed if he answered incorrectly.

One observed incident in Grade 0 that captures some transgressive behaviour I refer to as the 'Sex on Hands Incident'. Although Jason was not the only one involved in this incident, when children were in trouble he was most often at the centre of it. In the controlled space of the Grade 0 classroom children's behaviour was carefully monitored and, on the whole, the children's interactions with each other were respectful, with few comments or actions that could be construed as bullying. In the space outside the classroom the situation differed. Leaving the protected space of the classroom to play is both a time of freedom and the entrance into what can be a dangerous space for Grade 0s who share the playground with all the other Southside children. At the end of one break, Jason and three of his friends returned with a commotion from the other Grade 0s that alerted Lisa. Written in thick purple felt-tip on their hands was the word 'sex'. Lisa was very angry with them and asked them if they knew what was written on their hands. None of them did. They also could not tell her what sex was when she asked them. In conversation with Lisa afterwards she explained why she was so angry. It worried her that the boys had allowed someone to write something on them that they did not understand. She felt this left them open to other forms of abuse. If they let this happen what else would they let people write on them? She wanted to protect the children by teaching them to protect themselves by being aware of what was done to them so they could say no.

The incident reveals the boys as illiterate subjects – although they knew the letters of the alphabet and could work out some words by blending the sounds, they were unable to do this with the word 'sex'. They had consented to this word being inscribed on their bodies in ignorance. While Lisa's concerns are valid, I think something is revealed about their state as emergent literates. There is something powerful about letters and words. Many of the children were beginning to display a great interest in writing and were trying to form letters although this was never a formal part of any lesson. They had to wait until Grade 1 before the secrets of writing would be revealed. As such there was probably a fascination with a child who could wield a pen and write for them. On the playground their bodies became a canvas – but for someone else. While the motives of the writer cannot be known, the innocence of the boys is clear – the word was written on the top of their hands, in clear view, and not hidden. It is also highly probable that the word 'sex' caused all the consternation, keying into adult fears about the sexual abuse of children. If the writer had written the boys' names on their hands Lisa's reaction would probably not have been so strong.

Space–time/time–space and practice

Several key points emerge about how time is organized in the early years classrooms. As a general framework of activity the **timetable** is organized across all the grades to include large chunks of curriculum time. Unsurprisingly the quantity of these blocks of time increases from

Grade 00 as the school day gets longer. The fact that these blocks of time exist is very important for early literacy training. Various *occupations can be imposed* within these blocks but occupations are not allocated precise units of time. Time is not so tightly regulated. Rather, these larger chunks of time allow children to master tasks. This is where the **temporal elaboration of the act**, the **correlation between body and gesture** and the **body–object articulation** come into play. Children need time to learn how to co-ordinate the movements and gestures required to perform a task, correctly sequence gestures the body needs to make, and use the body to manipulate objects. Learning to manipulate a pencil to draw, colour in, and write on paper and in books is crucial. So too is learning book-handling skills: beginning readers need to learn how to hold books the right way up, that the right page is turned over to continue a story, that we read from left to right and top down. **Exhaustive use** needs to operate so that over time and with much practice these skills are internalized. These are foundational skills that are required for all school subjects children will be exposed to in later years. Without them children cannot access new knowledge and skills.

A shift in the organization of time that does occur is related to the *cycles of repetition*. Routine is the central organizing principle in the preschool. The repetitive nature of daily routines provides a sense of stability. Along with the knowledge children acquire, these routines function to create school subjects. Preschool children learn that there are times to complete tasks, the 'rules' for completing them and that this should be their sole focus. When they enter primary school they understand the institutional rhythm of a day. The highly structured daily routine begins to fall away as children are expected to be able to manage themselves (i.e. eating and excretion should be separate from curriculum time). A greater variety of tasks are scheduled into the chunks of curriculum time. They do not have the same predictable regularity as the preschool. One day may begin with a writing task, and the next day with numeracy. Whole-class teaching begins to be replaced by individual task completion. Spaces for spontaneous play become increasingly limited as children move grades.

When one looks at spatial organization, this shift in the amount of time children spend working and learning as a group compared to working and learning as individuals is reflected by the amount of time they spend at their desks. While time remains relatively constant and open enough to extend activities if children need additional time, space shuts down. The movement flow diagrams indicate this pattern clearly. The spaces that have the greatest potential to be used creatively, and for children to be creative, like the carpet and Reading Corner, are the ones that are shut down. In this environment, acts of resistance emerge. Children create and exploit gaps that open up in curriculum time. They may 'play the docile subject', looking studious while engaged in unsanctioned reading or writing. They may find excuses to get out of their desks and move around. They may forget the school space and create a new imaginative one where their school identities are subsumed by their real or aspirational out-of-school identities.

In light of what has been presented, it is necessary to return to the point made at the beginning of the chapter that space and time are interlocked and explore how the relationship between space and time can contribute to a greater understanding of classroom order. I'd like to think about this in three ways: what it means to *impose occupations*, rethinking the **rule of functional sites** for classroom spaces, and what it means to *accumulate time* by applying these to examples discussed previously from the research classes and with a fictional lesson plan for Grade 3s.

We know that one of the functions of a **timetable** is to *impose occupations*. The previous discussions have shown that the imposition of regular and repeated occupations in the early years classrooms functions not only to impart knowledge but to train children in the skills they need in order to continue their schooling. Some of what they learn reflects the norms and values of a school and society. But what Foucault does not cover in his discussion of the temporal are the practical aspects needed to successfully impose occupations in classrooms.

Very often these practical aspects are in fact invisible. They are the result of teachers' experience and intuition. They are also often small things that can have a big impact and when not 'second nature' require some thinking to unpack. How is it that the children in Dawn's Grade 00 class move so easily from one table to another to complete new tasks? One answer is that the equipment is already set out for the children. Each task has particular implements, for example, the right quantities of magazines, paper, scissors, and glue are provided for the children who will be cutting and pasting. The fact that Grade 0s come back after break to work at their desks means that, for a task that requires more resources than just handing out a worksheet, Lisa has time to set this up when the children go out for free play. There is little chaos when Helen reads with small groups of children on the carpet because she has two tasks planned in one block of time – perhaps the whole class is working at their desks in their numeracy books that day. Children are used to the routine practice of breaking away to read and then returning to their desks. The fact that the children are ranked according to ability and sit in groups reflecting this means that it's easier to move one group to the carpet than a number of dispersed individuals. Reading with a similar ability group saves time in the long run. The fact that Thulisile's Grade 3s can read means that children can hand out books quickly for the next lesson if she is busy with something else.

Ultimately, what these examples point to is an ability on the part of teachers to plan successfully. They are planning their lessons on two levels. The first is at the level of content – what information or knowledge or skills will be imparted over a set period of time and how this will be conveyed. This level would also reflect the aims or outcomes of the system of education set out by government. The second level of planning is often invisible. It deals with spatial and temporal management. This is something that is generally not dealt with in a systematic or detailed way when we train student teachers. It is not hard to integrate the use of space and time in lesson planning. This can be done by thinking about the following questions:

- How will X occupation be imposed?
- When will it be imposed?
- Where will it be imposed (in what space/s)?
- For how long will it be imposed?
- How will tasks/aspects of the lesson be sequenced?
- If resources are going to be used how will they be dispersed?
- What planning needs to be done to ensure this happens?

Figure 3.13 takes these questions and uses them to construct a lesson for Grade 3s. The lesson is on transport, which was a theme in Thulisile's Grade 3 classroom, although the lesson is not the same. The time allocated to teach the class aligns with the Grade 3 timetable outlined in Figure 3.8.

The questions about how an occupation/task will be imposed, its sequencing, and the use of resources highlight the importance of thinking about transition. The transitions between activities in a lesson or between lessons are important to take into account. Often when one part of a lesson is complete and a new section of work begins the process is uneven. Or if the children in the example go to their desks first before they come to the carpet, their movements need to be managed twice. Entering the classroom and moving from desks to the carpet is an inefficient use of time and space. When children move back to their desks if they are required to fetch their books to begin the individual task, but these books are located in a corner at the back of the class, time will also be wasted. When time is not used efficiently to make the move from one part of a lesson to another, gaps in curriculum time can emerge. In these unfocused moments children become restless and distracted, and it is often hard to restore order. This affects the pace of a lesson.

Grade 3 Lesson Plan

A Grade 3 teacher plans to teach her class of 30 a lesson on transport. It is part of a theme that will integrate literacy and numeracy outcomes. She wants children to be able to identify different types of transport systems (sea/rail/road/air) and their associated vehicles. This will be a whole-class discussion. Then she wants children to compete individual tasks. These will then be extended across the week.

- How will X occupation (the transport lesson) be imposed?
There are two occupations that will be imposed:
A Class discussion
B Individual task

- When will it be imposed?
Between first and second break – this is 1 hour and 35 minutes.

- Where will it be imposed (in what space/s)?
2 spaces: the carpet and then the children's desks

- For how long will it be imposed?
1 hour 30 minutes
(5 minutes to settle the children after break and get them inside the classroom)
30 minutes for class discussion
1 hour for individual task

- How will tasks/aspects of the lesson be sequenced?
1 Children move to the carpet as they enter the classroom.
2 Class discussion will begin generally and then move to specific identification of different types of transport with the use of visuals.
3 Visuals to be displayed on the wall/blackboard. (Who will do this? Teacher or children?)
4 Teacher to give general instructions for completing individual tasks.
5 Then children to move back to their desks. (How? Boys then girls, or one group at a time?)
6 Children complete individual task.
7 Task to be collected by group leader and placed on teacher's desk.

- If resources are going to be used how are they to be dispersed?
2 sets of resources will be used:
Transport pictures:
These need bluetack so they can be stuck on the wall/blackboard. But sticking them up before the lesson is likely to distract children from the discussion. Should the pictures already have the bluetack stuck on them or should this be done during the discussion?
ADVANTAGE: With bluetack already on the pictures. Saves time for presenting visual stimulus.
DISADVANTAGE: The pictures may stick together and waste time. If the pictures are not laminated the bluetack could damage them as re-usable classroom resources.
Putting the bluetack on during the lesson:
ADVANTAGE: If the pictures are not laminated they won't be damaged.
DISADVANTAGE: Can be time consuming and distracting. But children could be asked to help.

Where is the best place to store the pictures so they can be used efficiently if this lesson is on the carpet? How close is this place to the board?

Task 2 Individual task
Worksheet will be divided into 6 per group and placed on children's desks before they come in. Children in each group will distribute worksheets between themselves. Children know this routine needs minimal instruction.

Figure 3.18 Taking space and time into account when planning a lesson.

The distribution of resources is just as important as the distribution of children. This also has an impact on the pacing of lessons. For example, placing enough worksheets at each group of desks limits time wastage. A teacher may make this decision because her classroom is very small and movement between desks/groups is difficult. She may decide to have them within easy reach and hand them out while the children are settling down at their desks because she knows that being in the same space as the children has a greater disciplinary effect. Decisions need to be made about space to store resources and when they are needed should be anticipated. It also means thinking about how children can be advantageously distributed in space alongside the resources. For example, to display the transport pictures quickly, one or two children may be tasked with sticking them up. Children can be given the responsibility for collecting the individual transport worksheets. If a classroom space is to be reorganized the time it takes to do this, whether it is practical, if children need to move into or out of the reorganized space, and whether the space needs to be rearranged for the next lesson, or the next class, all need to be considered.

The pace at which children work is another consideration. When the Grade 0 children finished their work quickly they redistributed themselves to the carpet space. When the Grade 3s completed their work they stayed in their desks, watching, waiting, and often disrupting the other children. A hole opens in this curriculum time which children can use for their own purposes. This may not be conducive to classroom order and other children's learning. These times can be filled by having extension exercises ready. I am not arguing that every moment should be filled with work. Children do not have unlimited concentration spans – having a short play time and a space in which to do this was valuable for the Grade 0 children. There were clear rules about how free time was utilized and children moved with little fuss into engaging with the new task that followed in curriculum time.

Time is also an important element in viewing spaces as multifunctional sites. If spaces are to be used creatively in the classroom then there needs to be an understanding of how children can be moved through space and time efficiently. In getting the fictional Grade 3 class to move efficiently from outside to the carpet for the transport lesson, they need an understanding of **the temporal elaboration of the act** and the **correlation of body and gesture**. They also need to have done this often (**exhaustively**) to know what the appropriate behaviour is. Just as learning to read and write requires practice so does moving children through space and organizing spaces. Routine is fundamental – making children do group work, or spend free time on the carpet waiting for the next task will never be successful unless it becomes part of a regular routine.

Ranking is important in spatial distribution. In allocating groups to spaces questions need to be asked about how groups will be constituted (e.g. by gender or ability) which is based on teacher knowledge. In the transport lesson the teacher may decide to leave one group on the carpet to work with her because she knows they need additional support. That said, mixed ability groupings can assist in peer-sharing. What is important, though, is that teachers are aware of why they rank groups in particular ways. In Chapter 2 the issue of class size and higher numbers of children was presented as a challenge to spatial distribution. In such a class, where the children are older, small groups (of three or four) could regularly be given a space to work over a period of time. They might even be allowed to use the teacher's desk, or work there with her. Redistribution does not need to take every child into account in one timetabled period.

Disciplinary time is supposed to heighten productivity and efficiency of individuals in a system. This requires that time be accumulated rather than lost. Two common issues were present to a greater or lesser extent in all classrooms. One was that of managing behaviour when gaps in curriculum time opened up and the children were no longer engaged in tasks. The second was the problem of children copying each other's work. Children who are unoccupied become bored and can be difficult to manage. Their disruptions have a knock-on effect on the productivity of the whole class. Too much copying works against mastery. School knowledge is organized so that it builds on previous knowledge and increases in difficulty. If full mastery is not attained at the beginning of sections of work then time is wasted as children take longer to complete harder tasks.

If both of these problems presented themselves in the Grade 3 class how might these be alleviated if a knowledge of space and time were drawn on? The class consists of 30 children. The desks are arranged in five groups seating six children each. Of all the classrooms discussed in the research perhaps the general workings of space and time in the Grade 00 class are most helpful. One of the most powerful operations in the preschool is routine. These routines have been clearly orchestrated and their regularity means that children know and internalize the behavioural norms expected from them. The question to ask is when occupations are imposed in the Grade 3 class are there regular routines that set up a framework of expectations in which work takes place? The presence of routines implies a level of consistency. For example, if it is sometimes acceptable for children to talk to each other after they have completed their work and at other times not, there is a level of inconsistency. Children who have been in the school system for any length of time and understand its workings will manipulate it as far as possible for their own ends which are predicated on pleasure rather than work. Establishing consistent routines that remain the same through **exhaustive use** is one way curriculum holes may be closed. In addition, thinking about the general functioning of routines, the teacher needs to consider the transitions made between lessons/activities. If the overall pace of her lessons is too slow or the move from one section to another is drawn out then classroom order is eroded.

Another principle that can be applied from the Grade 00 class is the scheduling of several tasks in a set time period. In the present disciplinary climate just reproducing the Grade 00 spatial distribution would create havoc. There are too many children in the Grade 3 class to move from one group of desks to another to complete tasks. Instead of spatially distributing the class, a series of tasks could be developed so that each child in a group would be allocated a different task. For example, there could be a numeracy exercise calculating the load trains were carrying; a creative piece about what they would like to drive/fly when they are older; an exercise on the advantages and disadvantages of using different types of transport; the compilation of a list of causes of road accidents; a comprehension on aeroplanes. The children could not copy each other because the tasks are not the same. A variety of possibilities then exists: each child may be required to complete all the other tasks over the next few days. The jigsaw method could be implemented: all the children who did the specific tasks could gather together to compare notes. Rather than copying, they could consolidate information. Individual groups could disseminate this information to the rest of the class. The mode of reporting back would need to be considered – it could be written, a poster, or an oral presentation. The allocation of these tasks could also be strategic. Drawing on her knowledge of the children who finish their work quickly and are then disruptive, the teacher could give more challenging, or longer tasks to these children. They could also be engaged to help with administrative tasks that may be generated by such an exercise.

Ultimately, for this to be successful, careful planning of the lesson is needed that takes the tasks, overall routines, and spatial and temporal organization into account. A little experimentation and flexibility would also be required. Such tasks cannot be a once-off occurrence. If a group of 4-year-old children who are at the beginning stages of their inculcation into the practices of the school are able to complete a series of tasks within a period of time, distribute themselves within the classroom in order to do this, and not create anarchy, then the same possibilities exist for older children.

What also needs to be considered is the space and time required to train teachers in these skills. How do teacher trainers find ways for students to reflect on the use of space and time in classrooms? How much time is needed in real classroom situations, in controlled limited spaces such as a micro-teaching environment, if such a resource is available, and in lecture and tutorial time when existing curricula are usually already full?

Chapter 4

Managing and regulating bodies

Managing populations: a case study of apartheid South Africa

One of the ideas underpinning this book is the importance of **regulation**. With **regulation** comes particular ways of understanding and being in the world. In order for schooling to be effective, children need to be managed in particular ways, and to be taught to manage themselves in ways that are socially acceptable. One of the objectives of mass schooling is to produce citizens whose productivity, skills, and values are fundamental to the economic and social stability of the country in which they live. Apartheid South Africa presents an interesting case in point about how the management of the population worked to construct particular kinds of subjectivities. These subjectivities are proving a challenge to reconstruction in a post-apartheid world.

To illuminate the ways in which people are managed and regulated, and the ways they resist regulation, this section presents a case study of the apartheid system and its management of populations. This case study aims to do two things: it locates the educational institutions in my research in a broader and complex context and it begins to show the ways in which South African subjects have been constituted. In order to do this, Foucault's understanding of how power works to govern populations needs to be briefly outlined because it is through this lens that the apartheid state will be read.

Underlying all of Foucault's work on power is a preoccupation with how subjects are constructed and construct themselves. He says that modern power is marked by the rise of **bio-power**. **Bio-power** operates on two axes (see Figure 4.1 for a visual representation). The first is the '**anatomo-politics of the body**' (Foucault, 1978: 138). This simply means that power is directed at individuals and onto their bodies. Directing disciplinary techniques at the body increases its capabilities, especially its economic utility, and ensures docility. Learning to write is an illustration of this. The techniques for learning to write require mastery of the body (e.g. sitting upright, holding a pen). Being able to communicate through writing is a requirement to function in a modern economy. This is the focus of the second part of this chapter – the regulatory techniques that teachers use to manage their classes.

The second axis of **bio-power** is the '**bio-politics of the population**' (Foucault, 1978: 139). The welfare of the population is central here. **Bio-politics** addresses the social, cultural, geographic, and environmental conditions under which people are governed. **Government**, for Foucault, is not just about state management and political structures; it is also how individuals govern themselves and how groups are directed. **Government** is a means of shaping our behaviour according to a set of norms. If we are going to govern ourselves and shape the conduct of others we need to think about *how* we do this. The way we think about governing is referred to as **governmentality** – the mentalities of government. This thinking is influenced by knowledge and belief systems of our communities and societies. These thoughts become

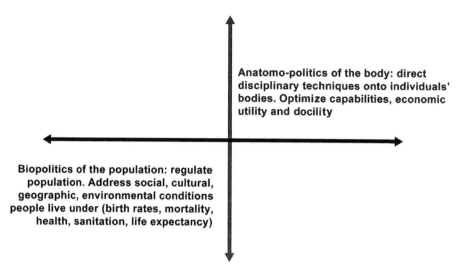

Figure 4.1 Bio-power's axes.

embedded in practices and institutions, like education, that shape our conduct. The way we govern is based on what we take to be true, but we also produce new truths in the way we govern.

But, what we believe to be true may not be in the best interests of everyone in the population. This is where an important point about power needs to be made: it is dangerous and full of possibilities, 'the instrument of oppression and of liberation' (Gallagher, 2008: 147). Dean (1999) talks about one form of oppressive power manifesting itself as **authoritarian governmentality**. **Authoritarian governmentality** sees certain citizens as being deficient, lacking responsibility, and needing close management, as opposed to liberal forms of governing that assume people are free and have the ability to govern/manage themselves, as well as to take part in the collective as responsible citizens. The apartheid state is an example of **authoritarian governmentality** where **bio-political racism** manifested itself. Dean (1999: 140) puts it starkly when he explains that bio-political racism is 'a way of thinking about how to treat the degenerates and the abnormals within one's own population and prevent the further degeneration of the race'.

Bio-political racism affects how individuals are managed (**anatomo-politics of the body**) as well as how a population is broken down into racial groups to be managed differently (**bio-politics of the population**).

Managing the South African population (the apartheid way)

The knowledge and beliefs entrenched in Afrikaner nationalism manifested itself in legislation. These programmes and legislation reveal the presence of **bio-political racism** whose aim was to segregate populations, and in the case of Black South Africans, physically remove them from integrating with White society, reducing their 'contaminating' effect on the White population. Much of the management of the population took place through legislation. Some of the groundwork had already been laid by much earlier colonial legislation. For example, the spatial separation of groups was embedded in the Natives Land Act of 1913. The Act prevented Blacks from buying land in 'White' areas, and overcrowding and communal tenure in Black areas severely limited land ownership. After the National Party gained power in 1948, a slew of legislation and amendments to existing legislation was passed in the next four decades concerning land owner-ship, access to land, and the distribution and control of people in residential and commercial spaces. This spatial distribution was underpinned by the ways in which people were classified. The Population Registration Act in 1950 conferred a racial identity on all South Africans. Divid-ing the South African population into several population groups predicated on race required the management of separate population groups. The Group Areas Act of 1950 segregated popu-lations by allocating different race groups separate places to live. There was a mass of legislation about influx control because cheap labour was needed in White areas. A particular subjectivity was conferred onto Blacks – cheap, docile labourers whose presence was key to a establishing a strong economy for the dominant group. These were workers not citizens. Blacks who moved into or worked in White areas were controlled through the Pass Laws. Influx control led to the homeland policy which purported to give political rights to Africans that would be practised in 'independent' homelands. Its real aim was to eliminate an entire population group from South African territory. Or, as the Minister of Bantu Affairs in 1978 expressed it, 'If our policy is to be taken to its logical conclusion ... there will not be one Black person with South African citizen-ship' (Bindman, 1988: 25).

Conferring a racial identity onto people and reinforcing difference through spatial distribu-tion and segregation are powerful ways in which to entrench an ideology. Despite the efforts of the apartheid state to construct particular subjects, people resisted them. Dominating strategies of power always give rise to tactics of resistance (Gallagher, 2008). The bio-political imperative of optimizing the lives of one population group on the basis of race over all other population groups was patently unjust. It affected the entire population as the apartheid state was forced to introduce more and more repressive measures to maintain its policies as people resisted this differentiation.

Education was a key area in which this contestation took place. The racist and segregationist policies of the apartheid government were applied to education in the hope that two different subjects would emerge: a docile and subordinate Black subject, and a patriotic, docile, White subject. The Bantu Education Act of 1953 was constructed to

> prepare blacks for their special place in society. This involved a differential syllabus with greater emphasis on practical subjects, the use of vernacular instruction throughout the primary school, and the simultaneous introduction of both English and Afrikaans, not only as subjects but as media of instruction, in the lower secondary school: in other words, edu-cation for subordination in the workplace.
>
> (Davenport, 1991: 535)

The Act created a great deal of resistance. Teachers were involved in boycotts. The African National Congress (ANC) defied the act by keeping many children out of school. They began a 'Resistance Against Apartheid Campaign' in 1954 in which education was one of the key issues.[1] As the years progressed, opposition to unequal schooling continued. The watershed moment of the 1970s was the Soweto Uprising in 1976 that led to other disturbances across the country. Tension and violence continued into the 1980s. Students complained about unqualified, immoral teachers, the quality of education, educational facilities, insufficient textbooks, and costly school uniforms. They called for a single education department, believing it would create equality in the education system.

On the other side of the racial fence, Whites received funding and resources no other popu-lation group received. But White education was also tightly controlled. The National Education Policy Act, limited to Whites, reveals the vision of Christian National Education (CNE). A CNE institute founded in 1948 had explicit aims: 'We want no mixing of languages, no mixing of cultures, no mixing of religions, and no mixing of races. The struggle for the Christian and the National school still lies before us' (SPROCAS in Christie, 1991: 174).

White children were classified linguistically and English- and Afrikaans-speaking children went to different schools. From this education system 'patriotic christians' would be produced. Christian principles permeated through all aspects of schooling. Although education was to 'have a broad national character', the notion of the nation was limited to Whites, and Afrikaner nationalism (Christie, 1991: 176–178).

Within schools, two programmes exemplify the subject whose morals and values reflected the teachings of CNE: youth preparedness (YP) and moral preparedness (MP). YP was heavily influenced by military thinking. The presence of military thinking was not unusual in a country that had to increasingly call on its police and army to quell resistance. A gendered and patriotic subject was constructed who would willingly undertake compulsory national service, protect his country from internal threats coming from the townships and homelands, as well as the perceived external threats that emerged when colonial governments were replaced in all of South Africa's neighbouring countries. YP also manifested itself in cadet training where boys and girls were taught to march. Students attended MP classes and were taught to manage themselves in ways appropriate to apartheid ideology. Obedience to and a respect for authority were strongly emphasized. The ideal White subject was obedient, compliant, unquestioning, and respectful.

The effect of **bio-power** can be seen to have operated on the White population. An **anatomo-politics of the body** was directed onto White children's bodies to ensure docility. The allocation of adequate resources for all aspects of a population's welfare ensured little resistance. Creating and targeting a belief of the superiority of the White race through education created a sense of entitlement and a patriotic subject who would protect his country. This subject construction was not uniform and there were Whites who joined the struggle. Prinsloo's (2002) discourse analysis of Matric (grade 12) examination papers reveals the Afrikaner subject whose concerns are national, the global English citizen, and the narrow, localized concerns of the Black subject.

Apart from White schooling, education came to a standstill in many areas in the 1980s. In 1985 the government declared a state of emergency and the ANC released its slogan 'Render South Africa Ungovernable'. It called for a 'People's War' in which people would fight

> in every way possible using … Molotov cocktails, spears, petrol bombs, and small arms seized from whites.… We are talking about rent strikes, we are talking about bus boycotts, we are talking about the overthrow of the township councils of the puppets and the creation of the people's organs of power, the people's courts and so on.
>
> (Kane-Berman, 1993: 41–42)

With such actions came the realization that anti-apartheid movements had lost control of their followers, particularly Black youth. Serious questions arose as to how a society can be governed when its institutions lose power and its citizens become unregulated. Black writer, Nomavanda Mathiane, wrote:

> Political organisations have created monsters they cannot control. In the interests of mobilisation, they gave the children the power to disrupt life – they used them to enforce boycotts, work stay aways, etc. etc. and having tasted that power, they are not about to give it up. These children are now a threat to democracy.
>
> (in Kane-Berman, 1993: 88)

This was indeed a serious concern. Not all Black youth were ungovernable and nor was there a complete collapse of order. The overall political handover and first democratic election in 1994 were relatively peaceful. As the site of much of the struggle the education system has unquestionably been severely affected by the restricted, inferior disciplinary knowledge transmitted to students and the erosion of social control. Most children attend school and schooling has been relatively uninterrupted since 1994. But the political upheaval and its legacy have resulted in 'the development of a school culture which is inimical to learning and teaching' (Christie, 1998: 285) in many schools.

Creating a 'culture of learning and teaching' implies the re-establishment and/or reconfiguration of **bio-power**. Providing for the basic well-being of the school-going population requires the adequate provision of material and social conditions and functioning management structures like school governing bodies. Basic management of resources is not enough. The operation of disciplinary power is essential if South Africa is to create an environment of sound learning and teaching for all students. What leads to loss of control is 'a breakdown of rhythmical, disciplined learning and teaching, formally structured in time and space' (Christie, 1998: 289; 2001). It is thus the invisible, mundane disciplinary practices like keeping registers, having timetables, allocating classrooms, maintaining rituals like school assemblies, requiring punctuality and a respect for authority, that need to be actively reinstated in order to control populations and maintain order.

This means that apartheid subject constructions have to shift. Identifying oneself in terms of race as a fundamental marker of who one is, where the racial classification is informed by apartheid thinking, is inimical to building a more tolerant society. Overly docile subjects who are obediently patriotic and unthinking about what they are taught, or overly resistant subjects who will not be taught, cannot function optimally in a democratic society. Subjects need to be docile enough to submit to the rules a society sets down so that it can function. These rules need to be applied equally to all. Subjects who manage themselves responsibly create a society in which others, by implication, benefit. Driving in South Africa is a case in point. Responsible drivers who drive carefully take care of their own lives and in doing so protect the lives of other road users. With the huge number of road deaths every year, South Africans would do well to internalize this lesson. But subjects cannot be mindless in their docility. They need to be critical enough so that they do not submit unthinkingly to unjust, authoritarian regimes. A critical subject knows when to resist rather than using resistance as an immediate response to not getting one's way.

A new vision of the South African subject is encapsulated in a new education system and a revised curriculum. 'Curriculum is a disciplinary technology that directs how the individual is to act, feel, talk and "see" the world and "self". As such curriculum is a form of social regulation' (Popkewitz in Cannella, 1997: 91) that filters down through principals and teachers in schools. This new vision of the world as expressed by the Department of Education (DoE) desires 'a prosperous, truly united, democratic and internationally competitive country with literate, creative and critical citizens, leading productive, self-fulfilled lives in a country free of violence, discrimination and prejudice' (DoE, 1997b: 47).

It is these new beliefs that shape how South African school populations are to be governed. But it is the presence of daily disciplinary practices that Christie (1998, 2001) discusses that is crucial. The scope of such practices is often invisible but it is through their functioning that disciplinary power operates and education happens. In a close reading of Foucault, Gore (1995: 103) identifies eight practices that are integral to the functioning of disciplinary power:

Surveillance – defined as supervising, closely observing, watching, threatening to watch, avoiding being watched
Normalization – defined as invoking, requiring, setting, or conforming to a standard, defining the normal

Exclusion – defined as tracing the limits that will define difference, boundary, zone, defining the pathological

Distribution – defined as dividing into parts, arranging and ranking bodies in space

Classification – defined as differentiating individuals and/or groups from one another

Individualization – defined as giving individual character to, specifying the individuals

Totalization – defined as giving collective character to, specifying a collectivity or a will to conform

Regulation – defined as controlling by rule, subject to restrictions, adapting to requirements, invoking rules through sanctions, reward, or punishment.

It should be noted that the operation of these disciplinary practices is not the same in all schools or classrooms. The ways in which they are applied reflect a broader notion of what it means to produce a schooled population. Thus what counts as normal and how children are regulated are never neutral. They may be used oppressively or positively. Schools will take up this vision differently and traces of apartheid ideologies remain embedded in many schools (Dornbrack, 2008; Dixon & Dornbrack, 2010). With this point in mind, when analysing the operation of these disciplinary practices it should be noted that they do not work in isolation but often happen simultaneously or may be a result of another practice. For example, **surveillance** may result in **redistribution**. **Normalization** and **exclusion** could happen together as the abnormal is invoked to define the normal. Many of these practices are targeted directly onto the body. Their operation will be explored in several examples of classroom events in the following sections.

Regulatory techniques in classrooms

Is this the way you draw? Normalizing Grade 00 behaviour at the drawing table

Drawing is one of the tasks the Grade 00s complete on a daily basis. The content of what they draw is controlled by the children but the activity is under close teacher **surveillance**. By watching the children carefully Dawn **regulates** their behaviour, invoking rules verbally and physically. Several regulatory rules are associated specifically with literacy and reveal literacy **norms** for this classroom. The operation of these disciplinary practices is presented in a literary event at the drawing table. It takes the form of a photo story and accompanying transcript:[2]

> There are five children at the drawing table: three girls and two boys. Two girls have started to draw; Sibonelo is talking to one of the girls, holding a glue stick. He has not started drawing but is still sticking his symbol down (the children cannot write their names and are given symbols to identify them instead). Siphiwe has no symbol either but Chantal does. At this moment, Julia, who has finished her first task at the cutting table and is on her way to the puzzle table, stops here. She starts to tickle Siphiwe and then whispers in her friend Chantal's ear (Figures 4.2, 4.3). She tickles him again and then tells Chantal to do the same: 'Tickle him Chantal, tickle him.' Chantal leans over the table to tickle Siphiwe (Figure 4.4). There is giggling and laughing. Dawn who is supervising Friday baking at the next table reprimands them: 'Chantal is this the way you draw? Build the puzzles, Julia. You are sitting watching other children.' Chantal immediately sits down and picks up her felt-tipped pen and Julia sits down at the puzzle table (Figure 4.5). Chantal begins to draw but Siphiwe sits up on his seat, leans over and takes another pen from the container (it is wooden with separate holes to hold the pens). He begins to sing: 'pa chumchum ch chum chumchum da da da di di di didit.' The song gets progressively louder and he takes more pens out of the container until he is holding

Figure 4.2

Figure 4.3

Figure 4.4

Figure 4.5

Figure 4.6

Figure 4.7

about four (Figure 4.6). Dawn walks past the table to her desk and reprimands him: 'Siphiwe I see no work there by you. I see nothing. I hear noise all the time.' He starts to laugh like Donald Duck and continues to do so until Dawn comes back. She looks at Sibonelo who is still holding his symbol but his page is in front of Siphiwe. She then leans over and takes the pens from Siphiwe's hand and the rest in front of him that he has put down and replaces them in the container saying: 'And I want them to stand on their head. Lungelo you can't

Figure 4.8

Figure 4.9

Figure 4.10

Figure 4.11

Figure 4.12

Figure 4.13

draw with gloves' (Figures 4.7, 4.8). She then moves back to the table she was originally at. Lungelo takes off her gloves (Figure 4.9). Siphiwe now has the glue stick to glue his symbol on the page but he waves it in front of Chantal's face and starts to sing the letters of the alphabet: 'ABCDEFG'. She gets annoyed and she either pokes or smacks him on the leg (Figure 4.10). 'Hey Chantal!' he cries out, which prompts Dawn to look up and see Sibonelo has still done nothing: 'Sibonelo I see no picture coming.' Chantal continues drawing, carefully placing the pens back in the container. She also has Siphiwe's page underneath her own and Siphiwe tries to take it back while she holds down both pages (Figure 4.11). In doing so she knocks a pink pen that has been precariously placed at the edge of the table onto the floor. Sibonelo has finally stuck his symbol on his page. Siphiwe takes his page back. Dawn sees the pen on the floor: 'Chantal there is a *khoki* [felt-tipped pen] there on the floor by your chair.' Chantal bends over to pick it up and starts to put it back but the holes closest to her are full and she makes a general movement in the middle but does not find a hole and the pen falls (Figure 4.12). Dawn says: 'Chantal put it in nicely.' She takes the pen she was drawing with and carefully replaces it and then does the same with the first one (Figure 4.13).

In this event every child is disciplined for some infraction. Each of these infractions reveals undisciplined bodies from Julia and Chantal's expansive tickling to Lungelo's glove-covered hands. These children are not being deliberately naughty, rather there is a tension between the ideal schooled and literate subject and who the young children are, they have only been at school for a few months. Thus in this class there is a need for quite intensive **regulation** on Dawn's part.

A number of **norms** and regulations can be extrapolated from this event. The first is the injunction for children to stick their symbol onto the page before they begin a task. All the children, despite Sibonelo's slowness, have internalized this. The symbols reveal the operation of **classification**. By identifying their work as their own it can be **ranked** and Dawn can tell what progress they are making. Another rule points to **distribution**. In moving to another table it is not appropriate to stop off and disrupt children working, as Julia does. Neither is it appropriate to be too noisy. The practice of **individualization** is present here because Siphiwe is called out by Dawn when she comments on his lack of progress and that she 'hear[s] noise all the time'. In this particular event the individualizing is strong as Chantal, Sibonelo, Siphiwe, Lungelo, and Julia's indiscretions are directed at them and for all the class to hear. **Totalization** does not operate in this instance because Dawn does not comment on the lack of progress of the group as a whole.

There are clear rules that emerge as to how literacy implements are managed: children must use one pen at a time; they must be put back in the container with the lids facing down; each pen must be placed in a hole in the container so it can stand up; if anything falls to the ground it must be picked up and put in the correct place; drawing can only happen properly if hands are unimpeded by clothing; children need to stay on task.

All of these regulations directly involve the body – where the body should be located in space and time and how bodies work with literacy implements. The imposition of all these regulations is set in place through **surveillance**. I would argue that **surveillance** is the most powerful disciplinary technique in operation in this event. The power of Dawn's gaze is evident in the way she expresses herself. It is very clear that these children are being watched closely. She tells them: 'Siphiwe I *see* no work there by you, I *see* nothing'; 'Sibonelo, I *see* no picture coming'. This is not just a powerful seeing gaze, it hears as well: 'I *hear* noise all the time.' The repetition of the word 'see' reinforces to the children that they are being watched. During this activity the power of the watcher is located solely with the teacher. The power relations work top-down in this instance. Julia cannot sit 'watching other children'. She needs to work.

When Foucault talks about **surveillance** emanating from the panopticon, one of the points he makes is that 'it is permanent in its effects even if it is discontinuous in its action' (1977: 201). Its power lies in the fact that individuals know they are being watched but cannot verify when this happens. In not knowing whether they are watched or not, the individual begins to monitor their own behaviour, internalizing the disciplinary gaze, becoming both the watcher and the watched. So the process of **self-regulation** begins. The fact that it is impossible to watch individuals constantly does mean that some incidents slip through the **surveillance** system. Chantal is an example of a partially self-regulating subject. As a literate subject she abides by most of the rules but she is also easily distracted and cannot stay on task. When Dawn asks her 'Is this the way you draw?' she refocuses and begins to draw. She continues doing so until Siphiwe distracts her and then loses all control and retaliates by hitting him. Unsurprisingly Dawn misses what is a quick reaction and reprimands Sibonelo instead who has made no progress. If she had seen this, then **exclusion** as a disciplinary practice might have come into play since hitting other children is an action beyond accepted norms. One could argue that Chantal is not a totally resistant subject – hitting out is an immediate unconscious response that would have happened whether Dawn was watching or not. She does not look to see whether Dawn is watching her before she acts. To become a successful schooled subject Chantal needs to learn to control herself and her reactions so she can concentrate on her work.

Alongside verbal commands, Dawn's physical presence also works to discipline the children. When she walks past the table and sees Siphiwe singing rather than working she reprimands him verbally. On her return, nothing has happened so she physically removes the pens in his hand and replaces them in the container. She explains how she wants them to be managed which is an oblique reference to not doing the work. The fact that he has had the pens taken away by a stronger more powerful body reinforces the verbal message to do some work. The type of literate subject being constructed here is one who can manage resources so that everyone at the table has access to them. Using one pen at a time considers the collective.

The last comment I want to make here is a broad one. A productive learning environment is created at the tables. This is a literacy-rich environment that the children are immersed in. There are very few reprimands for the noise children make – unless it is loud and obvious that they are not 'on task'. This 'lack' of **regulation** is in fact productive. There are lots of conversations among the children both about what they are doing and other issues related to their personal lives. These conversations take place in a number of languages and seem to be dependent on who the conversants are. Speakers who have the same mother tongue use it to talk to each other. They switch to English to communicate with other children. In this multilingual classroom code-switching appears for the most part to be co-operative and about accommodation rather than exclusion.[3] The close proximity of small groups of children at the tables generates conversations in which a vast amount of learning takes place. This is in contrast to the Grade 00 class who complete the tasks at their desks in silence. This silence becomes embodied in a performance where children are told to lock their mouths and throw away the key before they begin work (see Chapter 6).

Reading bodies, reading texts: the Dippy Duck lesson

The literacy event described here took place in Helen's Grade 1 class and is also represented in the form of a photo story. The children had been at school for just under a month when this was captured. It shows the symbiotic relationship between learning to read and the disciplinary control exerted over the body to enable a particular form of reading to take place.

From this event five forms of disciplinary control that target the body can be extrapolated:

- spatial distribution of bodies
- disciplinary control signalling transitions to capture attention
- reinforcing behavioural norms
- training of the **linguistic habitus**
- signalling behaviour of participants of 'the Literacy Club' (Smith, 1988).

These five forms of control are not exclusive to Grade 1 and are present in various approaches teachers use in the other Grades.

Figure 4.14

Figure 4.15

Figure 4.16

Figure 4.17

Figure 4.18

Figure 4.19

Figure 4.20

Figure 4.21

Figure 4.22

Figure 4.23

Figure 4.24

Figure 4.25

Figure 4.26

Figure 4.27

Figure 4.28

Figure 4.29

Figure 4.30

Figure 4.31

Figure 4.32

Figure 4.33

Figure 4.34

Figure 4.35

Figure 4.36

Figure 4.37

Figure 4.38

Spatial distribution of bodies

Before this reading lesson took place the children were involved in another task at their desks. Helen needed to relocate them to the carpet. The children need to learn to get to the carpet in an orderly manner and where to distribute their bodies. The process begins at their desks. First, Helen organizes space in relation to time when she tells the children to clear their desks in preparation for the numeracy task they will do on their return. Helen tells them:

> Pack away please I don't want anything on the tables.... Now I am asking you again – Come to the mat but you are going to do it quietly – uh, uh, go back.

The act of packing away involves children having to be retold to put their things in their chair-bags (cloth bags which fit onto the back of the children's chairs in which they store books, readers, pencil cases, etc.), and the move to the carpet is far from orderly, as the children do not move together (Figure 4.14). They also do not move in the same way. Amy takes the opportunity to add a performative aspect in the move from one space to another. In the relocation, Helen's attention cannot be focused on every child and thus **surveillance** is limited; in this gap another space is created as Amy's body is no longer a schooled body but reflects the body of a ballet dancer. As she moves to the carpet her carriage is upright and her arms reflect the arm positions of ballet dancers (Figures 4.15, 4.16).

While Amy is in the process of seating herself, Helen's attention is on the opposite side of the class where the children have distributed themselves incorrectly (Figure 4.17). Before she can begin the lesson she has to reorganize several children (Figure 4.18). **Individualization, totalization**, and **classification** all operate here as individuals are named, groups are referred to and gender and height are organizational categories:

> What is the matter here? It is supposed to be boy–girl. Why do you sit like that?... Move up Vicky. Move up Vicky. More Vicky. Where you [inaudible] You are at the top of her.... Move a little forward. Kim where are you supposed to sit? Is she supposed to sit there, Steve? Is she supposed to sit near Stephanie? Who must sit behind you?

> I don't think you're supposed to sit there Tshepo because you are not supposed to be anywhere near Vukani. Now move a little bit back please Steve…. Bongani come and sit in front of Tshepo please. Move back a bit Steve.

> You guys move up there, space yourselves out please. Lungelo *skyf*[4] a little bit shiver, shiver, shiver, come a little bit forward here. Move back James. MOVE BACK JAMES. A little bit more James. More. Thank you. Tshepo are you sitting nicely? Are you sitting nicely? Bongani, cross those legs. Khanyisa are you sitting in the right place because I know you are taller than André?

Sitting on the carpet for reading means that everyone sits in an allocated place, from shortest to tallest in each row, with boys alternating with girls (**classification**). There also needs to be enough space for everyone which Helen communicates in a variety of ways: in English, Afrikaans (*skyf*), with repetition, and with varying levels of volume. Children also need to 'sit nicely', which reveals a behavioural **norm** whose bodily translation is 'sitting with crossed legs'.

With Helen's attention on reorganizing the class, the close proximity in which the children find themselves can be both frustrating and also very tempting. Throughout this event there was shoving and pushing and hitting as children got too close to each other, venting their frustration when they would not be seen. Unlike Chantal these children are **resistant**. They know how they should behave but choose not to when they know they are under limited **surveillance**. Nqobi, sitting behind Claudia, succumbed to temptation by leaning forward while Helen was busy, to poke her in the back (Figures 4.19, 4.20). The result is a public reprimand, and Nqobi's body language indicates the public shaming:

CLAUDIA: Miss, Nqobi is poking me on my back.
HELEN: Nqobi, is Claudia your wife? [He puts his head down and shakes it.] Is she your child? [He shakes his head.] Is she your girlfriend? [He shakes his head again.] Leave her alone please.

These comments also reveal particular norms about personal space. Helen intimates that because Nqobi does not have an intimate sexual or familial relationship with Claudia he is not allowed to touch her. Learning to respect the boundaries of personal space, however they are culturally construed, is important in a country where rape and child abuse are endemic.

Disciplinary control: signalling transitions to capture attention

Signalling that a lesson is to begin or a new element is to be added is often conveyed verbally by teachers. In the research classes this was sometimes accompanied by a change in the teacher's body language, by clapping her hands, using a whistle, or changing spaces by moving to the front of the classroom. In Helen's class, gaining attention involves controlling the bodies of the children before the lesson can either begin or resume. In this event it is the control of bodies that operates as a structuring element as the lesson shifts from one text to another.

Helen gains the children's attention by signalling with her body. She lifts her hands so they are just below shoulder height and keeps them open, then she closes them to make a fist. This is the signal for the children to repeat the rhyme she has taught them – that will also allow for the final element of what constitutes 'sitting nicely' – folded arms. Once she has caught several children's attention she begins the rhyme – the class joins in and follows her actions (Figures 4.21, 4.22, 4.23, 4.24):

Open them shut them, open them shut them.
Give a little clap and fold them in your lap.

She then introduces the class to the letter 'd' and reads them the Letterland story about Dippy Duck (Figures 4.25, 4.26):

> Right I am going to read you a story about a friend of mine who wants to come and visit you guys. Do you think we should let my friend come and visit you? Do you really think so?... You must listen carefully to the story.

At the end of the story there is a question and answer session relating to the letter 'd', the pictures in the book and words that begin with 'd'. When Helen has finished talking about Dippy Duck she then moves on to talk about *Mo the Monkey*, the first class reader. Once again this shift is accompanied by drawing attention to the body in moves reminiscent of the game 'Simon Says' (Figures 4.29–4.36). Helen makes the children copy her movements, even using the commands of the game 'do this', 'do that'. The focus is not just on the children responding, but on their responding correctly, particularly to the movements that require fine motor co-ordination:

> Right I want you to put up your hands. Uh, uh. No don't make that noise
>   Sit down my dear.
>   I'm not holding my arms so wide. I'm not holding my hands in her face.
>   No, (to Kumo) you are going too far.... Do this (movement) and that (and that) and down and up and up.... I'm not moving my arms I am moving my hands.

The children's movements are not a perfect mimicry of Helen's as several struggle with them. Figure 4.32 shows the overextended arms of one child. Figure 4.34 shows Helen correcting another child's gestures, and Figures 4.35 and 4.36 indicate that some children are a second behind Helen's gestures: they still have their hands on their heads while her arms are raised. But in having to follow her movements the children refocus their attention, making it easier for Helen to introduce the next part of the lesson.

Reinforcing behavioural norms

Throughout the interaction Helen reminds the children how they are expected to behave. Once again these instructions are directed at the body. The reminders are directed to the whole class (**totalization**) when she knows there may be an over-enthusiastic response:

> Right, don't shout at me – I want you to tell me what colour is Dippy Duck? Vukani?

Or to individuals (**individualization**):

> And Bongani cross your legs please. Where did you see the dragonfly Bongani?
>   That's lovely Vicky but put your hand up hey.
>   Everyone is pinching you today. What's wrong with them?

These comments serve as a gentle reminder of class rules. The use of 'please' and the follow-up question to Bongani, and the reinforcement of Vicky's answer mean that the discipline is not foregrounded, rather the children's interactions with the text are.

When the interaction does not centre on the text, disciplining is forceful. During the discussion, another teacher walks into the class. Helen prompts them to greet her and the class responds to her cue. While her attention is focused on the other teacher the character of the class changes. The noise level does not alter significantly but the relative docility of bodies alters rapidly to encompass a variety of movements that involve rocking against each other, hair pulling, and hitting. A comparison of Figures 4.26, 4.27, and 4.28 demonstrates the point. In the first Helen is reading to the class and the children are sitting still, listening. In the second picture she is interrupted by another teacher and by the third the scene has changed. Front left of the photograph one girl is leaning back into another. This girl's hair will be pulled by the girl sitting behind her. In the middle of the picture a boy is headbutting the boy in front of him. This boy's head, in turn, is pushed back to touch the 'headbutter's' head. On the far right of the picture two more children are smacking each other. I think that it is necessary to point out that while some of these engagements are a result of anger or frustration, some are merely physical games the children indulge in without malice. Touching one another is more a desire for affirmation (and a reaction) than anything violent.

Helen's response, on the other hand, is forceful. Her tone changes completely and she demonstrates the power of a panopticon – even though she was not looking directly at the class, she has seen them. They are all in trouble and individuals are picked out and **classified** as having broken the boundaries of acceptable behaviour. She brings their bodies back into line, literally and figuratively with her final comment:

> Right – No I am not happy! I am not happy with your behaviour! Bongani turn around and face the front. Tshepo move back please there is enough space. But you want to sit right up against him. Put your hands on your laps.

Linguistic habitus

An area of competence these teachers assess in reading is pronunciation. For a phonics-based programme to work, children need to produce the correct sounds. Helen goes beyond making the connection between the letter–sound correspondence to demonstrates how the sound itself is produced. When asked to identify something in the picture other than Dippy Duck, one girl points to a capital D. Helen immediately distinguishes between the sound of the capital and lowercase letter by asking what sound Dippy Duck makes. She asks Kurtis, who struggles to identify the sound, and so she emphasizes it for him:

> Oh, the capital letter D ('dee') – Dippy Duck's door. Right. But what sound does Dippy Duck make? Does she say 'dee'? What sound does she make Kurtis? 'd' -ippy 'd' – uck What sound does she make?... When I say Dippy Duck what sound do you hear? I know ducks make quack, quack but Dippy Duck is special like Annie Apple. Can apples really talk? [Class shakes their heads.]

Once the sound is identified Helen makes the class practise it. She makes the class listen to the sound as she models it, emphasizing the plosive nature of 'd' for the class and then they repeat it. She also draws their attention explicitly to how this consonant is produced:

HELEN: Listen, listen 'd'. Listen, listen 'd'. Say it
(Class says 'd' several times)
HELEN: When you say 'd' where is your tongue?
CLAUDIA: On your palate

HELEN: Yes it is on your palate at the top of your mouth. It's just behind your teeth. Put your tongue there, 'd', no, no, like that straight up you must feel it press up 'd', 'd', 'd'.
(Class makes d sounds)
HELEN: Wow, so many dippy ducks. Thank you

'D' is a lingual alveolar consonant, but Claudia produces an impressive technical term that Helen does not discredit as incorrect but refines her answer by adding 'It's just behind your teeth', but in doing so she also provides information as to how the sound is made.

In the previous sections, disciplining the body has primarily been associated with the body in general. But here training of the **linguistic habitus** is taking place. Bourdieu (1992: 86) points out that language is a body technique that has a marked impact on how one negotiates one's way through the world:

> The sense of acceptability which orients linguistic practices is inscribed in the most deep-rooted of bodily dispositions: it is the whole body which responds by its posture, but also by its inner reactions, or more specifically, the articulatory ones, to the tension of the market. Language is a body technique, and specifically linguistic, especially phonetic, competence is a dimension of bodily hexis in which one's whole relation to the social world, and one's whole socially informed relation to the world are expressed.

The teachers in this study have their own **linguistic habitus** tied to their identities beyond the school. An example of this is reflected in the pronunciation of the word 'says'. In extended utterances Helen pronounces 'says' with a short vowel sound [sez] but in shorter utterances and most noticeably in sentences like 'Dippy Duck says...' 'says' is pronounced with a diphthong [seiz]. The use of the diphthong indicates a dialectal variety of English rather than standard South African English pronunciation. At no time did any children in the class question this pronunciation and, when repeating after her in the reading lessons, all the children copied her pronunciation. I do not want to argue that all the children in the class will take on this particular pronunciation because that would be dismissing the influence of children's linguistic communities at home, in the media, and within their peer groups. Some children will take this speech pattern on because it is reinforced outside school, and for others it may be a speech pattern related to school practices.

With English perceived as a powerful language in South Africa that is closely connected to social and economic mobility, there is a strong desire on the part of many parents for their children to be educated in English (De Klerk, 2002; Kamwangamalu, 2003; McKinney, 2007; Mda, 2004). Accent and pronunciation are important markers in the linguistic market Bourdieu refers to. Speaking with a 'White'[5] English accent is seen to be the ideal – and students who speak fluent English without the intonations of African languages are often referred to as having a 'Model-C accent'. This comes at a cost and in the townships these students are often labelled as 'coconuts' (black on the outside white on the inside) who have sold out.

Joining the 'Literacy Club'

Frank Smith (1988) argues that for children to be competent readers and writers they need to belong to a community of language users that he calls the 'Literacy Club'. He details eight characteristics of learning through participation in the club, namely that learning is: meaningful, useful, continual, and effortless, incidental, collaborative, vicarious, and free of risk. While much of this learning takes place outside school, teachers have a role to play. He writes:

> Teachers should facilitate and promote the admission of children into the literacy club. Children who come to school already members of the club, who regard themselves as the kind of people who read and write, should find expanded opportunities in school for engaging in all the activities of club membership. Children who have not become members before they get to school should find the classroom the place where they are immediately admitted to the club.
>
> (Smith, 1988: 11)

The notion of a literacy club is helpful and also resonates with what Gee (2003) describes as affiliation groups and networks that people join and learn through. What is important here is the recognition that some children have already joined the literacy club, and others are introduced to it at school. The way the Dippy Duck reading lesson operates is that while there is formal instruction, these children are also introduced to a notion of reading that goes beyond word recognition. The body is incorporated in particular ways as a means through which children are invited to participate in the literacy club.

Being a member of the literacy club in this class requires that certain content be mastered. Rather than the teacher just teaching letters and sounds, she incorporates a story to help facilitate this learning. Not only are children in the process of learning to read, they are also being read to. This implies that stories can function as pleasurable and learning experiences. All the aspects of story time and books that the preschoolers learn during story time are reinforced, or for those who have not been to preschool, introduced for the first time. Smith's (1988: 11) assertion that stories should not be viewed as 'extras, rewards or frills' in classrooms but rather should be integrated as meaningful reading activities is present here. In terms of facilitating a growing understanding of texts, Helen also explicitly indicates the metaphorical level that stories work on by drawing the children's attention to the fact that Dippy Duck is a fictional character. As such Barton's (1994: 81) assertion that 'one of the most important aspects of learning to read is the spoken language around a written text' is realized.

Helen works out levels of participation and understanding of the children in the literacy club by asking them what they know.

HELEN: Who knows Dippy Duck? Do you know Dippy Duck Khanyisa? Hey? Have you seen Dippy Duck before?
[Khanyisa answers in the negative.]
HELEN: You haven't seen Dippy Duck. Who else hasn't seen Dippy Duck? You haven't seen Dippy Duck Maxine? Hey shame. That's so sad. OK, I am going to show you. Put your hands down; close your eyes so that everyone can see at the same time. Close your eyes. OK open your eyes. [She turns the books around to show the class the picture.] Right, can you see Dippy Duck?
CLASS: Yes

Helen's understanding is informed by the children displaying how much they know via their bodies; they raise their hands – several have never been introduced to the letter 'd' or its concomitant character Dippy Duck. She indicates that this is a sad state of affairs, but it is not shameful. Her use of 'Hey shame' is a colloquial indicator of sympathy. The fact that the children raise their hands to admit their ignorance is an indication that the reading environment is a safe one. As an experienced member of the club, Helen can alter this for them. She does this in a collaborative way by involving the whole class. She makes them close their eyes so that they can all meet Dippy Duck together, although the learning experience may be new for some or reinforcement for others. Making the children close their eyes adds an element of excitement to the event and emphasizes the power of the visual in stories. This is a subtle way of getting the class to conform (**totalization**) to a particular conception of reading that operates in a positive way as opposed to marking out deviant behaviour.

Texts in this class can also be a springboard for affirming children's life experiences and adding to their knowledge. The initial exercise after Helen read to the class involves identifying pictures from the book – while it is a labelling exercise it is also an exercise in application. Can the children do more than recognize and say the letter 'd'? Can they work out the initial letter in words? Once the word has been identified Helen asks the children to talk about their interaction and experience – in this case dragonflies. Elwin's answer creates an opportunity for incidental learning as Helen tells the class why a dragonfly's habitat is aquatic.

HELEN: In the tree. Let me see there is someone else I wanted to ask – Elwin have you seen a dragonfly before? Hey? Have you seen it, where did you see it?

ELWIN: By my cousin

HELEN: By your cousin, where was it [jokes] on your cousin's hair, where? (touches her hair)

ELWIN: By the river

HELEN: By the river OK. Put your hands down guys. Let me tell you, dragonflies love to be around water. 'Cos you know why?

[Vicky says something about eggs.]

HELEN: That's lovely Vicky but you put your hand up hey. They lay their eggs in the water. They live by the water because that's where they catch a lot of their food, OK, by the water some of the insects fall down there on the water and the dragonfly zooms in [Helen makes a sucking sound] and he [continues making a sucking sound] it up. Hey Kumo. OK what else do we see in the picture, Adam?

This interaction is playful as well as instructive as Helen uses her body to become a dragonfly, swooping down on Kumo sitting in the front row to demonstrate how a dragonfly finds its prey. Stories can be a springboard for validating experience, additional instruction, and play. Helen further reinforces the latter by drawing in the whole class by physically demonstrating another word that begins with 'd'.

HELEN: Ja we've got daisy. Something that your body can do

[She starts to dance.]

STUDENT: Dizzy

HELEN: Diz – oh you can also get dizzy [she demonstrates with her body by pretending to almost fall off the chair]. What else can your body do? What am I doing?

CLASS: Dancing

HELEN: Can you do … [Class begins to dance.]

The class giggles as they do this, finding a rhythm and enjoying themselves (Figures 4.37, 4.38). This interaction demonstrates Helen's understanding of who the children are in her class. The majority of these children come from cultures where dance is an important element of identity and cultural expression. Reading is not something divorced from who these children are, but a way into this knowledge, and a validation of it. Reading, like dance, involves a particular set of bodily postures that convey pleasure. An understanding of the space is also implicit. In this interaction no one stands or moves away from the carpet – it is a big enough space to contain the expansiveness of the movement while also clearly demarcating the boundary in which it can exist.

Literacy as a disciplinary tool: writing lines and writing names

Literacy can be harnessed as a tool in the workings of disciplinary power. The most obvious form of this is disciplinary writing that captures individuals and records their abilities and behaviours. In the second example described here writing is used as a means to record trouble-makers through **peer surveillance**. Power in this instance operates laterally as children develop a system for monitoring each other's behaviour. In the first example, drawn from Catherine's Grade 1 class, writing is used as a form of bodily punishment. The section questions the effectiveness of this technique in Grade 1.

Writing lines: 'I must behave'

For many children the process of learning to write neatly and correctly may be a punishment to be endured. In the incident discussed here writing is harnessed as a form of punishment. Several children were talking in class and were given lines to write out. Since corporal punishment was banned in South Africa alternative means to punish need to be applied. This form of punishment does not reveal the wrath of the teacher descending on the body of the child and disciplining through public humiliation, rather the external power of the teacher compels the body of the child to punish itself. Writing out lines requires a docile body to complete the mundane and repetitive nature of the task. The subject may internalize the crime (talking) and the punishment (writing lines) and regulate future behaviour. If the task is sufficiently long the pain of cramped fingers may serve as an additional reminder of the offence. Like other disciplinary practices, writing out lines functions as a punishment marking out an offender. But writing in itself is powerful. If the message written out is negative the writer is constructed in a negative light (a talker, a disruptive element, a subject who cannot/will not complete work). By writing the message over and over the offender takes it on – he or she is complicit in the judgement, it is acknowledged as truth. In addition, with young children in this study the effects of harnessing the body does render it docile. Once children are engaged in a task which requires focused body movements they are seldom able to multi-task and engage in other forms of disruptive behaviour.

But, how does this disciplinary technique impact on the subject if they cannot decode the message? Figure 4.39 is what one boy, Sivuyile, produced when the class was unruly and he was given lines to write out. At the top of the page, written in red pen by the teacher is the boy's name and below it the words 'I must behave'. In fact this message is rather ironic because Sivuyile was one of the quieter boys in the class and better behaved than many others. The page reveals a number of things about the kind of literate subject he is. There is evidence of varying levels of mastery. The first point is that as a child in the beginning stages of learning to read and write (in a language other than his mother tongue) he is probably unable to decode this sentence and it is thus meaningless. The orthography does indicate that deciphering the combination of letters and words is probably beyond him. The misspelling of 'behave' as 'behawe' reveals a possible lack of familiarity with the letters 'v' and 'w', an inability to distinguish them, as well as a possible unfamiliarity with handwritten messages and their stylistic vagaries.

Sivuyile has internalized a number of other requirements needed to write – there are consistent spaces between the words. He has also written the sentence in relatively straight lines on an unlined piece of paper. It does seem that writing out 'I must behave' became a strain for Sivuyile whose previous writing tasks involved copying lines of one letter of the alphabet, and the occasional short sentence. This is illustrated by the shifts in letter formation: the 'u' in 'must' begins to look like a 'y' towards the middle of the page; the 'h' in 'behave' sometimes looks like an 'n'; the spatial arrangement of the final 'behave' is cramped with the 'a' overlap-

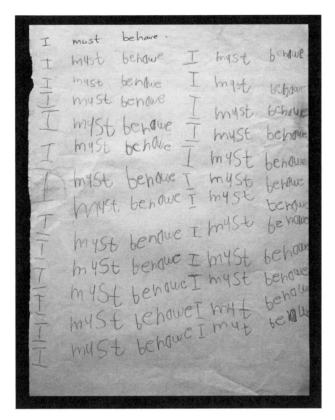

Figure 4.39 Writing lines.

ping the 'h'. There is only one other spelling mistake besides 'behawe' – the 's' in 'must' has been left out in the final two sentences which probably reflects fatigue. Sivuyile has mastered directionality. Rather than writing the sentence as a list he has written the sentence twice to reach the end of the line. (Had he written one sentence per line he could have completed the job faster.) In terms of the spatial arrangement of words on the page, he has written literally right to the end of the page instead of leaving a small margin. The final sentences on the right-hand side become increasingly cramped and this may account for the upward tilt of the sentences towards the end of the page so that all the letters can fit in. In a task that required more concentration than many of the other short class work tasks Sivuyile demonstrated an ability to go beyond the limits of class tasks.

The answer to the initial question has still not been addressed: if this is a meaningless task because Sivuyile cannot decode what he is copying, what power does this disciplinary task have? The initial goal of writing out lines was met, and that was to stop children misbehaving; the effort and time that it took to write this page out for a beginning writer imply a docility and focus on the task at hand. But such a punishment meted out too often is possibly dangerous for children learning to write, and its mundane onerousness could be associated negatively with all other forms of writing – particularly since at this stage of schooling these Grade 1 children had very little control over what they wrote. Rather than creating a docile subject as the task was intended, a resistant (non-) writer may be produced.

Peer surveillance in Grade 3

Earlier chapters alluded to the limited use of the carpet as a space in Grade 3. It is a site of disciplinary power though. Classroom control is, on the whole, managed by the teacher who teaches, gives instructions, and reprimands here. Although present to an extent in all grades, by Grade 3 **peer surveillance** increases in both occurrence and organization. Children are placed in charge by the teacher to maintain order. The choice of child is random: they may be model students or naughty ones; they may have finished their work, or simply be the first child in view. The first thing they do is appropriate the teacher's space by **redistributing** themselves on the carpet. This is accompanied by a shift in subjectivity as the schooled subject who is supposed to be docile and under the authority of the teacher now gains greater, although transient, power and status as an enforcer of discipline. Their movement becomes freer as they pace along the carpet. In the younger classes the children sit on the teacher's chair on the carpet. Their demeanour shifts – they sit straighter and look sterner; sometimes they point their fingers or talk in a firmer voice.

It is in the Grade 3 class that this officially sanctioned peer-regulation occurred in a way that brings literacy, **surveillance**, and **regulation** together. Without fail, the Grade 3 'surveillance officer' took their chair from their desk, placed it in front of the blackboard, and stood on it to gain a better vantage point. The blackboard, a traditional medium of literacy, is a literacy resource but it also represents the power of the teacher. It is the space where she writes, the space where children are expected to look in order to carry out tasks assigned to them. They do not write on it themselves. Being put in charge means that the student can commandeer this sacred space of writing. The board is no longer something to be read; for a short while, sanction has been given to write on it. The board represents both a record of those who misbehave and the success of the watcher. In Grade 3 it is a highly visible record because the height of the chair allows for the names to be clearly displayed. The presence of a child's name on the board implies three things – the first is a public shaming; if this does not bring shame, then the threat of punishment when the teacher returns to take control should. These two elements combined should motivate others to regulate their own behaviour (and there is a move from **individualization** to **totalization**).

But commandeering a space of power does not imply success. Peer-regulation relies on a number of other factors. If discipline is to be successfully enforced then the child in charge has to regulate his/her own behaviour. The gazer is enmeshed in a network of real disciplinary gazes. The children often abuse this position by talking themselves, making concessions for friends, or being harsher on children they dislike. Once this position is compromised, there is no shortage of children willing to report infractions. Arguments often break out, with various groups presenting their own version of 'the truth'.

The disciplinary gaze in the Grade 3 class is gendered. In this class the gender divide is spatially demarcated – the girl and boy 'surveillance officers' write names on opposite ends of the board.

What is essential is that the external control of the teacher is effectively and consistently used. When it is not, the success of peer-regulation is undermined. Children may behave themselves because they are being watched and they fear punishment; if there is no punishment, the behaviour is seen to be condoned. In several classes, the taking of names as a disciplinary practice was unsuccessful in maintaining complete control of the class. It seems that when there were no consequences to behaving badly, taking names lost its disciplinary power. This was coupled with the frequency of using peer-regulation as a means to control the class. As a technique, this appeared to be more successful when it was implemented less frequently, and the teacher reprimanded the children. The power of this technique is also lessened when the list of names grows. The child put in charge can undermine the success of peer-regulation. When they overstep their authority and assume more power there is almost immediate resistance – and an increase in noise levels. The child is still a peer and not a teacher. When the child keeps complaining to the teacher about what the others are doing it displays a loss of control. This often results in a reprimand by the teacher. Once the child 'in charge' is reprimanded, their power over their peers is lost and the power shifts.

'We must all be in charge of ourselves.' The self-regulating subject?

> The Grade 0 children are waiting on the carpet in their places for the Language Ring to begin when Lisa is called to the office. As soon as she leaves the children move away from their places although they are still seated. Then Jason, Tshepo, and Keven stand up in the middle of the carpet and begin what looks like a gumboot dance (a dance originating from the mines, where miners jump and rhythmically slap their gumboots), lifting and stamping their feet. The rest of the children who are still sitting on the edge of the carpet get caught up in the dance, banging their hands on the floor to create a rhythm for the dancers. The external eye of surveillance is closed with Lisa's absence and the action of the children who break 'rank' draws the others in, making them all part of the performance. Although not completely installed, the disciplinary gaze has begun to be internalized by some of the children. One of them asks: 'Who's in charge?' The reply is 'No one'. This response opens up a space for the children to continue their performance because they are not being watched. Then Zama responds: 'We must all be in charge of ourselves, then we tell on ourselves.'

This incident, taken from fieldnotes, is fascinating for a number of reasons. It verifies Foucault's point that power is not static, it circulates, as do the Grade 3 **peer surveillance** practices. It also makes a point about **regulation**. This incident would not have happened with Lisa in the classroom because, as the teacher, she holds most of the power the majority of the time. As she left the classroom the power dynamics shifted. They did not shift to me although I was the adult left in the classroom. I maintained my role as silent observer. The power was taken up by the three boys with strong personalities who took control of the carpet. Had the dance turned into a fight then one of the other children might have stopped it or, because I was the adult in the class with the ear of the teacher, I could have wrested power from the boys.

The incident also reveals the kind of classroom environment that Lisa worked hard to create. This class has been taught to work together as a collective and to support each other. This notion of the collective remains part of the class's individual subjectivities but is transformed without the presence of the teacher. It is not just the dancing boys who transgress, it is the entire class who get caught up in the performance. They urge the dancers on by creating a rhythm for them to dance to. While the act is transgressive – they are supposed to be sitting quietly not leaping around or banging on the carpet – it works to hold the class's attention.

Such a performance is unsustainable and several children realize this. As 'watchers' of the dance they realize what they are witnessing is not acceptable. As participants in the dance they are watching themselves. The internal regulatory gaze comes to the fore. They realize that the power relations have shifted in such a way that there is no one left in charge. Lisa did not hand over her power to someone else. If the answer to who is left in charge is no one, then the responsible subject is required to take charge of their own behaviour. Zama's internal regulatory gaze acknowledges that the external gaze does not need to be permanently present when there is an internal gaze. There is also the recognition that when one transgresses one needs to take responsibility for one's actions by confessing.

Of course just because Zama had come to this realization did not mean that the dance came to a halt and the entire class **regulated** their behaviour. Some children halted and others continued to gain a little more illicit pleasure from unrestrained freedom of movement that the carpet allowed. The tables turned, sentries were posted to watch for Lisa's return.

Docility, resistance, and self-regulation

Foucault talks about man being a confessing animal. The religious confessional has been assimilated into a secular world. The deluge of talk-show confessions is certainly evidence of this. Alongside Zama's desire to confess, this section contains my confession about making generalized assumptions and adjusting my thinking about **self-regulation**. Larger questions about the kind of society South Africans live in have been important in trying to understand the environment in which education takes place, and the effect that education has on subject formation. Living in a country where people are not always highly regulated and can be ungovernable requires an understanding of how this is so, the reasons why, when generally regulated people become ungovernable, and the role of education. The answers are complex and they have to do with the ways in which we have structured our society and are attempting to restructure it, and the ways in which individuals respond to this. A recent example illustrates this complexity. Lecturers at a tertiary institution in Gauteng damaged property by breaking windows and throwing stones. Their CEO, who had been accused of corruption, nepotism, and maladministration, had kept his job after an inquiry. After destroying property and causing teaching to come to a halt, they later went to the police station to hand themselves over to the police (Karolia, 2010a, 2010b). In the first half of this incident the angry mob-like behaviour is indicative of resistant, **ungovernable** subjects. In the second, a level of **self-regulation** emerges as they know they have broken the law. As responsible citizens they hand themselves over to the police. Hitting out in a violent manner is not sanctioned in a Grade 00 classroom like Dawn's and Chantal will learn that hitting other children is wrong. But when educators behave in this way the disciplinary power they hold diminishes and undermines the power for others.

I am aware of this complexity but did not take it into account when, at the beginning of the research, the question about levels of **self-regulation** over time emerged. I had assumed that the longer children were exposed to the disciplinary power of the school, in a school that is considered functional, where disciplinary practices operate, levels of **self-regulation** would increase. The reality is of course far more complex than that. In several cases it was not **self-regulation** that increased but **resistance**. Thinking in binaries is too simplistic because the opposite of a docile subject is not a resistant one. In our own lives we know we are not just one or the other, sometimes we are docile and sometimes we resist norms and rules. Sometimes we resist out of a sense of justice and sometimes our attitude is one of 'because we can' even though we know better.

In retrospect the issue of **self-regulation** over time needed careful consideration with regards to the relationship power and **resistance** have with one another. Foucault expresses quite clearly that where there is power there is **resistance**. A nuanced understanding of power sees it not as a purely negative force. It is something that shifts because people have agency, they make decisions and act. Power can shift in people's favour in both oppressive and democratic systems and everything in between, through small acts and large. When power circulates and relations change it is not possible to claim that **self-regulation** increases over time without considering the role **resistance** plays.

This point is important in considering the power relations, **regulation**, and management across the grades. If I were asked which classes were the most and least regulated my answer would be the Grade 0s and Grade 3s respectively. The answer indicates that there has not been an increase in self-regulation over time. But this is deceptive. The answer gives the impression that the Grade 3s were naughty and badly behaved. This is not the case – there were a number of docile, ideal school subjects in the class, there were some who were less so, and on certain days there were some really disruptive children. But they were not incessantly disruptive, nor were their acts of resistance always publicly disruptive. And, as is clear from the gumboot dancing, the Grade 0s were not model citizens either. So how else can **regulation** be thought about?

Part of the answer, I think, is that resistance is not a monolithic whole, there are different ways of resisting and different degrees of resistance. This is inextricably linked to subjectivities. I use the word in the plural deliberately because as individuals we are not one-sided. We are multi-faceted and our identities are shaped by numerous people, places, events, communities, and knowledge we are in contact with. We are not the same in all spaces; sometimes we are experts, sometimes we are novices. Sometimes there are tensions between our view of the world and other people's views. Sometimes what we know in one domain is in tension with what we've been taught by our communities. The training and knowledge we receive mean that we can take up multiple subject positions.

In light of the classroom events presented here several degrees of **resistance** can be identified. Chantal, Julia, and Siphiwe are not docile subjects. But they have been at school long enough to know what kind of behaviour is expected of them. They are at the beginning of the training regime that results in a schooled subject. The lack of regulation on their parts is indicative of a tension between a schooled subject who has to complete tasks in a specific way, in a certain period of time, and an unschooled subject who is free to play when they want to. The fact that Julia and Chantal never look to see where Dawn is before they act indicates subjects who have not internalized all the norms of the schooled subject; they are partly regulated. They act first and think later. The rules and norms they have learnt at home also play an important role. The ways in which children are disciplined, or not, and the rules they are taught, may or may not be in alignment with school's formal regulations. Thus the construction of a schooled subject may be a fluid process because a new subjectivity is built on a foundation of similar home practices. Or this may not be the case, and the outward manifestation is **resistance**.

Hunter (1994: 57) argues that a reflective person can only emerge after they have been 'initiated into the arts of self-concern and self-regulation'. There needs to be an awareness by the subject of his/her conduct. Then, through processes like self-examination the subject attempts to conduct him/herself responsibly. In taking up the bodily position required when she is told to draw, Chantal shows some awareness of what she should be doing. Her initiation has started. Zama is further along and she demonstrates a capacity to examine her own behaviour, and realizes that it is not appropriate in this classroom space. Schooling is one of the places where children are initiated into the arts of self-concern and self-examination. But, knowing what one *should* do does not necessarily mean that it will be done. The wriggling bodies of the Grade 1s on the carpet are evidence of this. Many of the children sitting there conduct themselves appropriately. But, several do not. They are well behaved under the force of Helen's power. When her attention shifts their unschooled bodies emerge as wriggling, touching, headbutting subjects. For some of these children Grade 1 is the beginning of initiation into becoming a **self-regulating** school subject. For others, knowing what should be done and subtly challenging norms so as not to self-regulate are acts of **resistance**. It is a desire to be a child in control rather than a schooled subject. The children who look first to see who is watching them before they act know what they are doing will be deemed inappropriate. They choose to act in other ways, displaying some agency.

Compared to the younger grades, the Grade 3s are old hands in the school system. They understand how it works, what they can get away with, and what their teacher will let them get away with. There are several reasons why they are possibly less docile than the younger children. One is a chafing against being positioned as the babies of the school. They have outgrown this space. At the end of the year most of these children want to 'move on' to Grade 4 and escape the strictures of the Foundation Phase.

Some of the resistant acts were possibly connected to the ways in which they were managed. The management styles of the teachers differed. The teachers whose management style was underpinned by organizing principles appear to have more obedient classes. This also translates into a greater management of time and space. The issue of power arises here again; when disciplinary power is maintained and embedded in classroom routines with clear rules and consequences for action, then greater docility prevails. When this is not the case, the power relations shift. If one can get away with more in one classroom than another, then it takes a highly self-regulating subject not to be tempted to do less work and have more leisure time. There is also power in numbers – when all the children resist for whatever reason, teachers can lose control. When whole communities resist, the result can be angry mobs.

The final aspect has to do with what children get out of what they are learning. Children who are interested in what they are learning, who buy in because they get pleasure out of the experience, should be easier to manage than children who are bored and frustrated. This point is directly linked to thinking about discipline in the two ways in which Foucault explains it. Discipline is a means of social control which this and the earlier chapters have taken up, but discipline is also a body of knowledge. Teachers need a full, deep disciplinary knowledge to run alongside disciplinary control in their classrooms. As adults, we are unlikely to be docile for hours and hours over a sustained period of time if we are 'taught' by individuals who themselves do not understand the knowledge they transmit, or are not committed to the task. Expecting children to be compliant in the same situation is a double standard. When disciplinary power fails in the classroom is it because teachers have insufficient knowledge and experience in implementing disciplinary practices? Is it because the way in which disciplinary knowledge has been transferred is poor, inappropriate, inadequate, or patently incorrect? Or, is it a combination of both? The transmission of disciplinary knowledge is the issue the following three chapters take up. They look specifically at the teaching of literacy as a body of knowledge, and show that the way in which reading and writing are conceptualized constructs a particular kind of literate subject that has long-term implications as children move through and beyond schooling.

Chapter 5

Reading bodies

> Models of reading have been based in models of the social order and how the literate person can and should fit into that order. Ways of reading are not neutral but are indeed correlated with issues of identity and cultural and political power, access to capital, and contemporary configurations of gender, ethnicity, class, and citizenship in the late capitalist societies.... Reading practices that are developed in schooling contexts are not accidental, random, or idio-syncratic. Rather they are supportive of the organisational needs of schooling and the stratified interests within social organisations.
>
> (Freebody & Luke, 1997: 191)

This quotation by Freebody and Luke can be extended to other models that are entrenched in education systems. Writing can be substituted in the above passage because it too is not neutral; the way in which people are taught to write and what they write tend to reflect the interests of dominant groups. Several centuries ago, reading and writing were thought of and taught as completely separate skills. A person could read but not write. Today reading and writing are viewed as interconnected and a different literate subject emerges where readers write and writers read. This interconnectedness means that models of writing are directly influenced by the ways in which reading is enacted in schools. It is worth thinking about how reading is practised in schools and how this impacts on writing practices in the formation of the literate subject.

The reading practices at schools are also influenced by prescribed curricula. Although the curriculum is a means of social control, the ways in which schools choose to take up its prescriptions fit in with the world view of individual schools. South African schooling is in an interesting position. The fact that South Africa is a society in transition attempting to overhaul a racist segregated past does not mean that the 'old' ways, including 'old' models of reading can be easily erased. The traces of old practices remain despite the implementation of a new curriculum.[1] This is in part because teachers' professional training and practice are embedded in past ways of thinking. They also speak to ways in which retraining does (or does not) take place. Models of literacy thus exist in tension with one another and it is worthwhile to compare curricular visions of literate subjects, teachers' understandings of literacy, and the way these are played out in practice when thinking about the construction of the literate subject at the beginning of schooling. It is not possible to describe every reading lesson across the grades; rather specific reading events that are common in the different classrooms are discussed in detail in this chapter.

Teacher and curriculum views of literacy

In attempting to address educational inequalities, before it came into power the African National Congress proposed a number of educational changes in the early 1990s. An overhaul of the curriculum was one of these. A new curriculum, known as Curriculum 2005 (C2005), was implemented in Grade 1 classes in 1998. It was subsequently reviewed in 2000 and a revised, more reader-friendly version published in 2002, entitled the National Curriculum Statement (NCS). The new curriculum represents a complete paradigm shift from apartheid curricula. It draws on progressive learner-centred education, outcomes-based education, and an integrated approach to knowledge (Review Committee Report, 2000).

The understanding of literacy set out in the NCS attempts to incorporate the shifts in thinking that have taken place in the field of literacy. It reveals a move away from viewing literacy as purely skills-based and decontextualized to one that acknowledges the importance of the social context in which reading and writing are situated. Literacy practices are valued differently by different groups and communities: sending a text message may be seen as a normal way to invite people to a social engagement by one group or completely inappropriate by another. In line with a growing body of work in early literacy, the curriculum acknowledges that literacy does not begin at school but emerges from early home and social interactions with texts. Children's literacy learning has a strong social basis that takes place through regular, repeated activities and active participants. The knowledge of these interactions is internalized and built upon (Barton, 1994). Literacy teaching at school should support emergent literacy. The NCS defines emergent literacy as:

> a child's growing knowledge of the printed word. Children see print in the environment and begin to understand its purpose. They may have stories told or read to them and they learn how stories work and what books are. So even before they come to school they often know a lot. They may try to write their names using their own ideas about letters and spelling (i.e. emergent spelling), and they may try to pretend to read a book (i.e. reading-like behaviour). This is the beginning of children's literacy.
>
> (DoE, 2002: 137)

It sees its approach to literacy as balanced and justifies it as such:

> It is balanced because it begins with children's emergent literacy, it involves them in reading real books and writing for genuine purposes, and it gives attention to phonics. These are things learners need to know and do in order to read and write successfully. In reading, this means moving away from the 'reading readiness approach', which held that children were not ready to start learning to read and write until they were able to perform sub-skills such as auditory discrimination and visual discrimination, and had developed their fine and large motor skills to a certain level.
>
> (DoE, 2002: 9)

Despite the promising nature of the curriculum, there are a number of contextual factors within educational practice that are far from ideal. The influence of 'reading readiness' and skills approaches to reading have been pervasive in teacher education and informs the daily practice of many South African teachers (Stein & Prinsloo, 2004). In contrast, a balanced approach takes three elements of reading into consideration – it 'begins' with what children already know and then 'involves' them in reading and writing for specific purposes and 'it gives attention to phonics'. But, the placement of the phrase 'and gives attention to phonics' at the end of the sentence emphasizes the teaching of phonics. This is a common and deeply entrenched practice in South Africa. What is less common is teaching literacy using a wide reading approach, where children have access to lots of reading material, or from a sociocultural perspective, that takes children's cultural contexts and builds on literacy valued in these communities. For teachers who were trained under the apartheid system these newer approaches to reading were either peripheral or absent.

Although the approach to literacy sets itself up as balanced there is no explicit statement requiring these three elements to be integrated. Phonics teaching is still highlighted; the next section in the NCS entitled 'Encouraging Practice' states:

The curriculum says that it is necessary to:

- Encourage and support learners to do wide reading
- Give learners frequent opportunities for writing and for developing their vocabulary and language use, and
- Help learners to discover techniques and strategies that unlock the code of the written word, for example:
    - The development of various word recognition and comprehension skills such as phonemic awareness (sensitivity to the sounds of language)
    - Knowledge of letter–sound correspondences (phonics), and
    - Knowledge of blending (the putting together of two or three letters to make a sound)

(DoE, 2002: 10)

When wide reading and reading and writing for specific purposes are two practices that have had little to no exposure in many classrooms and may be entirely new concepts for some teachers, it seems strange that phonics teaching is explained in more detail. It also means that teachers are likely to draw on what they know and foreground phonics. Nevertheless, there is a definite move away from a narrower definition of literacy that does allow for more holistic approaches to teaching. Access to a variety of texts should result in greater access to knowledge and, coupled with writing experiences, increase children's abilities to identify and reproduce genres alongside the development of language. If these practices are continued throughout schooling, the literate subject should be well read and able to communicate appropriately in written and oral forms that are necessary for functioning in a modern society.

My interviews with the teachers yielded relatively conventional views and in some cases limited views of literacy. It appears teachers do not have an extensive understanding of literacy as there is often a mismatch between what they believe literacy to be, and what they do in their classrooms. As expected Dawn and Lisa's understanding of literacy is slightly different from that of primary school teachers. Dawn sees literacy as:

Preparation for reading that is my main concern and language as the most important issue for learning – that is literacy in my view. In the Grade 00 class … we regard that as very important and it's preparation for reading and learning. The new curriculum asks us to um implement recognition and um of the symbols for reading, getting 'a' for an apple, but we don't teach it we just introduce it.

(Interview 27 June 2002)

Lisa says:

Literacy for Grade 0, um I'd say teaching them how to use proper sentences instead of because they go from baby language in Grade 0 to speaking fluently so using correct pronunciation that kind of thing um in general teaching them about everyday life, so it's general knowledge … generally for me is when you're communicating with kids, and with teachers, adults.

(Interview 26 November 2002)

For Dawn in Grade 00, the constraints of the curriculum are felt especially when some children want to go beyond letter recognition. Although there is a supposed move away from a reading readiness approach, the fact that she is preparing children for reading and cannot teach them to read in any formal way, implies that learning to read for these children can only happen when they are older and 'ready'. This preparation is underpinned by phonics, since children are taught to recognize the letters of the alphabet. Although Dawn's definition of reading is influenced by curriculum requirements, her practice is broader than this and comes close to a balanced approach to literacy. Of all the classrooms in this study it is here that there is a space for child-driven wide reading. This is also underpinned by environmental print: posters, words written on cards identifying objects in the classroom, children's artwork, and the availability of books that change regularly to support children's emerging literacy.

One of the common threads that run through the majority of the teachers' understandings of literacy is its connection to language. For several teachers literacy and language are conflated. This is understandable when, for many teachers, what used to be language teaching has been renamed the Literacy Learning Area. While a knowledge of language is needed in order to read and write, and the teaching of language is intertwined with the teaching of literacy, they are not the same. In addition, different literacies are often conducted in different languages (Barton & Hamilton, 1998). The language used to read religious texts at home may not be the language children learn to read in at school. The English reading and writing practices of early schooling at Acacia and Southside do not reflect the home language and literacy practices of many children. For many of them this is where they acquire English. So it is understandable that one of Dawn's main concerns centres around language acquisition and that Lisa reveals a preoccupation with language (speaking fluently, pronunciation, proper sentences).

Lisa also comments on the connection between literacy and 'everyday life' where context comes into play. Although the themes that are discussed are chosen by her, she attempts to draw out what children know and extend their knowledge. While the social aspects of learning are highlighted in Lisa's explanation, a substantial amount of time spent on literacy in her class is skills-based, with a strong phonics emphasis. What is absent from preschool discussions around literacy is (emergent) writing. If the children are not formally taught to read, the implication is that they are not writing either.

By Grade 1, writing is mentioned as part of literacy and Catherine gives the conventional definition of literacy:

It's to do with language, and the understanding of the English language. That's what I understand literacy … to be literate, to read and write.

(Interview 14 May 2003)

Helen's understanding of literacy is more detailed:

Literacy for me is learning to read and write, um its comprehension. Like they must be able to understand what they're reading, they must um, identify their different sounds, there's something else I wanted to say. It's reading, writing communicating orally and they need to communicate orally, so for me once a child by the end of the year, by the end of the third term this child that has come to school and hasn't understood anything I mean if you give it instructions and the child just looks at you and smiles and by the third term they can do what you ask and I mean they don't speak English at home for me that's excellent so I feel that we've achieved something along the lines in literacy. Literacy is just for me communicating through reading, writing, spelling, things like that.

(Interview 21 May 2003)

Here literacy is set up as a meaning-making exercise integral to communication. Although children 'must be able to understand what they are reading' this understanding is the result of skills-based instruction because the children must 'identify their different sounds'. Helen acknowledges the challenge of learning in English for many children. In this Grade 1 class discussion is encouraged when the children are learning new concepts, and communication feeds into the reading and writing they are expected to do. Helen's final comment that literacy is communication through 'reading, writing, spelling' also reveals a particular conception of literacy. Her inclusion of spelling, which is only one aspect of learning to be literate, indicates what types of knowledge are privileged in the teaching of literacy and the perpetuation of social norms. Clark and Ivanic point out that 'the insistence on "correctness" in spelling, punctuation, and sentence structure has a disciplinary, normative, and discriminatory role in social life' (1997: 187). This construction can also be applied to Lisa's concerns about correct pronunciation and use of proper sentences. Thus, what counts as literacy in the move from Grade 0 to Grade 1 is underpinned by standardized notions of correctness transmitted through repetitive skills.

This preoccupation with spelling continues and re-emerges in Grade 3. Thulisile's understanding of literacy is also connected to issues of language proficiency that go beyond the school into children's home worlds. But her specific example of competency revolved around spelling:

THULISILE: To me, I think it's to try to learn to communicate because it's about the language if you don't have enough language you can't communicate so I think it's very important because they have to communicate with me and even outside the school, so I think it's language.

KERRYN: What do you teach for literacy?

THULISILE: Like the spelling part last week we … it was about real life it was Usher is coming to SA and stuff about J. Lo.

(Interview 27 November 2002)

This spelling lesson reveals an attempt to make aspects of the children's worlds relevant. In this Grade 3 class popular music was important for many of the children but rather than work from this interest into new spellings, spelling words were decided on beforehand and the children's interests were grafted on to it.

But Grade 3 literacy is not purely skills-based. Gail, the Foundation Phase HOD, talks about 'creative literacy'. In discussing literacy with her, a detailed picture emerges about how she conceptualizes Grade 3 literacy teaching:

Well literacy is your entire language programme, poetry, writing, creative. As you know I did the stories of the [inaudible] and that was the creative literacy. You teach the grammar you teach the rules of spelling but in a creative way it's not just that's the rule and you learn it. You try and implement it and get them to implement it in their own writing and that forms the whole holistic child.

Grade 3 specifically is the creation of their own work.… It's them trying to formulate their own opinions, write their own decisions, debating. Grade 3 literacy is exciting because you're actually taking the child and making them form their own decisions and then writing it down, so it is not, you're not giving them the point of view, you are telling them, 'What do you think?' and they have to form their own opinions.

(Interview 6 March 2002)

Gail's emphasis is on writing. The reference to 'creative literacy' is a project her class undertook at the end of the year when children made their own books, writing and illustrating their stories. Gail spent time with the class emphasizing the features of books because many children have limited access to books. Literacy, in this example, goes beyond skills and includes an application of spelling and sentence construction, knowledge of the genres of stories, and the design features necessary to produce a book. Literacy becomes a means of empowering students by which they are able to take on an identity as producers of knowledge and makers of books. There is also an assumption operating about the developmental level of Grade 3s who are now able 'to form their own opinions' and transfer this into writing.

The interviews indicate that, while there are various elements of a balanced approach to literacy, none of the teachers' explanations can be said to completely follow a balanced approach. There is a preoccupation with issues around language and basic communication. There is also a shift in what is emphasized as literacy teaching across the grades. In the preschool the emphasis is on preparing children to read. In Grade 1 both reading and writing are important elements of literacy with the teaching being underpinned predominantly by a skills approach. By Grade 3 writing is foregrounded with the assumption that reading has been mastered sufficiently. This of course is not to say that reading does not take place during teaching, but rather, its absence reveals a shift that prepares children for Grade 4 where the majority of the reading done will not be for pleasure but for information related to new disciplinary knowledge. What is significant is that none of the teachers mentions using books in the teaching of literacy. Although books are present in classes they cannot be said to represent a wide reading programme. The same point can be made about writing because, apart from Gail, no teacher mentioned writing for specific purposes.

Reading practices in the classroom

Grade 00: Reading Corners, reading bodies (a photo story)

There is an abundance of texts in the Grade 00 classroom. The class is full of the children's artwork and posters. Children are exposed to a number of reading practices each day, with Dawn reading their names from the register, the staff in the kitchen reading the Lunch Book to provide the correct amount of lunch, notes from other teachers, and books. The children are often read to. Dawn uses a children's Bible to tell Bible stories on most mornings. Although it is a children's Bible the language is often complex for the children. Dawn both reads and paraphrases the stories. She also makes space for the children's own books. When a child brings a book from home Dawn reads it aloud to the class. Thus an unwritten rule operates that if a book is brought to school, time is made to read it aloud.

This section examines one unsupervised reading event in detail that took place in the Reading Corner. It is interesting for several reasons, specifically with regard to how the children's bodily positions reveal their understandings of literacy. In order to analyse this incident, Hamilton's framework (2000: 17), developed for analysing literacy practices and events from photographs, was useful as a way to read the body in relation to the setting (where it happened), participants (who were involved), artifacts (what literacy resources were present), and activities (what was done/performed). I had initially moved from the tables to watch some boys who were actively playing with cars on the carpet. It was then that the scene in the Reading Corner unfolded. There was a clear gender division as remarked on by Gregory and Williams (2000) as the boys continued to play while the girls read. Although there was some dialogue between the girls, the noise from the boys often drowned out what they were saying.

A discussion of this interaction runs alongside a photo story. This interaction demonstrates the fluidity and openness of space not present in the other classrooms, and allows for the children to negotiate their reading space and the reading practices on their own terms that are revealing of the kind of readers they are learning to be. There were a number of reading interactions that took place as different children entered and exited the space. This interaction involved five girls. Ntombi, already in the Reading Corner, was joined by Nomfundo who was then joined by Thandeka. Nomfundo left and Lungelo arrived. Ntombi left and Thembi arrived. The event ended with Lungelo and Thembi reading. Both Thandeka and Lungelo arrived at the beginning of the year with a limited knowledge of English and this interaction also serves to illustrate their growing acquisition of the language.

The first part of the interaction begins with Ntombi sitting on a cushion with crossed legs, her back facing the shelves with an open book on her lap. Nomfundo stands in front of her with two books tucked under one arm, while she leans with the other arm on a cupboard next to the Reading Corner watching Ntombi, possibly waiting for her to move (Figure 5.1). Ntombi is engaged in her book. The book is an illustrated book for early numeracy. Each double page depicts what appears to be a country scene with small pathways and hills. On the left-hand side is an object (e.g. four trees) and printed on the right-hand side the number of objects that can be counted in the scene. As the book progresses the picture becomes fuller, incorporating the objects from the previous pages. Ntombi's engagement with the book is indicative of several of the elements Snow and Ninio (1986) refer to as the 'contracts of literacy' for emergent readers. First, Ntombi is acquiring book-handling skills. Her turning of the pages is clumsy – she holds several pages up and then tries to turn them from this position so that sometimes more than one page is turned and she has to page back (Figure 5.2). The content of the book leads the reading event. Ntombi demonstrates her ability to make meaning from the text – she stops at the number four, pointing and counting on the page. One of the elements of an emerging reader is repetition; Ntombi repeats her pointing and counting for the number four. This episode also reveals directionality as another aspect she has learnt. Even though her page turning is not perfectly sequenced, she counts the objects from left to right.

Nomfundo then sits down opposite Ntombi, her books still tucked under her arm, and leans forward to join in Ntombi's reading. She points on the page with Ntombi, then takes her finger away letting Ntombi count, nodding her head as Ntombi says each number aloud, mouthing them quietly with her (Figure 5.3). There is something wonderfully tactile about this experience. Nomfundo is interested in what Ntombi is doing and Ntombi lets her into the reading space she has created. Nomfundo then leans back, says something to Ntombi, stretches her

Figure 5.1

Figure 5.2

Figure 5.3

Figure 5.4

Figure 5.5

Figure 5.6

legs out and crosses one over the other. The books are on her lap and her initial gestures suggest she will begin reading. The interaction shifts from reading that is shared between the two girls, to what would have been individual reading, when Thandeka enters the Reading Corner. She leans across Nomfundo and takes another book off the shelf; off camera she opens the book on the title page (Figure 5.4). Nomfundo takes the book out of Thandeka's hands and says, 'I want to', places it on her lap, and keeps it open and looks at the title page (Figure 5.5). Thandeka makes an aggrieved sound, closes the book Nomfundo is now holding and tries to take it from her. She fails and then leans right over so that she lies on Nomfundo's legs and takes another book entitled *My Book of Colours* off the shelf. This book is set out with each page depicting a specific colour with objects representing this colour. At this moment there are no books left on the shelf, they are on the floor or being held by the girls. A tacit rule has been played out about access to the books. Ntombi, who was in the Reading Corner first, is not challenged for her book or her sitting space, but Thandeka has arrived after the other two and thus they have first choice of the books. But the fact that Thandeka has not fought over the loss of her first choice gains her entry into the circle because Nomfundo then says something to her and smiles. At this point Ntombi draws Nomfundo's attention to something in her book and both girls look at what she points to.

Thandeka demonstrates her understanding of reading. She opens her book, sits on her haunches and begins to read aloud (Figure 5.6). This action reveals several things. Her book-handling skills are not consistent. While she opened the first book on the title page; this book is opened randomly on the 'orange' page, with pictures of a cup, carrot, and orange. I would argue that the fact she sits up on her haunches and reads aloud are linked. She reads in quite a loud voice. Thandeka's reading behaviour demonstrates an understanding that stories are read aloud. This reading behaviour is possibly modelled on what she has seen Dawn do. But the situation shifts from what Dawn does because there is no audience she is reading aloud to – she is reading for herself. Furthermore she reads aloud in English:

> One day, the carrot, the apple, and the cup…

Stories in the class are read aloud in English and Thandeka demonstrates Barton and Hamilton's (1998) point that different literacies take place in different languages. These girls informally communicate with each other in Zulu. Story reading for Thandeka, whose English proficiency is limited, is predominantly an English activity. This is further illustrated by the mistake she makes by identifying the picture of the orange as an apple. She demonstrates an understanding about the structure of stories and their concomitant linguistic patterns by beginning her story with 'One day' and turning the apple, cup, and carrot into characters. But, since this is a children's book as opposed to a children's storybook,[2] Thandeka, possibly lacking the vocabulary and ideas because the layout of the page represents only objects, cannot continue as she began. Barton (1994: 145) points out that children's first books frequently have no story 'and are often just pictures and first story times may consist mainly of the adult naming unconnected pictures'. This would indicate that Thandeka's interactions with and handling of books for children have been limited. It may not be an incorrect assumption to make that the naming and labelling of these 'unconnected pictures', identified as middle-class practices (Heath, 1983), are something Thandeka has not had exposure to at home. It also points to a limited knowledge of the different genres that can be represented in books.

Thandeka then moves to sit next to Nomfundo and leans against the cupboard with her legs crossed. Nomfundo is reading her book with her legs raised and the book propped up on them. Ntombi has changed posture by this stage and is sitting on her haunches with her book in front of her, half on her legs, and half on the cushions, bent over the book looking closely at the pictures, absorbed by her counting. The girls change postures, sitting in ways they find comfortable to read the books. Thandeka's reading triggers a response with Nomfundo who opens her book on the last page and also begins to read aloud and begins her story with 'One day' in English (Figure 5.7). By this time both girls are reading aloud and the noise from the boys behind makes it difficult to hear what she is saying but her gestures in themselves are extraordinarily expressive and indicate that Nomfundo takes on the identity of storyteller. With her book propped up on her legs and anchored by her right hand she gestures with her left. Her identity as storyteller is further reinforced by what appear to be performative gestures that take on elements of characterization. It appears that she is telling a story about a mother and baby. She lifts her hand to her head on the first page as if to say 'Oh dear look what has happened' as she reads (Figure 5.8). She pauses, turns the next page, and begins again with 'One day'. This time she lifts her hand again which is accompanied with a 'wooo' and opens and closes her fingers as she continues, moving her body and head. It seems as though Nomfundo's hand becomes one of the characters, moving with the dialogue as a puppet would. The cadence she adopts clearly mirrors that of a conversation between two characters as opposed to an extended piece of story, which is indicated by her reading of the third page (Figures 5.9–5.13):

Figure 5.7

Figure 5.9

Figure 5.8

Figure 5.10

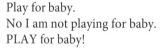

Play for baby.
No I am not playing for baby.
PLAY for baby!

Just before Nomfundo begins this page she moves her head sideways to Thandeka and quietly tells her, 'Thula' (keep quiet) as Thandeka is laughing loudly at what she has just finished reading in her own book (Figures 5.14–5.15). Thandeka's laughter indicates that reading in this space is a pleasurable activity. Nomfundo's quiet reprimand does not remove the pleasure, but merely serves as a reminder that there are other readers present. Nomfundo's reading is brought to a halt as Dawn calls her to ask if she has painted. She shakes her head and gets up.

This is fortuitous, for Lungelo has arrived and moves to sit between Ntombi and Nomfundo. There are no books left and she tries to take Ntombi's. Ntombi refuses. Thandeka replaces the book she read on the shelf – a **regulated** subject who has internalized the rules of the Reading Corner. Ntombi leaves and Thembi comes to sit next to Lungelo who has chosen a book. When she has finished with the book she replaces it on the shelf and takes the book Ntombi had.

Figure 5.11

Figure 5.12

Figure 5.13

Figure 5.14

Figure 5.15

Figure 5.16   *Figure 5.17*

Thembi and Lungelo sit quietly on the cushions looking at their books and then Lungelo moves off the cushions to lie down. As Thembi sees this, she moves over Lungelo's legs to lie flat on her stomach to look at her book. They continue reading by themselves (Figures 5.16–5.17). In this moment the space of the Reading Corner is extended into the more open carpet space, and the children's bodies reflect reading postures associated with reading for pleasure as opposed to the disciplined posture of the child reading aloud or reading for information that the other children in the study display. Although emergent readers, reading subjects in Grade 00 have time to learn to handle real books, use them to perform the act of reading, find pleasure in them, and create a community of other readers which is in contrast to Grade 0 readers discussed next.

Grade 0: indirect reading

Activities relating to reading in Grade 0 are still located on the carpet, and although there are some similarities with the Grade 00s in relation to the end of the day story time, the first major shift is evident in the way reading is controlled and the impact that this has on children's bodies. It is only at the end of the day that children move from their allocated places on the carpet to sit close to Lisa for the story. This is encouraged by Lisa. This rearrangement of the children that results in a greater proximity to the teacher, and each other, can be seen to work to create a more intimate environment which points to Lisa's understanding of how story time should operate. Story time at home is often a time when children and adults sit in close proximity to each other and it is possible that Lisa is drawing on practices of the home domain and transferring them to her classroom.

At the same time this level of intimacy cannot be replicated with an entire class and story time also contains a level of discipline. In two incidents of story time, drawn from fieldnotes, Lisa's storytelling was interspersed with comments all directed to the children's behaviour and by implication to undisciplined bodies:

> Sit flat
> Sit. If you carry on talking I am not reading.
> Do you want to get out?
> It is always the same children who are naughty during story time.

Stop picking your nose.
I am not going to ask you questions because you are not listening.
Sit on your bum, fold your legs.
Put your shoes on.

The general rules for sitting on the carpet apply, even though story time is supposed to be a more relaxed time. Children have to sit properly and not move around. While it is important to allow everyone enough space to see the book when Lisa shows the pictures, it still has a regimented element. The prescribed dress code is maintained the entire day. This is different to the Grade 00 class where both Nomfundo and Thandeka were wearing their socks in the Reading Corner. Reading is no longer an activity where one can lie back and kick off one's shoes. It has become more serious. The most important rule for this literacy activity is to listen and not talk. Story time is about listening well so that one can demonstrate through answering questions that one has remembered the story. It is interesting that Lisa sets up the asking of questions as a privilege that can be taken away if the children do not listen.

The second shift is a far more explicit pedagogical practice in preparing children to read. Instead of just exposure to print in the classroom environment and some lessons on letters of the alphabet in Grade 00, 'indirect reading' takes place every day in Grade 0 as part of the first ring time. Since my observations of this class took place at the end of the year, the children had already been introduced to the letters of the alphabet and were currently learning two and three letter words. The texts that were used for indirect reading consisted of Letterland Letters, stuck up below the blackboard, as well as Dolch words. The placement of the letters and words below the blackboard was at an appropriate level for the children to read when they were sitting on the carpet. Lisa also had flashcards. Children were introduced to a new word each week. The reading approach in this class is a bottom-up one (Jackson, 2000; Wray & Medwell, 1991) where Lisa teaches the children to 'unlock the code of the written word' (DoE, 2002: 10) by creating a phonemic awareness through repetition of the sounds of the letters of the alphabet. Sometimes the children also sang along with the Letterland tape. Lisa makes the link between letters and sounds and blending of words as prescribed by the curriculum.

How is this type of reading lesson organized? There are two classroom arrangements depending on whether Lisa uses the flashcards or the words and letters stuck below the blackboard. Because reading is a part of the first ring, all the children sit around the edge of the carpet with their legs crossed. When they have to read, the girls sitting on the carpet next to Lisa move to sit in front of her so that they can see. Reading is no longer the tactile experience of the Grade 00 Reading Corner – Lisa controls the flashcards, and the letters on the wall are only to be looked at. Reading is predominantly about memorization and testing.

The following is a typical reading lesson, reconstructed from fieldnotes:

The children read the words stuck up on the wall as a class.

Lisa introduces a new word and asks if anyone knows what it is. This day it is *pot* and Tshepo puts his hand up and identifies it correctly.

She sounds it out, '*p-o-t is pot*' and the children repeat after her. She makes some attempt at defining pot by saying: '*Mommy cooks from a _____, Daddy eats from a _____*', the children respond with '*pot*'.

She then goes around the class showing flashcards of the following words that each child has to read: *on, at, us, up, as, if, in, it, is, am.*

Lisa tells the class that if they get all the words correct they will get a star. When the children read all the words correctly the class claps for them. The first seven girls read the words with little trouble.

Vukani then makes one mistake and Lisa announces that he will also get a star because he only got one word wrong.

Busi is told to take her hand away from her mouth when she reads. She makes a mistake reading *it* as *at*. Lisa questions her about her sounding out: '"I"–"t" *says at?*' But the class is told to clap because she has tried.

Faizel who reads well, reads his words very quickly and receives an overenthusiastic clap.

Before Zama reads Lisa compliments her on her new earrings, asking if everyone has seen them.

Damon, who battled with two words, but eventually got them is annoyed that the class did not clap for him and demands that he gets his clap.

After getting halfway through the class the children become restless. From this point on until she finishes Lisa keeps having to reprimand them: '*Will you stop moving now?*' '*Nicci do you have ants in your pants?*' '*Right, fold your arms. You are distracting her. Dipuo what does it say?*' '*Fold your arms.*' '*Tshepo do you want to get out?*' '*Fold your legs.*' '*Talk now and see what happens.*' She sends Damon, who is habitually restless, to stick up a picture that has fallen off the wall – but he begins to chat and is told to '*shush*'. Towards the end of the lesson she says, '*I know we are restless but the others have been good at waiting for you.*'

The last child to read is Jason who has to sound some words out. He struggles with *at* and uses the Letterland names '*Annie Apple says "a", Ticking Tess says "t" – [long pause] – at.*'

The children who got the words right are given a star and told to flatten them on their foreheads. Nicci makes a suggestion that the other children should get a star on their hands for trying hard. Lisa gives another five stars out to be stuck on children's hands.

A particular conception of reading impacts on the construction of the Grade 0 reading subject. Reading functions not as a meaning-making exercise but as a demonstration of decoding skills. Choosing to focus on decoding skills may in part account for Lisa's emphasis on pronunciation – the children need to sound out letters correctly so they can be blended and then read 'properly'. This impacts in several ways on the bodily disposition of the children. Reading is a public act that takes place in front of peers and a teacher. A reader reads aloud and enunciates each word clearly. What counts as enunciated clarity and projection are of course culturally loaded concepts further complicated by children whose **linguistic habitus** is moulded by their home language and not the medium of instruction. Sometimes it is the body itself that works against enunciation. At the time of this study Jake had lost his front teeth and had a great deal of difficulty pronouncing words with the letter 't'. 'T' is a lingual alveolar consonant to pronounce where the tongue is placed on the upper gum ridge but the teeth may help support the tongue on the gum ridge and the absence of teeth may impede pronunciation.

Other issues around children's ability to decode are also raised as Jason's attempts to work out the word '*at*' illustrates. He goes back to naming the appropriate Letterland letters, indicating that he has worked out the sound–letter correspondence, but naming the letters as Annie Apple and Ticking Tess makes blending them an arduous chore. While the Letterland characters have been devised as a memory aid to learning the alphabet, they can present a barrier to sounding out words.

English is Jake's and Jason's home language, but for the children who speak other African languages using phonics to teach reading can present serious problems. For example, there are a number of sound–letter correspondences that differ between English and isiZulu. Since the letter 't' was problematic in both these examples I will illustrate my point using it. The letter 't' is an ejective plosive in isiZulu. This sound does not occur in English; it is shorter and sharper. It could be compared with the final sound in 'that' but is not aspirated (Taljaard & Bosch, 1988). A transfer of this knowledge can result in mispronounced words. Possibly more confusing is [th]. In English [th] as in 'that' is a voiced, continuous, lingual dental consonant. But in isiZulu it forms part of a group of aspirated consonants which are voiceless, lingual, alveolar plosives 'which are followed by a short period of voicelessness before the voicing of the vowel starts' (Taljaard & Bosch, 1988: 8). Distinguishing the ejective from the aspirated 't' is crucial for meaning: *tuba* means to soften but *thuba* means to become darkened (Doke, 1990: 10). For children encountering English for the first time, producing the correct sound–letter correspondence and then blending them correctly can be a bewildering experience. Thus Busi's mistaking *it* for *at* may in fact be influenced by the fact that there are seven vowel sounds in isiZulu which affect how she hears the 20 vowel sounds in English.

Although the spatial arrangement of bodies in a circle does create unity within the class, individuality is stressed during reading lessons where individual children need to identify letters and words. In addition there is a subtle message that operates as to what constitutes reading that the children will encounter when they reach Grade 1. When the children are required to read a list of words they stand. A standing body clearly marks out levels of competence. In another lesson, the class was made to stand and on correctly identifying the word they sat down. By the end of the round the children left standing were the ones who did not know their words and did not get a star. But reading aloud in the later grades will require more than the identification of decontextualized words.

The awarding of stars is another element of how the body is literally marked as a reader. Giving stars to children is an outward sign of their competence. Although the children use their bodies through clapping to encourage and acknowledge success, the sounds fade, but the materiality of the star carries more significance. It is a reward from a teacher, not peers, and thus holds greater symbolic value and reveals a compliant subject. The placement of the stars on the forehead is a clear indicator that success has been achieved and indicates a body that performed a school task very well. Nicci's desire to recognize the work of her peers appears on the surface noble, but it also indicates a realization of hierarchical power relations. By asking for the stars for these children to be placed on their hands, which is not nearly as visible, she maintains her position as one of the clever and favoured children.

The time Lisa spends in disciplining the children by directing comments at their bodies makes the lesson time consuming. To stop the movement which results in general noise and talking, she reminds them where to place their arms. If their arms are folded and their legs are already crossed, their bodies are unable to move in ways that indicate restlessness. She also threatens to relocate children – spatial relocation is a means of punishment. When she says 'talk now and see what happens', having no recourse to corporal punishment, the next disciplinary tactic is to move the children. Sometimes she sends the children outside the classroom. She does relocate Damon, who could be very restless if not occupied with some activity, subtly in this lesson by giving him something to do.

An indirect reading routine was added when the children worked with magazines on two consecutive days, although this was not observed again. On both days the usual round of flashcard identification of letters and words preceded this task. Then magazines were fetched from the back of the class and handed out. On the first day, the children were asked to identify the letters 'o' and 's' (or in Letterland terms, Oscar Orange and Sammy Snake). The children were excited by this task and shouted out when they found the letters. They were reminded to put their hands up. To execute this task the class spread out on the carpet, leaning in various directions to read their magazines. Lisa walked around the carpet to check if they had identified the correct letters. The second day, the children were asked to identify the first letter of their own name and then the first letters of various children in the class. These exercises were short but the children seemed excited to flick through the magazines. Although they were still 'code-crackers' (Freebody & Luke, 1997) decoding alphabetic symbols, this exercise moved away from decontextualized reading, as such an interaction with the magazines created a way for children to become more print literate. This engagement can create an awareness of the design features of magazines. For example, different fonts can represent the same letters, and letters can be represented in either upper or lower case. Considering the children's limited interactions with texts, and the lack of use of the Reading Corner, this kind of exercise could have been expanded upon. Children could have looked to see if they could identify any of the Dolch words they had learnt. This would have expanded their understanding that printed words are connected in longer pieces of writing as opposed to being discrete entities.

Reading in Grade 0 is teacher-regulated and children have limited tactile experiences with real books. Reading is associated with a demonstration of individual decoding proficiency that will be a common practice in Grade 1. Children who demonstrate proficiency wear their 'badge of competence' by being awarded stars on their foreheads. There is limited meaning associated with recognizing words, and even during story time children are closely controlled.

Grade 1: the reluctant reader (a photo story)

Because a number of Grade 1s have had no preschool experiences, children are taught to read as if they had no background knowledge. The pace at which children are introduced to letters and words increases. Children who can already read receive their first reading book earlier and move on to more difficult books than those who struggle. This ability is monitored by assessing how children read aloud. The Grade 1s read aloud relatively frequently and were listened to either by their teacher or a teacher's aide several times a week. Reading aloud is managed in two ways. Either children are called individually from their desks to read or small groups of children are called to sit on the carpet and wait their turn. The groups consisted either of the rows or groups the children sat in. The children brought their homework books and readers with them. On being called to read for the teacher they would stand at her desk. She would take their homework book and open it to the back where a page was stuck in with a record of the title and number of books each child read. This was signed by both the teacher and parent each time the child read to them. The school called this a Fun Reading programme to encourage children to read more. The child who read the most books by the end of the year was rewarded with a prize.

After observing several of these reading aloud sessions, I would not characterize this form of reading as 'fun'. What was fun was what happened on the carpet while the reading aloud was in progress, when children talked, read, or played with each other. Essentially the focus of this section is to establish what counts as reading aloud and how bodily postures reflect whether there is submission or **resistance** to this. It is important to note that there are changes over time in how the children respond to reading. A comparison of videotaped samples of reading aloud after a month of schooling and again at three and a half months is an indication of this. There are several shifts, for example after being at school for a month, several of the children pointed with their fingers at each word when they read aloud (Figure 5.18). This may have been permissible early on (there were no comments from the teacher to indicate otherwise), but finger-pointing works against fluency. After three and a half months of school this practice stopped for most children. Engagement with the pictures in the books became increasingly limited and reading centred around the text only. Several children also revealed limited book-handling skills by opening their books upside-down or on the wrong page – for example, during one reading lesson Calvin did not make the association between reading and print as he covered the words with his arm to look at the pictures (Figure 5.19). Three and a half months later children displayed more control of their texts even if they were not competent readers.

Figure 5.18   Figure 5.19

Figures 5.20–5.28 chart Melany's experience of reading aloud. Her body language expresses very clearly how she feels about reading. She does not know how to read in a way that is required and her **resistance** stems from a lack of understanding. On her arrival at Catherine's desk she takes on the appearance of a reader, holding her book up, but when asked to begin she remains silent. Her book is then placed on Catherine's desk. While she looks at the pages her hands, first occupied with her nasal orifice, indicate a lack of engagement with the text (Figures 5.20 and 5.22). At no time does she touch the book; Catherine turns all the pages for her. Her hands are either up, or blocking her body (Figures 5.23 and 5.26). At one point she reads with her fingers in her mouth and is told by Catherine to take them out (Figures 5.24 and 5.25). In the third last picture she has her hands clasped and the expression on her face is one of distaste (Figure 5.26). In a moment there is a disturbance behind her. She quickly turns around to see what is happening (Figure 5.28). To end the ordeal she repeats after Catherine, but indicates no ability to decode the words she is reading. Each page of the book reads 'Is it in here?' 'No', until the final page of the story where 'it' is found. When Catherine is silent waiting for Melany to

Figure 5.20   Figure 5.21

Figure 5.22

Figure 5.23

Figure 5.24

Figure 5.25

Figure 5.26

Figure 5.27

Figure 5.28

read by herself after several prompts, she remains silent. Apart from her body language indicating **resistance**, Melany's gaze also reveals this. While she looks at the book, she does not look at the words she is supposed to be reading.

Catherine's actions, while meant to support Melany's reading, undermine it. She controls the text and thus the pace of the reading, turning the pages herself (Figure 5.21). She also demands a particular response from Melany – that Melany repeat what she reads aloud for her on the page as she points at each word with her pen (Figure 5.22). Reading is about word recognition. Reading aloud also requires clarity, and she both physically and verbally indicates to Melany that she cannot read with her fingers covering the text or in her mouth. Although she indicates to Melany that the words are the same on each page, this is as far as the interaction with the text extends.

Thus reading is a teacher-controlled activity with no sense of individual ownership until one can demonstrate enough competence to stand back and hide the printed word, relaying it orally. The book being read is predominantly visual, with the pictures spread across two pages. The visual is clearly laid out to support the text, and some engagement with the visual may have facilitated Melany's entry into this text. This kind of discussion is time-consuming if it has to take place daily with all the children in the class, but not impossible. As mentioned earlier reading often took place in Helen's Grade 1 class in small groups that had been ranked according to reading ability. In this sort of situation, reading in small groups at the beginning of the year, when some discussion can take place to facilitate the reading process, may be far more beneficial to children. It also constructs reading as a different activity that not only requires a performance of decoding skills but is a means through which an entire text can be engaged with on a meaningful level. The fact that, on one of the days when children were called to the carpet to wait their turn to read and talked to each other about their books, is an indication that children want to do far more than demonstrate they can read aloud.

Grade 3: sanctioned and unsanctioned reading

The final section of this chapter examines reading practices as found in Grade 3 at the end of the Foundation Phase. There are several key shifts, the most obvious one being the limited amount of time spent on story time. On an average day in Grade 00 several stories might be read to the class. By Grade 0 story time is a once a day event and by Grade 1, although the year begins with time for stories, this time diminishes until Grade 3, when it almost ceases to exist. The Fun Reading Programme remains, which is monitored by the teacher listening to individuals reading aloud. However, the frequency of these events also diminishes.

At the same time, several practices that have been set in place from Grade 0 continue. The clearest of these is the predominance of working in a phonics paradigm. This is demonstrated by the kind of activities and texts used and produced by the Grade 3s. For example, fieldnotes indicate the introduction of new spelling words for the week. They were written on flashcards and stuck up on the board. Thulisile pointed to each word with a stick and the class repeated the words:

part, starch, farm, tart, hard, bar, card, chart, start, charm, dart, hard, yard.

The children were then asked which words they do not understand and 'hard', 'starch', 'charm', and 'dart' were identified. Each group was given two flashcards and had to find the definitions in the dictionary, then write down the definitions and a sentence for each word. This exercise showed the children's lack of familiarity with dictionaries and an understanding of how to use them effectively. One group of girls received 'farm' and 'dart'. They struggled to find the word 'farm' because they were looking for farm under the fo- words. Children also did not seem to realize that words can have different meanings. They found their words, wrote out the first definition, and did not read further. When they were called upon to read their definitions and sentences this disjuncture was made clear. For example Vusi's group defined 'bar' as:

A long piece of wood or metal.

But their sentence read:

I went to the bar yesterday.

Given that children are not required to read extended class texts, it is not surprising that they did not read further than the first definition. Providing explicit information about how dictionaries are organized is important so that these children understand dictionaries as a particular genre. If children do not work with dictionaries often or they are not used in many homes, assumptions cannot be made that techniques for using them are obvious.

The choice of these spelling words is influenced by phonics where more complex sounds and letter correspondences are covered in Grade 3. Thus, improving and building a working vocabulary can be undercut by too heavy a reliance on phonics. Two days later the children were told that the words they would learn had the 'bossy r' in them. They were required to complete the following exercise presented on an overhead transparency (see Figure 5.29 below):

With reading aloud being limited and little reading for pleasure sanctioned, what texts are most commonly read by the Grade 3s? The most prevalent of all texts were worksheets. These were handed out several times a day to children, and, once marked, were filed by the children in their literacy files. The predominance of the worksheet is an effect of OBE thinking. When OBE was set in motion, and material from the previous curriculum deemed inappropriate, there was limited material available for teachers. Several workbooks were put together for teachers with material appropriate for the learning areas. The downside to this was an over-reliance on worksheets whose pedagogical soundness was variable. The reliance on worksheets is not limited to the Grade 3s only or to this school in particular.

While it may not be the case in every class, or every school for that matter, working with loose worksheets has the potential to undermine discipline in the class. This can be compounded by the types of worksheets that are utilized. What observations from this study have

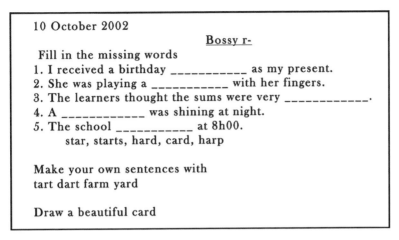

10 October 2002

<u>Bossy r-</u>

Fill in the missing words
1. I received a birthday _____ as my present.
2. She was playing a _____ with her fingers.
3. The learners thought the sums were very _____.
4. A _____ was shining at night.
5. The school _____ at 8h00.
     star, starts, hard, card, harp

Make your own sentences with
tart dart farm yard

Draw a beautiful card

Figure 5.29 Grade 3 spelling exercise.

reinforced is the commonsense notion that there are less likely to be disciplinary problems when children's attention is engaged. A key difference between working in a book as opposed to off worksheets has to do with pace. In a book, once one piece of work is completed, a turn of the page is all that is needed for the next piece of work. But access to worksheets is controlled by the teacher. The worksheet is not owned in the same way as a book is. It is not packed, carried around, and taken home; it is filed away and left in the classroom. When worksheets are handed out, discipline can slip. Since worksheets are handed out to each individual and require the teacher to walk around to achieve this, it means that there is time when children are not engaged with any task and thus their attention is not focused. The knowledge that teacher **surveillance** is lowered invites children to talk, move, and play.

This brings me to the second point about the kinds of worksheets chosen. Figure 5.30 is an example of a phonics worksheet dealing with the sound 'ph'. Children have to write the correct word next to pictures and then fill in the missing word. As is clear from Charmaine's answers, she has not read with any meaning at all. Next to the picture of a photograph she has started to write 'elephant', but the number of letters in elephant do not fit the lines so she ends with 'oph' writing 'elephanoph' – a nonsense word. She already has 'ph' from elephant so why end the word with 'oph'? The answer to this probably has to do with classroom layout and the fact that she was a serial copier of other children's work. What is more interesting is that the 'fill in the words' exercise requires that one read for meaning. Both the sentences and the words to be filled in have to be understood, as well as how an exercise like this operates. Charmaine demonstrates that this is a meaningless task for her – she copies the words she must fill in, in the order in which they are presented, creating meaningless sentences.

Worksheets have a place, but in excessive use they create a limited reader. Using worksheets means that reading is never an extended exercise. It involves limited problem solving and the ability to read instructions to decode what is required. Worksheets do not require any real discussion or engagement, which returns me to my point about sustaining attention. It is obvious from being in any classroom for a short period of time that children do not work at the same pace and some children may finish worksheets like these very quickly, while others plod on, distracted by those who have finished.

In the time gaps between worksheets being given out and being completed and taken in for marking in Grade 3, two boys demonstrated that other kinds of readers exist. The first boy sat at his

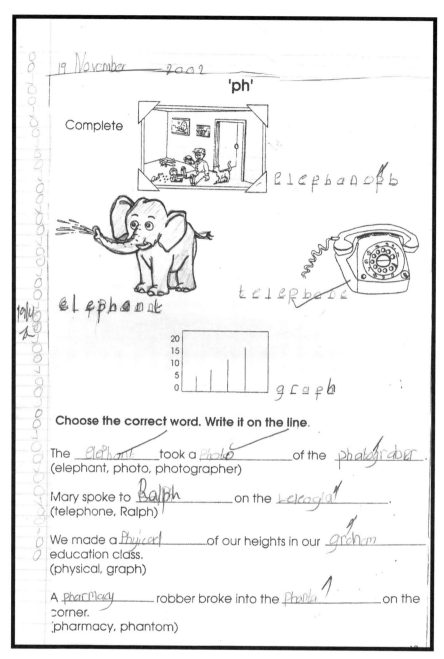

Figure 5.30 Grade 3 phonics worksheet. (From Pollard, B. (1992). *The Big Book of Phonics*. R.I.C. Publications. Reproduced with permission of R.I.C. Publications www. ricpublications.com.au)

desk reading a magazine. Unlike the surreptitious reading of magazines that often takes place in classrooms, this was clearly displayed on his desk. Unfortunately it was impossible to see what kind of magazine he was reading. The fact that this magazine was clearly displayed was unusual, given that no one else in the class had any reading material on their desks. The question to be asked then is why was it openly displayed? The answer lies in part in the lessening of controlled spatial distribution. The movements and distribution of resources in Lee and Helen's classes are more tightly controlled. In Grade 3 there is less **regulation** and there is also less regulated control over distribution, so children manipulate this. Movement needs to appear purposeful so they 'work' the system: trips to the dustbin to sharpen pencils, borrowing stationery from friends across the classroom, going to file worksheets. In these moments when several children are moving through the classroom, a child sitting at their desk reading is hardly going to count as a disruption.

The second reader is also interesting. Nhlanhla is a boy for whom 'purposeful' wandering around the class is a well-acquired skill. Nhlanhla sat in the middle group of desks in the front of the class. During the class he wandered around. While Thulisile was at her desk, in a move reminiscent of the Grade 00 Reading Corner he lay down on his back on the carpet, propping his head up on his schoolbag in what can only be referred to as a restful position. His desk at the front of the class, as well as the other bodies of the children at their desks, shielded him from Thulisile's gaze. He had with him several pages of full-colour advertising that had come from a newspaper. He had folded up the pages and they also were on his desk. Several times in between his wanderings he pored over the pictures of goods that were being advertised. This was not some casual reader paging through adverts, but a close reader who was reading with a purpose and possible pleasure (desire?). It is possible his fascination with these pages was elicited because it was nearing Christmas and he was scouring the pages looking for presents he would like to receive. His focus was at odds with the limited attention given to the work he was supposed to be doing. This is an example of reading a text from the real world, for a real purpose. Children's attention can be drawn to the design features of the text to make reading exercises more interesting and relevant. Even in resource-poor communities this kind of text could be used to great effect.

In thinking about the Grade 3s, I recall how the Foundation Phase teachers talked about how difficult the Grade 3s could become at the end of the year. While they were no doubt eager to move on in their school lives, a certain amount of boredom must have manifested itself in the sameness of the materials they were required to complete.

Filling in the gaps

If South Africa is to produce literate citizens then readers who are limited to filling in missing words, who have limited access to texts of their own choosing, and a limited variety of genres to read, fall short of the mark. If there are no spaces provided to have discussions about the books they are reading, then the prospect of producing critical subjects is narrowed. For many people in South Africa there is no culture of reading; it is not valued as it may be in many middle-class western homes. When resources are scarce, money cannot be wasted on books. This means that schools are tasked with the important job of teaching reading in such a way that it has value, and that people are able to read in a way that is useful in society.

This is a really difficult task. The majority of children in these classes will be able to read; they will read enough to get them through school. But the way they are being taught to read is the same way their teachers and generations of South Africans have been taught to read. Learning to read texts and the words in texts, when an ability to make meaning is limited, is insufficient for today's world. This is not a world which can support docile unskilled labour, neither can it support individuals who cannot solve problems and show initiative. When the ways in which literacy is used are changing so fast, the gap between these children and those whose literacy training incorporates technological developments and problem-solving will not be bridged.

I am not arguing that what children are being taught here is wrong. Research shows that early quality phonemic awareness interventions produce more successful readers and phonics-based programmes are used successfully internationally, but multidimensional programmes that address all aspects of reading are more successful (Wolf et al., 2009). Nor am I arguing that reading aloud, filling in missing words, and weekly spelling tests are not important. There is great value in 'traditional' methods. Nor am I blaming the teachers for what they do. The presentation of these events here hides the passion and commitment of these teachers. I do question their training and retraining. The new curriculum requires a major paradigm shift that has been mediated through short courses and a cascade model, where one person feeds back everything they have learnt to their schools. Ultimately this is the adult version of the children's game, Broken Telephone, but the stakes are higher.

Successful readers will be those whose home environments support their reading. They will surpass those who have little access to texts and do not know how to break the code beyond sounding out words.

Teachers become adept at taking on the language of new curricula, writing up their lessons in the way that is expected but not necessarily shifting their practice. Under government **surveillance** they play the game, and often know more than the people surveying them. But close classroom observation that examines what is said by the teacher and the students, the tasks given, the resources available and how they are used, the texts given to and produced by children, reveals far more about how the school subjects, in this case reading subjects, are produced.

The question that remains to be answered is, if the models of reading in schools are producing a traditional rather than a modern subject, what kind of subjects can then be produced by the disciplines across schooling? What exactly is the knock-on effect in other classrooms?

Chapter 6

Writing bodies

Taking into consideration how literate subjects begin to be formed, and the type of reading subject that emerges, this chapter focuses on the construction of writing subjects.

As in Chapter 5, it compares teachers' views of writing with the national curriculum and examines classroom writing practices. In examining classroom practices the spatial is again foregrounded. This is because writing is closely connected with the spatial. As a visual medium the emphasis is on space and spatiality rather than temporal sequencing, its internal logic is guided by spatial arrangements (Kress, 1997: 17–18). Thus it is through an examination of spatial relationships that an analysis of the construction of the writing subject can also be located.

Space is worked with in two ways in this chapter. The spatial distribution of bodies and the associated physical training give insight into early writing practices. Space can also be used metaphorically. Examining the spaces created by writing gives insight into the way in which children reveal aspects of their subjectivity. Kamler (2001: 54) argues that as an act, writing is 'never a skill but deeply constitutive of subjectivity'. This is closely linked to context and, to return to Freebody and Luke's (1997) contention, the model of social order in which understandings of writing are embedded. When writing is taught to young children within a skills-based paradigm, how and what children write produce different subjectivities from those where children have greater control over their writing. The same piece of writing can be considered an act of resistance or lauded for creativity or mastery of genre. What is produced and the response these texts receive give us insight into the ways in which the writing subjects are produced.

Curriculum and teacher views on writing

Luke (1996) argues that literacy training is affected by the ways in which theory and practices impact on people's different uses of writing. He goes on to point out that the history of literacy education is about power and knowledge; this is played out in the modern state by particular individuals who are placed in dominant positions and thus influence our understandings of what literacy is. This seems a useful place to begin this discussion on writing. In a state-constructed curriculum, what counts as early writing in South Africa?

In South Africa's Outcomes Based Education (OBE) system, writing is one of the outcomes set out in the NCS for the Literacy Learning Area:

> The learner will be able to write different kinds of factual and imaginative texts for a wide range of purposes.
>
> (DoE, 2002: 11)

Since children in this phase of schooling have not mastered writing, a further explanation is given:

In the Foundation Phase, learners work towards this outcome. They learn that writing carries meaning, and that they themselves are the authors of meaning. They develop their handwriting skills to be able to record their thoughts and ideas so that they and others can read them. They learn how to use writing conventions such as spelling and punctuation to make their writing understandable to others. They learn that writing is a process that includes pre-writing, drafting, revising, editing, illustrating, publishing.

(DoE, 2002: 11)

This view of writing is quite broad, and in order to meet this outcome, children need to understand or master three things: writing as making meaning, writing as process, and writing as mastery of skills and conventions. This view also recognizes the two aspects of writing that are contained in the word 'write': scribe and author (Barton, 1994). The writer as scribe has to master the mechanics of writing, having control and mastery over the implements used. This mastery is achieved through tasks like tracing letters and words, copying and reproducing texts, being taught to write between lines of varying sizes, even maybe writing out lines for punishment. The author, on the other hand, is a composer, someone who uses writing to make meaning, to communicate a message, to use writing to think, to be creative and to express him/herself. Writing can be seen to operate on a continuum with scribe on the one side and author on the other. A certain level of technical mastery is needed to make meaning. But levels of meaning-making vary. Consciously placing letters together to form a word is an act of meaning-making but may go no further. Writing for record keeping, or copying notes, may have a scribal element if they are not used further, but if they are used to compose another text then the scribal aspects of writing are integral to the process of authoring.

Thus when children are required to understand that meaning is embedded in writing and that certain conventions need to be mastered in order for this meaning to be conveyed in an understandable form, both forms of writer are contained here. One of the important aspects of emergent literacy is when children realize symbols (letters) represent meaning. They then need to master the production of these symbols and the conventions that go along with them (scribes) so they can make meaning (authors) in a conventional and understandable form. Writing has a communicative function whether it is to oneself or others. It is important to make the point that children do not need full scribal mastery to make meaning as authors. 'In learning to read and write, children come [to school] as thoroughly experienced makers of meaning, as experienced makers of signs in any medium that is to hand' (Kress, 1997: 9).

To become a meaning-maker who can communicate for a 'wide range of purposes', children need to be aware of a number of genres and their organizing principles. This can partly be gained through a wide reading programme. But it also speaks to a genre approach to teaching writing. Genre theorists teach explicitly, and students learn to produce and distinguish the structural, grammatical, and linguistic features of different genres, for example descriptions, reports, explanations, arguments, and different kinds of narrative (Maybin, 1993). Genre theorists argue that this approach provides marginal groups access to genres of power. This has some resonance because of the history of stratified and low-quality education in South Africa. But the genre approach has been criticized (Hyland, 2003; Kamler, 2001). The explicit pedagogy used to teach different genres can be mechanistic and teacher controlled. Although students may use the right words, grammar, and structures for the right purpose and audience this does not necessarily lead to critical appraisals, thus perpetuating unequal power relations embedded in dominant genres.

The third approach set out is the process approach to writing. With the emphasis on process as well as the finished product, this approach requires the writer to be both scribe and author. The approach is child-centred where children choose topics and are guided by the teacher. Feedback and writing conferences between teacher and student, or student and student, make writing a collaborative and social act (Calkins, 1986; Graves, 1982; White & Arndt, 1991). The writing subject is an author who takes ownership of his/her work. But the process approach's focus on the individual and the individual writing voice is problematic. Insufficient attention may be paid to linguistic features and genre (Christie & Rothery, 1989). Without interrogation the subject can remain limited to their own experiences, and uncritical of their (racist, sexist, ageist, etc.) assumptions.

Although historically these approaches have been set against each other there is an acknowledgement that both are valuable (Kamler, 2001). It is perfectly possible to utilize a process approach with the genre approach. If children need to write factual and imaginative texts for a range of purposes then access to both of these approaches should be beneficial in creating writers. But knowledge of how best to implement these approaches, and an understanding of their limitations, are needed by South African teachers who, on the whole, have had little exposure to them. Without them, teachers revert to what they know. The result is, as Kress (1997: 9) reminds us, that 'lettered representation' rather than broader forms of meaning-making predominate in schools. When this is the emphasis, the writer is largely a scribe.

For the most part a balance between these approaches is attained in the curriculum across the grades. This is present in the assessment standards children need to meet. For example, alongside the scribal aspects of learning to write by manipulating pencils and forming letters, Grade 0s begin to produce texts of different genres like lists, messages, and letters. More genres are introduced in Grade 1 alongside a process approach where drafting and revision take place through group stories. By Grade 3 children draft, revise, and publish their own writing. They become more accomplished scribes who can write greater quantities more rapidly. In observing early classrooms there is a disjuncture between policy and practice.

As with reading, the preschool teachers do not teach writing formally. The focus in Grade 00 is on drawing and developing fine motor co-ordination. Dawn talks about how cutting out and playing with dough are important in developing fine motor skills. She monitors children's development in terms of drawing and requirements for colouring in:

> At first they just scribble … they only draw you the head and feet; as they develop they get arms and legs and toes and hands but then they haven't got a baseline … as they develop they make a little ground or grass for the man to stand on … my whole goal with them is to use the whole page … they just draw with one crayon they don't mind the colours then you get Lungile, she uses the whole page and never stops colouring and it just flows.
>
> You can't tell a child to colour but we try and teach them to stay in between the lines and colour in one direction but they don't cover the whole picture they just start up in the corner and then they carry on.
>
> (Interview 27 June 2002)

The argument has been made that the roots of writing lie in drawing (Barton, 1994), and Levin, Both-De Vries, Aram, and Bus (2005) argue that scribbling can be the starting point for both drawing and writing. Vygotsky (2004) shows how writing builds on children's drawings. Drawing continues to be an important feature in Grade 0, with free drawing and set tasks alongside pre-writing exercises. Lisa also uses drawings to assess the children's maturity through the representation of body parts and presence of a baseline. The pre-writing exercises she does fits the curriculum's assessment criteria that revolve around letter formation:

> We'll do perceptual worksheets, for instance, drawing lines from the left side to the right side, drawing lines from up to down, doing dot to dot, um, you start … left top hand corner and go down … always from up, up to down um things like the patterns … zigzags and twirly whirly patterns, drawing the patterns … spirals.
>
> (Interview 26 November 2002)

The restrictions (real or perceived) about what it is appropriate to teach preschoolers affects pedagogical decisions teachers make. The children are taught to write their names but not letter formations because as Lisa notes, 'the Grade 1 teachers show them the letter formation, how to write letters correctly'. The influence of reading readiness approaches impact on teaching writing – although the curriculum refutes that there is a reading readiness approach, teachers' mandate is only *to prepare* children to read. Both preschool teachers expressed a reluctance to do more. But Lisa comments that the children all want to write and are displaying varying levels of emergent writing ('they squiggle from the left to the right', 'he had a big sheet of paper with a whole thing written on it', 'they'll write different letters next to each other, even on top of each other'). An illogical assumption exists that if children are not ready to be taught to read, then they can't be taught to write. As with reading there seem to be territorialized practices: Grade 1 teachers teach writing 'properly'. Encouraging children to write seems to overstep the invisible barrier of what Grade 0 teachers do. This thinking erroneously constructs preschool teachers as limited in their ability to teach literacy.

This kind of contradictory thinking reflects a level of uncertainty and traces of older beliefs about teaching literacy. OBE thinking encourages children to work and develop at their own pace and levels. But implementing this creates 'problems' when children arrive in Grade 1, where some children can read and write and others cannot. Children, who have had access to preschool, or come from homes where parents teach their children to read and write, are at an advantage. For children who have not had this exposure, 'catching up' can be an issue. Alongside this, **normalized judgements** are made: children who display a 'precocious' desire to read and write cannot be taught 'properly', unless it is by Grade 1 teachers. Such children then need to be 're-educated' by teachers because they have 'bad' habits.

There is some continuity between the preschool and Grade 1. The emphasis on developing fine motor co-ordination and muscle strength to write remains. As such the tactile experiences of playing with plasticine, and tracing their fingers over letters cut out in fine-grade sandpaper are 'an extension of preschool'. Drawing is no longer central; children should be able to talk about their drawings, and teachers expect some development in drawing over the year which meets curriculum requirements. Drawings are still used as indicators of children's emotional maturity and well-being. Helen talks about a boy in her class:

> If somebody's … deviating from what they are supposed to be drawing, I mean we had an incident with him who we shall not name, when he was drawing other parts of the body and then I spoke to the parents and they told me why.
>
> (Interview 25 May 2003)

Although most teachers are not trained psychologists, their ability to interpret children's drawings is important. It is through drawings that the literate subject begins to represent him/herself. These texts are subject to the gaze of the teacher, who gains knowledge not just about the child but the family background and circumstances. This **surveillance** can be positive in dealing with children's emotional well-being and regulating their behaviour sensitively.

What emerged strongly in the interviews was a focus on writing related to a mastery of skills. One teacher summed up what was important, when assessing writing, in the following way:

> If they are writing on the correct lines, the size of the letters, if they are writing the correct word, the word is not misspelt, or turned … reversed. They usually write the 's' the other way round, or the 'b' and the 'd' … yes, correctness in the letters, the size of the letters, the lines they write on.
>
> (Interview 14 May 2003)

Kress's (1997) comment about the spatial arrangements required to write resonate here. It comes through in the preoccupation with technical mastery which results in a particular set of **norms** for assessing writing. The fact that the curriculum explicitly states that children should work towards learning to write, rather than attaining full mastery, means that the curriculum can be interpreted as one where the technical aspects of writing are taught and mastered first, before writing as a meaning-making task can be taken into consideration. This thinking is in fact reflected in the criteria listed for writing in Southside school reports: spelling, sentence construction, and presentation (see Chapter 7). This is evidence of Barton's (1994) contention that there is a huge temptation to assess writing through identifiable aspects like spelling and neatness rather than more intangible aspects. This thinking is worrying because, as Clark and Ivanic (1997) argue, 'skills' is a prescriptive term and creates a deficit notion of individuals who need to acquire a desired skill. A focus on skills mastery also potentially constructs mindless subjects whose bodies mechanically complete tasks as opposed to authors who produce interesting texts with idiosyncratic spelling or messy handwriting.

This has other implications, since writing seems to be defined by Grade 1 teachers as predominantly handwriting. 'Handwriting is the most physical part of writing, the most connected to the body rather than the mind of the writer. It is consequently what Bourdieu (1977) calls the "**habitus**": the bodily disposition of a person' (Clark & Ivanic, 1997: 187). The construction of the **habitus** takes place through disciplining a body, and already the kind of writing subject that is constructed in the Foundation Phase is evident.

This construction continues into Grade 3 where writing continues to be interpreted as handwriting. When teachers were asked what activities are set for writing, their answers were limited to the cursive and print exercises set for handwriting. Children begin the year writing in print, and by the third term are expected to have mastered cursive. Writing is also linked to spelling words, letters, and sounds learnt during the week.

> We use spelling words … applicable to the sound and the letter that they're doing. And then they only use the texts once they've done the entire alphabet and they are applying the knowledge of their writing skills. They either write their news, copy a text, copy writing cards, so that's how they apply it.
>
> (Interview 6 March 2002)

The choice of spelling words is limited to a phonics paradigm, reaffirming the impact reading approaches have on the teaching of writing. Grade 1 sets the pattern for the Foundation Phase. The Grade 1 process of learning to write letters follows a regular pattern – after the letter–sound correspondences have been made explicit, practice of letter formation begins with numerous tracing and copying exercises until letters are clustered together to form words.

The alternative subjectivities set out in the curriculum are overshadowed in practice by classroom approaches where writer as author is subsumed by a 'technocratic skills model' (Luke, 1996). The following sections consider how these play out in practice.

Writing practices in the classroom

From drawing to writing: lessons from Grade 00

Research done on emergent literacy frequently stresses the connections between the drawing and writing of children through the combination of scribbles, letters, and representational drawings (Barton, 1994; Grundlach, McLane, Stott, & McNamee, 1985; Kendrick & McKay, 2004; Kress, 1997; Levin et al., 2005; Yang & Noel, 2006). Clay's (1975) classic study identifies the stages children pass through when working out the aspects involved in writing that require complex understandings of the functioning of sign systems. This section examines emergent literacy from a slightly different perspective by looking at the possibilities the classroom environment creates for children in relation to the training they undergo as emergent writers.

Whitehead (1990) discusses how the presence of gestures, language, and make-believe play in young children signals their ability to represent thought symbolically. She goes on to state that 'early mark making is highly dynamic and shaped by bodily exploration of space and the possibilities of materials.... This total bodily involvement is often accompanied by vocal sounds, single words or a brief explanatory narrative' (1990: 143). The connection between language and production is most noticeable in the Grade 00 classroom by the constant levels of egocentric talk (Vygotsky, 1962). Much of the background noise in the class is of children playing; emergent social talk is constant as the children talk to themselves and each other about what they are doing; they make repetitive and rhythmic noises and break out into song. It is only when the noise level rises and affects children's bodies, making their movements more exuberant and moving them from the confines of their desks, that they are reprimanded.

Drawing and writing take place at hexagonal tables. The preschool children do not have books. The majority of work is produced on loose sheets of paper, be it photocopied worksheets, scrap paper, or clean sheets. In the Grade 00 class all materials are provided for the children – each table has the necessary equipment for the particular task for the day: glue, paper, and scissors, felt-tipped pens, newspaper, paper, paint, paintbrushes. Materials are recycled as children transform everyday objects into art. In terms of writing implements, the otherwise ubiquitous grey lead pencil is absent – the children colour in and write with wax crayons or felt-tipped pens. While felt-tipped pens are often 'controlled substances' in classrooms because of the permanence of their ink, these children manage them with impunity. The presence of the felt-tipped pens reveals that children are not engaged with or being trained in the technical aspects of writing (with pencils), but that they are capable of handling implements that are viewed as 'dangerous'.

The Grade 00s complete different activities at their tables. These fall into two distinct categories. The first tasks set up by the teacher are perceptual or pre-writing exercises that are sometimes an extension of the class theme. (There are a number of perceptual tasks related to improving fine motor co-ordination in anticipation of the more formal kinds of literacy that children will be engaged with – like playing with plasticine, threading beads, making patterns with pegs, puzzle building.) The second task is free drawing where children determine the content of their pictures. Two literacy events are discussed here that fall into the two categories respectively.

Sticky fingers: implement mastery

This first literacy event, although not dealing with drawing or writing specifically, is interesting because it requires implement mastery. For this task children were given a photocopied picture of a frog and had to glue polystyrene chips onto its back (to show the 'rough skin') and then paint it. This event was analysed from videotaped transcripts with the primary focus on what children did.

The task was connected to the weekly theme where children were learning about the lifecycle of a frog. To complete the task, children were given a pot of liquid glue and glue brushes – wooden sticks with a hard plastic brush at the end with which to smear the glue. A great deal of control is needed for this exercise – the right amount of glue is needed, each polystyrene chip has to be glued with the brush and then stuck down. This was not completely mastered; several children put too much glue on the brushes which fell onto their fingers or the newspaper-

Figure 6.1

Figure 6.2

Figure 6.3

Figure 6.4

Figure 6.5

Figure 6.6

covered table (Figures 6.1 and 6.2). They then moved on to the painting table. A similar amount of control was needed here in judging the correct amount of paint needed for application. Although the grip used for a paintbrush, gluestick, and pencil differs, I would argue that an important learning process takes place here with similarly shaped implements. Children experiment with and master the different movements required successfully to manipulate all three objects. At the same time the stick-like shape of each implement requires fine motor movements that need to be practised in order to attain mastery. In addition, as literate subjects these children are exposed to different mediums in which to make meaning.

The spatial organization of this activity lends itself to controlling what could be a messy exercise. Two tables next to each other are set out – the gluing table and the painting table. This limits the movement (and potential levels of distraction) from the first part of the task to the second. It also means that a limited number of children will be engaged with gluing or painting, allowing for closer teacher supervision. The children are not free to do what they like but are disciplined to follow the exercise to its conclusion in preset steps that prefigure tasks they will encounter later in their schooling. Thus, several **norms** need to be internalized for the task so that all the children working at the table can use the materials; there are enough materials for every child, and that the space is clean enough for the next group. All the containers and brushes are placed in the centre of the table so everyone has easy access to them. The children's actions display an attempt to follow these norms – they tapped excess glue or wiped excess paint from their brushes. They replaced them in the containers when they had finished using them. Being under closer **surveillance** by Dawn meant that children are reminded of these norms ('use a little bit of glue at a time'), and that correct use of the implements is modelled for the children. Lesego needed some support. He sat at the gluing table watching the other children carefully. Dawn, seeing this, demonstrated what he should do: she took the brush from his hand, showed him how to apply the glue to the polystyrene chips and gave him the brush to try himself (Figures 6.3–6.5). At the painting table he again seemed unsure where he should paint or how to angle his paintbrush. The photographs show him move his paintbrush over the frog before he begins, watching the girl next to him carefully (Figures 6.6–6.8). The shape of the tables allows for learning through observation of peers who have mastered tasks.

Figure 6.7

Figure 6.8

Don and Mick's free drawing

Free drawing is a daily literacy event that has several important functions. To illustrate this, two drawings done on the same day by two boys sitting next to each other at the same table will be compared. The first picture, a figure of a woman, was drawn by Don (Figure 6.9), the second (Figure 6.10), is drawn by Mick. Mick's picture reveals an attempt to draw a similar figure to Don's, but is out of proportion. The head is too low on the page and too big for the body, the nose is too big, the eyes are not level and there are two lines for legs that are at odds with the head. In comparison Don's spatial arrangement is more sophisticated. He has used the whole page but has not represented the entire body, stopping at the waist but keeping the proportions correct. While his one ear is larger than the other he has included ears with earrings representing the gender of the figure. Mick, who was watching Don draw, was taken with this representation of ears. He has redrawn the ears which are the circles around the top of the head. He diverges from Don by adding a spider in the middle of the configuration of ears. While Mick's picture could be judged to be more immature, Don had a tendency to scribble or paint over his pictures once he'd drawn them.

The spatial configuration of the classroom allows for peer learning and teaching, even if it is not explicit. Don's influence helps Mick learn to draw (Anning, 1999). The fact that the children are allowed to draw what they like provides them with a space for experimentation and learning how bodies and objects can be configured on the white space of a page. At the beginning of my observation period Mick drew stick figures common in children's early pictures, but exposure to Don's drawings reveal a more complex rendering of how, in this case, the human body can be represented.

General requirements for emerging writers in Grade 00 are subtly reinforced and the children have access to a number of materials to experiment with, as well as the rules that

Figure 6.9 Don's picture.

Figure 6.10 Mick's picture.

accompany the use of these. They are given access to the genre of the worksheet which they will encounter throughout their schooling. These function to develop children's fine motor movements in anticipation of the need to form letters. In addition, and in combination with implement mastery, free drawing allows for experimentation and creativity. The children are also prepared for the practices around which formal school literacy will centre: time on task, the rules for using writing implements, spatial organization of the body and writing implements in confined spaces. It seems that these children have a level of control over their emerging writing because they are provided with the space to experiment, create, and most importantly to make meaning of the literacy events they participate in. One could not call them writers – they are not authoring stories, but they are being prepared as scribes.

Less experimentation, more structure: Grade 0

There is a sense of continuity in the move between Grade 00 and Grade 0, as many of the activities in Grade 00 are replicated. Prescribed activities are still related in some way to weekly themes. But perceptual activities increase while free drawing decreases. The majority of tasks are perceptual and pre-writing exercises where implement mastery is implicit. Basic numeracy tasks are also included, e.g. a worksheet asking children to count and colour in the number of fairies in a picture.

The Grade 0 children also work on loose paper. This work is collected over the year and stored in A4 files at the back of the classroom. At the end of the year the children take this record of work home. Not every piece of work children completed was filed; some of it was taken home. But, as an archive of Grade 0 school literacy, the choice of work included in the file is revealing of what is considered to be important by the teacher and the kinds of literacy that is valued (Ormerod & Ivanic, 2000).

All the children had the same work in their files. At the end of the year Amanda let me examine her file. It contains 57 pieces of work. The pieces were not dated but filed in what appears to be roughly chronological order, with the early pieces at the back of the file and the later ones in the front.

From the examples in this file a clear shift emerges from Grade 00. All the exercises in the file have a specific purpose. There are no examples of free drawing and minimal opportunities for individual expression that were not guided by a set task. There are only four examples of work where children were asked to draw their own pictures (a spider's web, a spring day, a form of transport, an octopus) guided by topic. A large number of pictures children had to colour in, which probably originated from colouring-in books (e.g. giraffe, a see-saw, a rocket). The majority of exercises in the file that did not involve another medium like paint, required some colouring in. Many of these focused specifically on colouring-in particular sections of a picture in different colours (e.g. a striped dress, a striped beach ball). This aligns with the emphasis in the class where instructions about colouring in between the lines and distinguishing different segments in pictures were given. It is tempting to argue that this emphasis on colouring in between the lines leads to conformity and does not allow for creative expression or individual exploration, especially since some exercises prescribed the colours to be used. But while there is a definite shift to formal work with precise procedures, there was space for free drawing and individual expression. The fact that these pictures were sent home is pertinent and a binary is set up. Creative work goes home, other prescribed tasks stay at school as a material record of a child's abilities. An archive is built that contains a record of a child in which their work can be measured, calculated, and judged. The predominant means through which children's literate subjectivity is constructed is through their ability to complete prescribed tasks rather than creative, original texts. Docility is valued over creativity.

This is evident because the majority of tasks in the file are perceptual exercises aimed to prepare children for the task of writing. These tasks were also more dominant in the early part of the year. The type of tasks included improving hand-eye co-ordination by completing a number of join-the-dots exercises. Identification exercises were also prevalent: identifying similar objects, looking for differences or absences, foregrounding objects superimposed over each other, matching objects by drawing lines. A number of exercises drew attention to the body and body parts. In one exercise children were given a blank face and had to place the eyes, ears, mouth, nose, etc., in the correct place. Later they were required to draw in the missing facial features of a clown. They did handprints and footprints in paint. The presence of body parts in these texts is representative of a general concern for the body. During Language Ring children were frequently asked to identify parts of the body, sing songs about the body, and practise crossing the midline.[1] This attention on the body is important because it is not only about naming, but it also draws attention to the body generally, its parts specifically, and how they are required to function in the classroom space.

The increase in formality is evident in how literacy events located at children's desks are structured. The fluidity of movement in Grade 00, where children shifted from one desk to another and often took up a half-sitting, half-standing posture to complete their tasks, gives way to allocated seating that restrains movement. This function makes possible 'the supervision of each individual and the simultaneous work of all.... It [makes] the educational space function like a learning machine' (Foucault, 1977: 147). Children become this learning machine – a group obeying a system of command that requires them to complete the same exercises together. The exercise to identify and count fairies exemplifies this practice. Lisa began the lesson by miming locking her mouth and throwing away the key which the children copied (Figures 6.11 and 6.12). The class was told that they could not talk and work at the same time. Tasks that involve drawing or writing no longer have an element of classroom community but focus on the individual, as Figure 6.13 illustrates.

This can also be seen in terms in the distribution of materials. In the Grade 00 class all materials are communal; they belong to the class and are shared by them. In Grade 0 children are required to have their own stationery with which to work. It is kept in the back storeroom and children need to collect their equipment for 'writing' lessons. Children are required to manage their own material resources properly, like packing pencils away, and replacing products like

Figure 6.11   Figure 6.12

Figure 6.13

glue. Once again, one of the elements of a literate identity in school focuses around respons-ibility. The shift in ownership of material resources from class to individual prefigures Grade 1 classroom practices, where materials for drawing and writing are not shared. Thus individually owned resources are used for individual writing tasks that are completed in silence, in contrast to the shared conversation and shared materials of Grade 00. The identity of a writer then is also bound up with individually owned equipment. This practice is resisted by children who resort to borrowing, which breaks the spatial separation enforced by allocated seating. This classroom practice has an impact on identity formation of children. Toohey (2000: 92) points out that:

> These classroom practices, so commonplace as to be almost invisible, contribute to instan-tiating the notion that the children's individuality must be established, reinforced, pro-tected. Children sit in their own desks, use their own materials, do their own work and use their own words. Knowing and staying in one's place, having good materials in one's own place, keeping track of and taking care of them oneself, having one's own 'things' to write and draw and say, establish each child as an individual, who on her own, negotiates class-room life.

I have argued earlier that the preschool classrooms focus on developing group relations (working and learning together and sharing) which shifts to a focus on the individual in the primary school. The spatial configurations of these preschool classrooms reflect this, with chil-dren spending more time at ring times on the carpet than locked into their desks. This pattern does begin to rupture in Grade 0, when one examines writing practices where the focus is on individual mastery. This rupture, which breaks with preschool conceptions, is in fact the precur-sor to the next 12 years when children will primarily sit at their desks completing writing tasks individually.

Commandeering fieldnotes: writing for a purpose

This section draws attention to child-writers in the Grade 0 class who reveal a broader under-standing of the functions of writing that go beyond decontextualized pre-writing exercises. In her interview, Lisa, echoing the words of Graves (1982), states that the children *want* to write.

Yet in this class, writing is constrained by prescribed views that focus on skills and mastery. These imply that writing is a serious endeavour where one strives for correctness. Yet writing is also creative; the act of writing (and rewriting) is a sophisticated meaning-making process (Kress, 1997) that involves both a mastery of skill and an exploration of identity. Several of the children demonstrated this exploration by writing in my fieldnotes.

A short explanation is necessary as to how this came about. During each observation session, including those that were videotaped, I had an A4 notebook and pencil. My practice of taking notes was observed and commented on by children in all grades. As such, a particular kind of writing was being modelled to the children. For the Grade 0s, who were discovering writing and exploring their own writing abilities, the presence of a 'writer' in their class was of interest. They would often cluster around to see the fieldnotes. Several children wanted to know what I would do with my notebooks. I told them that this writing had a purpose. I was a student at university and I had to do a project so I could pass. To do the project I needed the notebooks as a record of events because I could not remember everything that happened. When I had finished all my observations I would read the notebooks from all the classes and I would read some books. Then I would make more notes. Finally I would use the ideas from the books and notebooks and write my project.

The children were interested in several aspects of the writing process, which reveal a number of things about their knowledge of writing. First they were interested in the 'tool' used for taking fieldnotes, in this case an inexpensive plastic clutch pencil with an eraser at the top. This innocuous choice on my part was a source of amazement for many children in the study. The Grade 0s wanted to see this pencil, hold it, try it; they were confused that something which looked like a pen wrote like a pencil. It did not need to be sharpened and, when you pushed the top, very thin lead emerged from the bottom. And it had another function; by turning the pencil over, you could rub out mistakes. I was initially surprised that these children had never seen a clutch pencil before, but realized that it revealed their economic circumstances. The lack of resources at home had nothing to do with a lack of interest in writing. The Grade 0s were interested in the implements used to write and what writing could be used for. In the Grade 0 classroom where writing implements were restricted to pencils and wax crayons, the grey lead possibly held the promise of what they would encounter as writers at 'big school'.

Several pages of fieldnotes are covered with a number of the Grade 0s' drawings and writing. Between tasks, or when waiting for a new task to begin, a group of children would sometimes cluster around me and ask to draw. The organization of tasks and greater freedom of spatial distribution are two conditions that allowed this to take place. Although the Grade 0 day is more organized than Grade 00, if children completed their tasks quickly they went to sit on the carpet. The open space of the carpet allowed for greater movement, and moving from the desk to the carpet could entail a 'detour' past the fieldnotes. Interestingly the 'good' children would come to draw even though they knew they might be reprimanded, and both girls and boys wanted to draw.[2]

Ormerod and Ivanic (2000: 98) make the statement that 'while writing is always a physical act, it can take very different forms, leaving different kinds of physical evidence'. With this in mind I want to look at the physical evidence left by the children in the form of drawing and writing on one page of fieldnotes (Figure 6.14). Seven girls either wrote or drew on this page (the boys arrived later and their writing is on another page). For ethical purposes I have edited this page so that none of the children can be identified. The girls show a preoccupation with writing their names, which is not uncommon in this age group (Yang & Noel, 2006). Kress (1997) remarks on the fascination and mystique that writing one's name has for children, and stresses the sheer creativity of the activity. It also signifies a sense of self-worth and place in the world (Whitehead, 1990). Studies indicate that learning to write one's name may promote the development of writing in general, because a knowledge of letter-formations, letter names and letter–sound correspondences are learnt (Levin et al., 2005). The children asked me to write my name, which they copied. Next to my name are the names and ages of one of the girls, her brother and cousins. There are also four female figures. They reveal several interests of the girls – fashion, jewellery, and hairstyles. The figure at the top is wearing a crucifix around her neck and the bottom left figure has earrings on. Both figures have boots on. The girl who drew the top picture often included details like high-heeled boots in her other drawings, which the other girls tried to replicate. The bottom right picture also shows attention to clothing where the skirt is patterned through the use of diagonal lines. The girls have also all paid attention to the hairstyles that range from a bob to long hair.

There are several fascinating things happening on this page. This is a communal space for expression rather than the individual class writing tasks they are given. The children were happy

Figure 6.14 Grade 0 fieldnotes (with names removed).

to share this writing space and talk about what they were going to draw or write, and they had conversations about what they were doing. This harks back to how writing operates in the Grade 00 class. What surprised me greatly was their patience in using limited resources. There was one book and one (albeit rather prized) pencil. As the owner of the pencil, my word was law, and what emerged was a general rule that one's writing turn was dependent on when one joined the group. Apart from 'reminders' to me that they were still present and should not be forgotten, the turn-taking was orderly – a sign of the general discipline present in this classroom. Although this class was well disciplined and understood the principle of sharing, the children also knew we were doing something that was not officially sanctioned, and that this pleasure could be removed if they were not compliant. This may also have contributed to the way these interactions took place. This notion of a shared writing space is demonstrated by the word 'lady' written next to the bottom left-hand picture. The picture has been labelled in a manner consistent with school exercises, but the writer is not the girl who drew the picture. The writer is identifying in print what the other girls have represented in their drawings – these are little girls fascinated with women ('ladies'). These pictures are not representations of themselves. They are fascinated with beautiful and fashionable women, and western representations of women. None of the girls who drew on this day is White. One is Indian and the other three are Black. Apart from the Indian girl who had long hair, the other three girls had short hair and at this stage of the research were not wearing their hair in braids. When the girls in this class drew females they were distinguished from males by long flowing hair as opposed to short, curly, African hair.

At this point I want to make a comment by comparing the interest the Grade 0s showed around the fieldnotes with that of the Grade 3s in terms of literate subject constructions. The Grade 0s were interested in the act of writing and producing something meaningful that incorporated their social worlds. They took on the identity of emerging writers, discovering and exploring how they could make meaning. The girls used the notes to explore a gendered subjectivity in their idealized depictions of femininity. On the other hand no Grade 3 asked to write in the fieldnotes, rather they were fascinated with my perceived writing skills. Much of the discussion was not about what was written but *how* it was written: in cursive, with speed, a large quantity was produced. They looked at my sloping, messy cursive script, at odds with the carefully formed cursive they were learning. They did not try hard to decipher it – they asked what I had written and took me at my word. The contrast is stark. The Grade 3s by this stage have mastered the basics of writing and are more proficient readers, but their understanding of writing and who they are as writers is narrowed by viewing it as a skill. The fact that I wrote because I wanted to, that I kept a record because I was interested in what I saw, that I found pleasure in writing, that the fieldnotes were not monitored or marked, that they were not a final product to be handed in, was an alien practice to many of these children.

This is a stark contrast that speaks to the impact school practices can have on subject construction. Its origin for many children begins in Grade 1.

Having a hand at writing: Grade 1

Over 20 years ago Grundlach et al. (1985: 40) noted that literacy skills were mastered through didactic instruction where 'literacy equals the sum of the individual mechanical skills that go into putting words on paper' rather than it being a 'meaning making and meaning sharing activity'. In many ways this sums up the approach to teaching writing in the Foundation Phase. The result is that scribes, not authors, are produced and the body takes the full impact of this kind of training. Although mastery of these skills is vital and has a crucial place, children are not incapable of understanding and applying highly sophisticated writing techniques. Riley and Reely's (2005) study of children between the ages of five and nine who were taught to write argument, demonstrates this. Using excerpts from a transcript of a handwriting lesson which is supplemented with photographs, this section explores the intensive training that the body undergoes with this approach, and the need for high levels of teacher **surveillance**.

The lesson, taped at the end of the first month of school, began with several body exercises. These exercises are used to refocus attention for the start of a new task (in a similar way to the Dippy Duck lesson, see pp. 78–79), but they also work to prepare the children for the rigours of writing. Control of the body is fundamental in learning to write, and this lesson begins with children being made to cross the midline:

HELEN: Put your hands at your sides … Lift your left shoulder up.… Take your right arm and touch your left shoulder. Let your right arm touch your left ear … Stand next to the table. Don't lean on the table. Put your right elbow on your left knee.

Quick exercises to get the children's fingers moving were practised. Children were told to play the piano, flick their fingers to imitate the hazard lights of a car, make tight fists, and shake their fingers and hands. Observing these exercises is revealing – children who struggled to maintain their balance, or whose movements were unco-ordinated, struggled with their writing. Their difficulties included the general transfer of information from the board to their books and the spatial arrangement of information on the page as well as letter formation. The harnessing of the entire body through these exercises, and the focus on the hands, have an important role in helping children who are unused to writing.

The children are then told to sit down and take out their pencils. These are thick triangular pencils aimed at aiding pencil grip for greater control. I have a sense of unease about these pencils and question them – not in terms the efficacy of their function – but rather the impact that they have on how writing is viewed. The Grade 00s and Grade 0s managed a number of literacy implements. The writing the Grade 0s did with the clutch pencil is neat and controlled. These fat triangular pencils are not used in most homes. But when children get to Grade 1, in order to learn to write they are given a special pencil. This implies that school writing is something difficult that requires special equipment. The implements children have used to write with at home and preschool are 'incorrect' which implies there may be something faulty with what has been learnt. If, as Goodman (2001: 319) notes, children as young as three 'express the fear that learning to read and write will be very hard and can only be learned at school', then the use of specific writing implements may play into this perception.

Nevertheless, fat pencils in hand, the children are given instructions from their teacher, who also demonstrated on the blackboard what they had to do:

HELEN: OK open your book to today's work.… You see the four dots?
CLASS: Yes
HELEN: And today's date is the 28th of January. See where I write January – the capital letter goes over two spaces Grade 1s, alright?
CLASS: Yes
HELEN: Now you may start, you may write the date. I only want you to write the date nothing else [murmuring from class]. And when we work we work quietly. Maxine face the front please. Quietly Grade 1s, no talking please. And try to remember to touch your lines. Just start with the date. Please touch the lines.

The four dots referred to are in the margin of each child's book indicating where the children should be writing. For this exercise the children are writing the letters 'a' and 't'. Depending on their level of mastery some children had dots, others had letters written next to the dots to trace

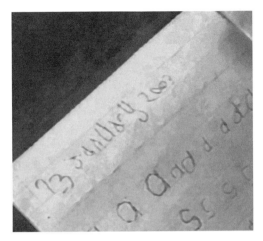

Figure 6.15   *Figure 6.16*

over. Figures 6.15 and 6.16 show Jason's previous writing attempt and the scaffolded writing where he has to trace over the teacher's writing. The following figure (6.17), indicates the first dot for this exercise which signals where the date should be written, the second dot indicates where the letter 't' should be placed, the third dot indicates the place for the letter 'a' and the final dot is for writing the numbers 1 and 2.

The transcript also reveals the structured nature of writing lessons. Structure is evident in the spatial arrangement of letters and words. The date is written in a specific place and the layout of the page is predetermined and marked by symbols (the dots). It is in these lessons that school writing conventions are internalized until they become invisible practices of habituated writers.

The teacher's comments work to regulate the pace of the lesson as children are only allowed to write the date. This reflects back to Grade 0, where class tasks are meant to be done together. Helen reminds the children to control their bodies generally (by being quiet, facing the front) and gives specific reminders about forming letters between the lines. The relaxed atmosphere of the Grade 00 class has been eradicated. Once the date has been written the internalization of bodily routine 'kicks in' as most children place their hands on their heads to wait for the next set of instructions. These are to write a row of 'a's and then a row of 't's. After this the children are given guidance in placing two letters together to form a word:

HELEN: (on her way to the blackboard) Wonderful – some people are using two fingerspaces, some people are not using a fingerspace at all. Right, now that was the 't' sound. What sound was that? And this word is written in your book already. I wonder who can tell me what this word is? Yes Amanda –

AMANDA: at

HELEN: at. And what sound is this, where do we get this sound from, who is this –

CLASS: 'a'

HELEN: in Letterland

HELEN: Who is this?

CLASS: Annie Apple

HELEN: What sound does she make?

CLASS: 'a', 'a'

HELEN: 'a'. What sound?

CLASS: 'a'

HELEN: Again

CLASS: 'a'

HELEN: Tina sit nicely dear, put your feet in front of you. And who is this again from Letterland?

CLASS: T/t/Ticking Tess

HELEN: Again

CLASS: Ticking Tess

HELEN: Ticking Tess. Feet together please Bongani, feet together. Bongani put your feet together. [His one leg is stretched out in the aisle.] Thank you. Right so we first write our Annie Apple, but remember she doesn't start on the line she starts below the line, she goes up, around, she touches the line, she closes and comes straight down [she writes 'a']. And next to her [continues writing] we are not going to make a big space, we write Ticking Tess. Trace over what is in your book. And we have your word: at.

CLAUDIA: Miss must we write 'at' on the whole line?

HELEN: Yes

HELEN: [walks around the class checking the children's work.] We go up, around, close her and come straight down.... Carry on you mustn't lift your hand you must go straight down to the line curling like you did the others. Ok. Yes. [Back at the board.] Now we are going to make the fingerspace – your two fingerspaces – make Annie Apple around, close Annie Apple, do the 't' and we have our word at ... [She walks around giving help to children struggling.] ...

HELEN: [at the blackboard] There are two numbers. You must touch your lines remember that. Kumo! You've got one, number one and a small little space and number two, right? You are going to trace over those and then you are going to start again, number one, number two. I only want one fingerspace between those, one finger not two. Then do a number one and a number two. Start. Remember number one is a straight line and you start at the top of the line and then you write down. These spaces are far too big Vukani ... [To class] Straight line down for number one, number two goes up, around, across and straight.... [To Xolani] Where is your fingerspace Xolani? [Figure 6.18] Put your finger on, next to the number, no, no, no, where's your finger? Use the left hand [Figure 6.19]. Put your finger down, use your

Figure 6.17

Figure 6.18

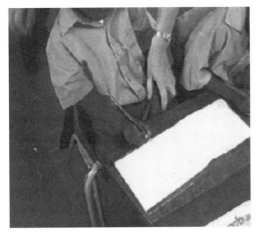

Figure 6.19

Figure 6.20

Figure 6.21

Figure 6.22

Figure 6.23

left hand, no, no, no, you are to write with this one. Put your finger like that [Figure 6.20]. Put it next to the number, make a dot, make a dot, alright [Figure 6.21]. Very good, now take your finger again, put it next to the number, right, now write number two, number two – this is number two, this one [Figure 6.22]. Uh uh you are making it a back to front Sammy Snake [Figure 6.23]. Do a finger space next to the number, next to the number do a dot and write number one. Wonderful.

The phonics approach to reading influences the writing lesson – reading the word 'at' and identifying the letter–sound correspondences. The letters introduced are influenced by the blends so that words can be produced by such a combination. This is illustrated by another exercise children had to complete. When they had learnt 10 letters (s, a, t, m, h, d, n, p, r, g) they had to combine them to write words they knew.

In terms of training bodies to write, the transcript and photographs reveal an attention to detail on the part of the teacher that is labour intensive. The primarily oral interaction that characterized the reading lesson is supplemented with increased bodily involvement on the part of both the teacher and students. The training required to produce correctly formed letters means that it is essential for the teacher to move around the class giving oral reminders and showing children where to place and move their pencils to form letters. She has to observe both what the children are producing, and how they are producing letters. Then she has to move into the space of those who need help and physically reposition them. At the beginning of a year, when most children have a limited knowledge of writing, this can be a challenge with a large class. Thus it is necessary for the children to be located in one space (their desks) and have their movement highly restricted. These practical issues may also indicate the constant underscoring of completing class tasks, one instruction at a time. The problem with this way of working is that some children finish sooner than others and have nothing to do while waiting for the teacher to go round all the children. The class also creates empty spaces that children fill with their own activities (talking, moving, playing). While intense **surveillance** is required on the part of the teacher, the children are required to watch and listen as she demonstrates and explains the movements required to write ('Annie Apple ... starts below the line she goes up and around, she touches the line, she closes and comes straight down'). Then they have to transfer what they have observed into their books. These instructions establish a **norm** that there is a correct and incorrect way to form letters. Forming letters as required by the teacher, and using her handwriting as a model to trace over (as Jason's book indicates), can have a homogenizing effect on the subjects targeted. Clark and Ivanic (1997: 192–193) argue that 'over-frequent insistence on neat handwriting – and sometimes on a particular style of handwriting – is in danger of having an homogenizing effect on the population and creating docile citizens: a political objective to which nobody would want to admit'.

This is a powerful argument to consider particularly if (neat) handwriting predominates in writing assessment. At the same time children need to be introduced to standard writing practices. Barton (1994) points out that young children's (experimental) writing often indicates a number of viable hypotheses: they may write in columns, or with no spaces between words, from left to right and then right to left. What children do eventually take on, through explicit instruction, are the norms of a particular system of writing that indicate membership of a specific society (Jones, 2000). A **norm** that appears to provide difficulty for a number of children is the spatial arrangement required to leave the correct amount of space between letters, words, and numbers. As the photographs of Xolani reveal, this is a complex task that involves careful co-ordination of the body (Figures 6.18–6.23), knowing how and when to use, in this case, the left hand to make fingerspaces and when to reposition it to give the right hand support to write. The finger provides an initial scaffold, helping the eye and the hand to judge the gaps so that they are uniform, until making spaces between words becomes part of the writing **habitus**. Children's movements are tightly **regulated** with the aim of producing **self-regulating** writers: they are managed so that they in turn manage their own writing.

Neatness can be a reflection of register revealing how the writer perceives him/herself as well as the reader (Smith, 1982). Giving children access to 'correct forms' is then important, since what they produce will later also be judged outside the confines of the school. At the same time, despite the initial tracing over teachers' words and letters, children's handwriting still develops its own individual characteristics.[3] But culturally accepted writing norms can be subverted. For example, teenage girls' penchant for drawing hearts over the letter 'i' instead of dotting it, may be a sign of **resistance** to the power of the school and teachers – and evidence of the constitution of a different subjectivity.

'Neatness, formation, and sharp pencils' or a technique of the self? Grade 3 writing

As is to be expected, Grade 3 is a culmination of the thinking displayed in the previous grades. The writing subject who has been carefully trained in a skills paradigm remains within it. Although writing takes precedence in this year as the means through which tasks are completed, there is no substantial writing for specific purposes or even for pleasure. The drawing and colouring prevalent in the preschool become marginal rather than meaningful in and of themselves. The majority of time is spent on worksheets. There are few opportunities for children to express themselves in writing. The genres available are constrained. Creative writing is almost non-existent. As the work becomes more formal and controlled, handwriting remains a constant. Each child has an A2 book with Irish lines specifically for handwriting, guiding children to form lower-case letters of uniform size in relation to capitals, and 'long' lower-case letters like y and g. The children have moved on to writing in cursive. Access to the tools of writing is decided via levels of mastery. Children who write neatly are allowed to write in pen, and those who do not retain their pencils.

It seems that writing in pen is a symbol and acknowledgement of a level of 'maturity'. The child who writes in pen is no longer stuck at the lowest **rank** (the Foundation Phase), but is able to take on the responsibility of producing indelible ink marks. This child is also ready to take on knowledge in its discipline-related forms. Denying the Grade 3 child access to writing in pen because they are not deemed ready is in fact counterproductive. Entry into Grade 4 demands pens. It would seem to make more sense that children who struggle need less practice with pencils. Thus the use and choice of writing tools are wielded as weapons of control and power and are inextricably tied up with **norms** of correctness and judgements about individual subjects.

The focus up until this part of the chapter is on spatial organization and its connection to training bodies to write. At the end of the Foundation Phase this training, while still present, is less important. The focus now shifts to looking at space on a more metaphorical level by examining the spaces created for writing. It works with Kamler's (2001) notion that writing is constitutive of subjectivity. It does this in two ways, first by examining sanctioned writing through teacher comments in handwriting books. This is set against the example of Travis's writing; he finds ways to insert his identity into both sanctioned and unsanctioned acts of writing.

'Your work is untidy.' Handwriting books

A sample of six handwriting books was examined (belonging to four boys and two girls who ranged in academic ability). At the end of the year children had the option of keeping their books or giving them to me. These are a small sample. The format of the handwriting exercises over the year is uniform; what differs is the letter being written. Each exercise is dated and then begins with a line of a specific letter in upper case, the following line repeats the letter in lower case, the third combines upper and lower case, and the final line consists either of words or a sentence beginning with that letter. Finally the children copy a pattern to complete the exercise, using coloured pencils (Figure 6.24). Handwriting is done twice weekly; on the first day children write in print, on the second in cursive.

What is revealing about these books is the interaction between the teacher and child writer. Foucault (2000c: 277) considers writing to be a technique of the self which is 'frequently linked to the techniques for the direction of others. For example if we take educational institutions, we realize that one is managing others and teaching them to manage themselves.' In his examination of writing as an element of the 'arts of the self' in Greco-Roman culture, Foucault discusses two types of writing, personal journals and correspondence (2000b: 209). I want to talk about the latter. Correspondence entails writing for someone who will read and respond to the writing. The writer also presents him/herself in a particular way. Although Foucault specifically mentions the content of letter writing, the representation of the self is not solely communicated through content but, as is powerfully shown by Thornton (2001), also through handwriting. Thus while the work presented in the handwriting books of a group of 9-year-old children does not have the same philosophical purpose as the writings of the ancients, it is work presented to another. This other is the teacher who comments on the work produced. The fact that some form of writing has been produced and has received a written response in return is, I believe, a form of correspondence. When this occurs a double gaze is present – the gaze of the self and the

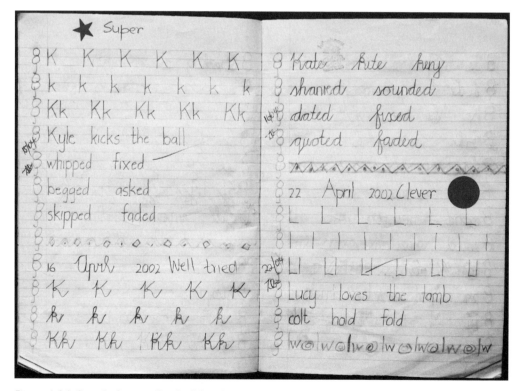

Figure 6.24 Sample from a Grade 3 handwriting book.

gaze of the other that the writer takes into account when presenting him/herself in a way that accords to the 'rules of a technique of living' (Foucault, 2000b: 221). In this case, the rules are those that have to do with the school as educational institution. In the contested space around handwriting, a link is made between handwriting and moral character. Handwriting reveals 'good work habits, respect of persons, an attention to detail and generally a "proper" attitude to life' (Clark and Ivanic, 1997: 192).

In the six books analysed, there were 40 different comments made by the teacher. They were presented in three different modes: handwritten messages in red pen, stickers with a picture and message, ink stamps with a picture and message. Each piece of work was signed and dated by the teacher. A frequency count of each comment showed that of the seven most frequent comments, five contained the verb 'try'. The most frequently written comment was 'tried' (22 times), followed by 'well tried' (18 times), 'try again' (15 times), 'keep on trying' (10 times) and the sticker version, 'keep on trying from [teacher's name]'. The use of the word 'try' varies in meaning depending on what it has been combined with. When it is paired with 'to' specific characteristics of the writer are stressed: 'try to improve', 'try to be neat', 'try to concentrate on your work'. Thus constant concentrated effort is of prime concern. The good writer strives to do better, pays attention to detail and presentation, and is focused. Put this way, the message indicates that there is room for change as opposed to the statement 'your work is untidy' which signifies a relational process ($x = y$). In this way many of the messages written by the teacher are encouraging, implying an understanding that attaining mastery is a process. This is in contrast to comments like 'tried', 'good try', and 'well tried' where the past tense nullifies this process. However, these comments do acknowledge effort. But the comment 'try again' is a euphemism for work that is below standard.

Neat handwriting is linked to intelligence as Figure 6.24 illustrates. This child was one of the more competent writers in the sample. For each exercise the teacher has written a message. The first comment, 'Super', with a star next to it compliments the writer's mastery of the exercise. The next piece of work receives 'Well tried' – which is not as good as 'super' but acknowledges effort. These two comments exemplify a pattern across all the books where children are more likely to receive positive feedback on the printed exercises than they are on cursive ones. On the whole children's printing is neater than their cursive, which looks laboured. The final comment is 'Clever', which points to the intelligence of the writer. But the exercise requires no application of intelligence, only an ability to copy.

The comments appear to have been internalized by the children. The compliant subject whose handwriting receives praise and thus validation from an authority figure does not want to slip in his/her teacher's esteem. When the writer of Figure 6.24, whose overall feedback was positive ('wonderful', 'excellent'), received a strongly worded negative comment ('I am not impressed') it seems the criticism was taken seriously. The exercise after this comment reveals a return to his usual standard of work which was praised as 'wonderful'. This pattern is also present in weaker students' work. Marcus was a student who resisted daily class routines by being disruptive. It therefore seems reasonable to assume that he would find the repetitive nature of the handwriting exercises cause for further resistance. But throughout his book messages of 'try again' are followed by 'well tried'. Granted, the constant reminders to 'try again' imply incomplete internalization of the requirements of handwriting – especially since he had a propensity to disregard fingerspaces at this stage in the Foundation Phase – but there is evidence of improvement in his work.

While the gaze of the teacher falls on the work of the students each week, the choice of message and mode is revealing. The choice of stickers creates an anthropomorphic identity for the teacher that is subject to the gaze of the child (and in this case the researcher). Many of the stickers used by the teachers are personalized. They are white squares with an animal and a

Figure 6.25 Examples of stickers in Grade 3 handwriting books.

typed comment. The messages on the stickers either begin with the personal pronoun 'I', or take on the genre of a letter by making a statement and 'signing' it with 'from [name of teacher]'. The teacher takes on a variety of identities through these stickers (Figure 6.25). In one she is represented in the form of a bulldog. It has heavy jowls and what look like a number of medals (representing victims?) attached to its collar. The message serves as a warning and contains undercurrents of force and violence – this is an attack dog. Thus the message is threatening and raises the question: Will the teacher, who has taken on the identity of an attack dog, use force if provoked? Another sticker, in contrast to the first, trades on guilt and manipulation. Children have a strong desire for validation and the sticker operates on this assumption. It depicts a small mouse holding a handkerchief and crying. The message reads: 'I'm so sad that your work is so untidy from Miss [name of teacher].' Rather than make her angry and 'bite back' the work is hurtful. The untidiness is linked to a lack of respect for the teacher who has been 'hurt' by looking at it. A third sticker, rather than representing the teacher reflects the teacher's judgement of the child. It depicts an ant rolling a nut with the comment 'Keep Trying from [name of teacher]'. The ant plays into the stereotype that ants are industrious and hardworking. The message is that persistence will pay off and that these are desirable qualities to internalize.

Handwriting then is not only about mastery through practice. It is the means through which particular values that are regarded as important in the school community are supposed to be internalized. Children need to be industrious and hard working, if the number of 'tries' the teacher has written in the books is anything to go by. This demonstrates explicitly how values are entrenched in the curriculum – it is no coincidence that the school's motto is 'Perseverance'.

Writing in the margins: Travis

> When we make space as crucial a component of that production as time, what results are embodied texts, where the body (sexed, gendered, racialised, classed) cannot be written out or ignored, where the body insists on occupying some space and will not be silenced. What results is an understanding of texts as processual – as a process of making which is profoundly embodied and disciplined, subject to all kinds of policy, institutional, private and power relationships.
>
> (Kamler, 2001: 5)

It is with Kamler's words in mind that this final section is written. This section looks at Travis, a Grade 3 boy, and who he is as a writer. In the mesh of curriculum choices, pedagogical practices, and complex power relationships, this is a body that has occupied a space and will not be silent. He is both a schooled subject and a rebellious one. As an individual subject formed by many forces inside and outside the school, Travis finds expression in the margins of his schoolbooks.

During my observations in the Grade 3 class I often sat with Travis's group. He was the unofficial leader of the group. Although quite small in stature he was a forceful presence. Academically he was the strongest child in the group. For the majority of tasks his modus operandi was to complete them as quickly as possible, with little regard for neatness and detail. This had a twofold result. His work could not be copied, and he had more leisure time. In this time he often distracted the others (not always purposefully) by talking to them. He was frequently reprimanded for talking and not paying attention. In many ways it seemed that Travis was bored. Schoolwork was a chore rather than something he was engaged in. Travis was often angry and frustrated, and could be quite aggressive. He never backed down from fights or confrontations. On one occasion he demonstrated his frustration by systematically snapping all his pencils, much to the annoyance of his teacher.

Popular music played an important role in Travis's life. He was particularly taken with many hip-hop artists and rappers and sang their songs to himself under his breath while working. Music was a frequent topic of conversation and he became extremely animated when he heard that Usher was coming to South Africa. We also discussed the merits of P. Diddy's then relationship with Jennifer Lopez. He questioned my taste in 'old school' music. Ja Rule, the American rap artist, was Travis's favourite musician and Travis sang his songs daily. His knowledge of this musical genre was demonstrated through his body as he would take on the movements embodied by these singers. Like the two Grade 1 boys who launched into their own performance, Travis could swiftly move from a Grade 3 schoolboy to a mini Ja Rule.

Dyson (1995) makes the point that commercial culture is often taken up by children who use it as a topic of their free writing unless teachers explicitly ban it. This argument assumes that free writing is a **normalized** classroom practice. It is not so in many South African classrooms. In these classrooms, forms of popular culture are not banned as topics for free writing because there is no free writing. There is no 'permeable curriculum', to use Dyson's (1993) phrase, where children's interests are seriously taken into account. The curriculum is tightly bound to include very narrow tasks. How then, when there is no outlet through sanctioned activities like free writing, do children express facets of their own identities?

In Travis's case it would be rebelliously – through subverting the genres that he has at hand and using a genre of defiance – graffiti. In the inside covers of his schoolbooks Travis, the lover of music, exists. In the back of his Life Skills book, written in pen, he lists the artists he considers to be important. He writes:

> R Kelly, Ja Rule, Tamia, Jeniffer Lopez, Usher, P. Diddy, 2 Pac, Alicia Keys, Jay-zee, mnm, Destiny's Child, Zola, Nelly, Nelly Fertado, Mr Bee, Janet Jackson, Buster ryms, Jay Dee, Celine Dion.
>
> (As original)

Writing this list clearly in the middle of the cardboard cover can be seen to be an act of defiance. He has defaced his book by writing about something that is not prescribed by his teachers. It is also a challenge to the thinking that we are not supposed to write in books – even if they are our own. But this love of music is hidden at the back of the book, placed in a marginal space. It is not listed or explored openly on the pages of the book. When Travis does inscribe this love on the pages of his books it is still hidden. In his handwriting book at the end of the year, given the space to draw his own pattern to finish the exercise, he takes the 'gap'. Instead of drawing the pattern, he has coloured three lines in yellow and written in green and yellow pencil. The word 'maxi' appears on the first line. The second line reads: 'Westside you [indistinguishable] dirty'. The third line reads 'H.L.K. and Hola'. By November R. Kelly, Ja Rule, Nelly, and Tamia appear in two more patterns.

Each week the children are required to report back on their 'Weekend News'. This practice begins in Grade 1, when children draw what they did over the weekend and begin to write sentences describing the pictures until the writing becomes central, and the pictures supplement it. In what is essentially a recount genre, there is very little room for creativity. In fact it is quite restrictive. Children are only required to recount what they *did* each weekend. Thus a list of activities is required. One of Travis's first entries for the year reads:

> I went to the glen [shopping centre] with my mother.
> I went to Gold reef city with my friends.
> I went to wimpy on Saturday.
> Me and my freind went to the swimming pool.
> I went to go and look at the church.
> I did play soccer with my friends.

> > (As original) (4 February)

Apart from playing soccer, every sentence contains the verb 'went'. This pattern continues throughout the year outlining where Travis went. This can create pressure on a writer, especially if nothing happened on a weekend or the child did not go anywhere or do anything. Thus fiction is created. Travis works to the expected formula that will mark him as compliant, but the content tells another story. On the 22 April he wrote:

> I went to suncity on Friday and had fun.
> I went to gold reef city for rides.
> We went to KFc to order a meal.
> We went to wimpy to eat lunch.
> I went to town to buy my new shoes.

> > (As original)

On a two-day weekend it does not seem possible that all this could have been accomplished. Sun City is a good two-hour drive from Johannesburg and priced for international tourists. It does not make sense to spend 'Friday' there to have what is vaguely termed fun. No doubt if Travis had been there the writing would have been filled with the activities offered at Sun City. In addition, a trip to Gold Reef City, which has theme park rides and is also expensive, warrants a day's participation. The inclusion of these two venues is perhaps the desire of a boy who covets such excursions. The final sentence jars. Apart from the question of how shopping was fitted into this 'full' weekend, it sounds like a sentence in an outdated reader. It is highly unlikely that Travis would have bought shoes in town when there are a number of shopping centres close by that feature prominently in his other descriptions of weekend news. Few people go to 'town' for weekend shopping excursions.

This writing is limited. Travis is limited by the restrictions of the genre – he can only talk about what he did. When he has run out of ideas he draws on his knowledge of other texts he has read. In this case the class texts and books he has access to are limited. The genre of Weekend News confines him to reality. So Travis subverts the genre and he makes up what he did. What results is a disjointedness to the sentences that sound like pages of dated readers. At this point there is no attempt to write cohesively, to form a paragraph, nor is there any understanding of these features of writing that are required in the following grades.

Travis does find a space to discuss another great interest, soccer. He writes frequently about playing soccer and we have some insight into how his soccer community works when he reveals he plays soccer for money and won R9.50 on one occasion. People who are interested in soccer are interested in the game and not just in playing it – there is a whole life around soccer – watching games, supporting teams, following scores and leagues, and having heroes. There is no place to talk about this in Weekend News but Travis finds a way to place his soccer heroes into this genre by replicating a team sheet for the Brazilian national side (Figure 6.26). He draws the team kit and writes the players' names and numbers on their backs in the same way that the team line-up before a televised game is represented. This is another life and literacy Travis has, that works its way into the gaps in his books.

At the end of the Foundation Phase Travis exemplifies the kind of writer that has been produced – a frustrated one writing himself into the margins of his books. Travis declares himself

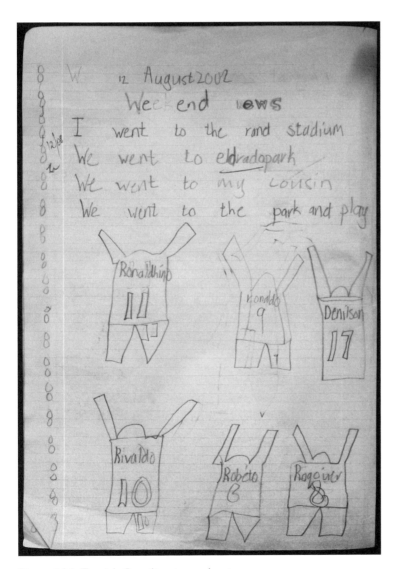

Figure 6.26 Travis's Brazilian team sheet.

in small spaces, and his identity, interests, and reading of the world are not acknowledged in the writing that he has to do. This has serious implications. If writing is constructed narrowly, then writers are also narrow. This narrowness will either create limited and docile subjects or alienated angry and resistant ones. Dyson's (1993: 33–34) words are worth considering:

> In a troubled world of poverty and violence, of racism and sometimes breathtaking indifference, we cannot pave children's way. But, as teachers, we can help. Within our classrooms, children compose texts that declare their existence in the world, but that existence is acknowledged momentarily completed, only by the response of the other (Bakhtin, 1986). In our own responses to the children, we help shape their understandings of what it means to be an educated person in our society. If our classrooms are not places for diversity of social action and a wealth of cultural materials, we risk sending messages of alienation, messages that say educated people are not rooted in their own histories, in strong relationships with people that matter.

Producing self-regulated writers

In the opening chapter I emphasized the connection Foucault makes that power and knowledge are joined through discourse and the way in which we see the world is shaped by the discourses we use. This point can be illustrated by the work of two educational psychologists who research the connections between writing and self-regulation (Graham & Harris, 1997, 2000). The way in which they understand and work with the concept of self-regulation is slightly different from the way in which it is used here; nevertheless, their conceptualization is useful. Graham and Harris (2000) separate transcription, which they see as a skill, from writing, which requires higher order thinking, and set out to prove a number of predictions. For example, 'skilled writers are more self-regulated than less skilled writers', 'teaching self-regulatory strategies improves writing', and 'transcription processes of skilled writers surpass those of less skilled writers' (2000: 4–8). Unsurprisingly they argue that 'the evidence reviewed in this article not only supports the claim that writing competence depends on high levels of self-regulation, but indicates that writing development is dependent on the mastery of transcription skills as well' (2000: 10). They provide evidence that if the mechanics of handwriting and spelling are not mastered then children cannot attend to higher order tasks like planning.

They provide a list of self-regulation strategies writers use:

> goal setting and planning (e.g., establishing rhetorical goals and tactics to achieve them), seeking information (e.g., gathering information pertinent to the writing topic), record keeping (e.g., making notes), organizing (e.g., ordering notes), transforming (e.g., visualizing a character to facilitate written description), self-monitoring (e.g., checking to see if writing goals are met), reviewing records (e.g., reviewing notes or the text produced so far), self-evaluating (e.g., assessing the quality of text or proposed plans), revising (e.g., modifying text or plans for writing), self-verbalizing (e.g., saying dialogue aloud while writing or personal articulations about what needs to be done), rehearsing (e.g., trying out a scene before writing it), environmental structuring (e.g., finding a quiet place to write), time planning (e.g., estimating and budgeting time for writing), self-consequating (e.g., eating ice cream as a reward for completing a writing task), seeking social assistance (e.g., asking another person to edit the paper), and self-selecting models (e.g., emulating the tactics or style of writing of a more gifted author).
>
> (Graham & Harris, 2000: 4)

The writer constructed here is able to perform a number of highly sophisticated tasks. A particular kind of writer emerges in the list of strategies and examples provided. This writer can produce extended texts, understands writing as a process, writes for a reason, and may write narratives. All of these strategies are important because they allow writers to produce texts that are valued in our world. But if we look at this from a Foucauldian perspective, which provides another 'disciplinary' lens, this notion of self-regulation is limited. It does not take the bodily training into account that is needed to 'make' a writer, to produce a writing subject. Apart from seeing the organization of space (environmental structuring) and time (time planning) which are regulatory techniques, most of the other strategies take place in the writer's head. The intensive work that teachers do with children's bodies to get them to write is demonstrated in this chapter. This training is invisible in Graham and Harris's (2000) article. A problematic binary emerges here, to refer back to Janks (2010); just as literacy is not a set of skills or a social practice, writing is neither the act of transcription nor higher order cognitive processes. It is both. The pedagogical power of the teacher is paramount. Graham and Harris (2000) show that when children are taught self-regulatory strategies and transcription skills, their writing improves. The point is we don't come to writing with these strategies already in place. The ways in which we seek information, keep records, and organize information require a regulated body with a set of embodied practices that have internalized why they are important and effective. Writers need to regulate their space, time, bodies, and minds to write.

The data presented in this chapter also work with this binary because the scribal aspects of writing are emphasized over authoring. Such an approach does not go very far in producing subjects who can use the self-regulatory strategies listed above to become writers who can construct and reconstruct their world. The question is how to balance the two in a system where one silences the other. We know that it is possible to engage young children in writing about their worlds. Dyson's research (1994, 1995, 1997, 2003) shows how children can write about their worlds creatively. Vasquez (2004), Comber and Simpson (2001) and Comber, Thomson, and Wells's (2001) work shows how literacy motivates children to make changes and take social action in their environments. In the projects studied, the children learn about written and spoken language, about making meaningful choices in their composition, about genres, and which genres are appropriate for communicating for a range of purposes, and about power. The possibilities of writing that goes beyond transcription produce subjects who have agency.

There is a plethora of research that shows the deep levels at which children can engage with and produce texts at all levels of schooling, using a variety of approaches. But so much of this is dependent on teachers. In thinking about models of reading and writing instruction it is worth considering how our own training has been coloured by particular models and approaches and the impact this has on what we really understand literacy to be. What literacy is at school for teachers may in fact be very different from the ways in which it is practised at home. For example, Gains (2010) gives an example of a teacher who reads with her child at home and interrogates texts with her but does not do this in her classroom. Janks (2010) discusses a teacher she worked with to produce alphabet books in a productive and successful series of lessons. While the teacher reproduces this project with her children at home, it is not part of her classroom practice. Making alphabet books and reading stories aloud take time. These teachers obviously think it is worth expending their leisure time engaged in these activities.

Locating enactments of literacy practice in time and space opens up ways to compare and interrogate how understandings of literacy can be multiple. But different understandings of literacy can be locked into specific spaces. When examined across spaces they may in fact be contradictory. These examples ask why an understanding of literacy is located in one space and not in another. Where does the disciplinary knowledge and ability to control children of these teachers limit pedagogical possibility, and where does their knowledge as mothers extend beyond this?

Thinking about space and time in relation to our engagement with literacy may be a useful entry point in interrogating points of contact and disjuncture. Questions focusing on the use of space and time are useful in identifying practices and drawing comparisons:

- How much time do teachers spend on reading and writing in their classrooms? Where does this take place? Why?
- How much time is spent individually/with small groups/with the whole class to teach reading? Where does this take place? Why? (What are the implications of this? Can these practices be changed?)
- How much time is spent individually/with small groups/with the whole class to teach writing? Where does this take place? (What are the implications of this? Can these practices be changed?)
- What texts are used in reading lessons? Why? Where are they? Why? Who has access to them? Why? How is access to texts controlled? How long can children work with these texts? Why? What do these texts enable children to do as readers?
- What texts are used for writing lessons? Why? Who has access to them? Why? How is access to texts controlled? How long can children work with these texts? Why? What do these texts enable children to do as writers?
- Do reading and writing lessons stand alone, are they integrated, or both, depending on the lesson? What does this reveal about reading and writing?
- Is time made available for children to write, to talk about their writing, and rewrite? How?
- Are spaces made available for children to write, to talk about their writing, and rewrite? How?
- Does a metaphorical space exist for children to take on the position of author to create imaginative texts? How is this space created? If it does not exist, what is in its place?
- Where do teachers (and their children) read and write in out of school spaces? How much leisure time is spent on reading and writing? How and why is this different or similar to classroom practice?

These questions are not exhaustive but, if part of a discussion, they open up ways for imagining possibilities to reread, rewrite, and rethink practice.

Chapter 7

Assessing bodies

Teachers are required to assess children's work, often in relation to numerous and complex outcomes set by education departments. Tests are supposed to reveal how proficient children have become by demonstrating their skills and knowledge. The methods of assessment teachers use should be aligned to what is taught in a classroom and how it is taught. From the beginning of schooling until its end, time is broken up on a daily, weekly, and yearly basis in which children are expected to master knowledge and skills. They are **ranked** by ability and move on to more complex tasks. Throughout their school career the **examination** is present.

Examination is the key term used in this chapter. It is not used as a synonym for taking tests or end-of-year examinations but as one of the techniques of disciplinary power. Its regulatory nature is revealed when Foucault describes it as a 'normalizing gaze' (1977: 184) that judges, classifies, and punishes. **Examination** allows for a constant exchange of knowledge: disciplinary knowledge transmitted from teacher to students, as well as a teacher's knowledge of students. What counts as knowledge is not neutral, and this impacts on assessment practices. Like models of literacy, assessment is also influenced and shaped by values, beliefs, and language and affects how subjects are constructed (Johnston & Rogers, 2001). For example, the positive descriptor 'fluent reader' may hold different meanings in different contexts. It may describe a child who quickly recognizes sight words on flashcards, where a skills model of reading predominates, or a child who reads aloud books of their own choosing, where wide reading is valued.

In this chapter the operation of **examination** provides additional insight into how the literate subject is constructed. Foucault breaks examination down into three key elements: *visibility, entrance into the field of documentation*, and *becoming a case*. These three elements structure the chapter. Examples of the ways in which children are made visible, documented, and recorded illustrate how these elements operate at Acacia and Southside in constructing a particular version of the schooled and literate subject.

Visibility: testing subjects

While the curriculum emphasizes the need for continuous and varied assessment, the focus is not on assessment techniques per se, but rather on how observation functions as a means to assess literacy. Teachers' observations of children are evidence of a normalizing gaze. Its function is to illuminate subjects, and the level and intensity of the gaze render individuals *visible*. Interestingly, from an American perspective, observation is foregrounded as the primary means through which children's learning should be assessed until they are 5 (Salinger, 2001). This is the primary means through which children are assessed in Dawn and Lisa's classes, as opposed to the multiple varied assessment techniques the curriculum calls for.

There appear to be three levels of observation individuals are subjected to. The first is a continuous general observation, where teachers literally watch the development of children throughout the year. This gaze looks to identify general patterns of development of both the group and individuals. The second is individual observation, where the gaze focuses on an individual. The third level combines the first two, and involves whole class testing. General observation is levelled at the entire class who are expected to internalize test writing rituals; these documented results allow for the scrutiny of individuals. **Individualization** and **totalization** work together here.

Testing in Grade 00 and Grade 0

In Grade 00 and 0 much of the examining takes place on the first two levels. This is partly because the children are not literate enough to write tests. They are continuously assessed on daily tasks with an emphasis on general mastery and school-readiness. The children are seemingly unaware that they are closely observed and judged. In discussing how she monitors the progress of the Grade 00s Dawn underscores the importance of observation:

> Observation when evaluating, only observation.... What I have been doing now is I've got them cutting pictures and colouring and drawing that I give the parents examples of. I attach it to the report ... so you keep back some of the artwork and compare it at the end of the year and see if there is progress. It's purely by observation, they don't write tests and things.
>
> (Interview 27 June 2002)

This kind of observation requires a level of knowledge, experience, and competency that the teacher has to draw on to make judgements. The fact that Dawn keeps back examples is the basis for entering children into the *field of documentation*. The Grade 0 file of work is also evidence of this. Individual progress can be compared over the year and is captured in a 'network of writing' (Foucault, 1977: 189). This disciplinary writing turns children into described, analysable objects that can be measured and compared.

General conversations with Dawn and Lisa reveal a focus on individuals' holistic development. In Grade 00 the emphasis is on how the children have developed rather than whether they met a specified norm. Dawn comments:

> Well we've got a written out report that we expect that they should actually be on that standard but as a matter of fact all children can't be on that standard because they are different ... to see if they develop we can't say I expect that – again they come from nothing or somewhere and they develop, as long as there is development during the year then I am happy.
>
> (Interview 27 June 2002)

The second level of observation is directed at individuals' engagement with tasks. An example would be requiring children to demonstrate left and right. There is no mention that 'testing' is taking place – often the task just seems like fun. For example, to meet one of the criteria in their reports, the Grade 0s were lined up outside their classroom where the squares and circles of a hopscotch game were drawn in chalk. Each child had to negotiate their way through it. The children treated this like a game – clapping and calling out encouragement to each other. The only indication that this was not a game was the presence of Lisa's mark book.

This observation of individuals also has a spatial dimension. The class needs to be distributed away from the testing site and occupied with a task. A **functional site** should exist where the teacher and individual are minimally disturbed. In the Grade 00 class one of the children's tables furthest away from the carpet was used. The rest of the children played on the carpet. This obscured the class's vision and limited distractions. In Grade 0 individual testing usually took place at Lisa's desk.

While testing is supposed to have a quantifiable, calculable element (Rose, 1989), testing in itself can be problematic. This is true of the vocabulary tests that were administered to the Grade 00s. Children were called up individually to a table and required to identify a number of objects. There were several problems with this test that Dawn was struggling with:

> We've got set out vocabulary words that we test them on so that we can have a guideline. Again there are English first language children and English second language. And then in my school there is an – an empty spot, we haven't got two reports for the different languages and now I intend to change that. So I evaluate cups and saucers, plates and dishes with all the children and it is not fair having the English first language and second language, but we're working on it … And I think it is underestimating an English first language child to ask 'What is this?' and it is a knife, so he can have much more. I think the report I have is for second language. I need a report for first language that is more advanced. They laugh at me if I ask them 'What is this?' and it's a cup.
>
> (Interview 27 June 2002)

Dawn is faced with complicated assessment issues. She has a multilingual school population. She also has to deal with parents who want their children to speak English. Despite the Language in Education Policy (DoE, 1997a) promoting mother tongue instruction, these parents have exercised their right to choose the language of instruction for their children.

The desire to have two reports, two sets of assessment criteria, is in itself complicated. Assessing second-language speakers in a way that acknowledges levels of languages proficiency means children are not disadvantaged by tests that operate beyond their level of attained English. The challenge lies in constructing such tests. These are issues that Dawn will have to grapple with.

What was interesting was how Dawn dealt with the testing environment. The cutlery and crockery vocabulary test referred to in the interview could have been administered strictly, but this never happened. Through her daily observations Dawn knew the levels her children had attained. The test became an opportunity for one-on-one learning. The vocabulary test does not reflect levels of intelligence, only language proficiency; some children identified the object in their mother tongue. I recognized *ummese* (Zulu for knife). Dawn first asked the children to identify an object, and if they could not, she named it for them. She then asked them to say it with her, to repeat it after her, and then she made them say it by themselves. She said the word again if they mispronounced it. Then she asked them to identify it again, often in conjunction with another object. To an extent this is a memory exercise and it is impossible to know how many words the children remembered later. But they received individual attention and help from their teacher, who patiently assisted them with the words they did not know.

The Grade 0s also receive teacher support during assessments. But making judgements on individual development is framed within a prescriptive set of norms related to school-readiness which is evidence of a particular type of **normalizing judgement**. Children become objects of knowledge, differentiated from the group. Lisa, commenting on her end of year reports states:

> Now it is more generalising … how do I put it – the child … do they fit the requirement of the class, [it's] not actually on the individual child, so it is more the class standard than the individual child.
>
> (Interview 26 November 2002)

Testing in Grade 1 and Grade 3

This section deals with the third level of observation evident in the class test. For class tests children are examined to assess whether they have attained a particular level and to assess individual abilities. The taking of the test requires a **spatial distribution**; children are required to **partition** themselves off from others to stop copying. The class works as a whole, following the commands of teacher, or the test itself. In order to do this the **control of activity** is necessary as individuals must have mastery of the **temporal elaboration of the act**, **correlating body and gesture** to take the test. If not, they will not complete it in time.

Two transcripts taken from videotape, one from Grade 1 and the other from Grade 3, are used to illustrate how subjects are constructed and how children resist constructions. Transcripts are not used in conjunction with photographs because the focus here is on how the discursive practices of the teacher positions subjects. The Grade 1 test was given at the beginning of March. It was their first 'spelling' test.[1] To address the limited **temporal elaboration of the act**, these children were given a piece of paper with a column of words on the left-hand side: *sat, fat, rat, hat, mat*. They were required to match these with corresponding pictures on the right-hand side of the page.

CATHERINE: You all should know how to read by now. We've done these words before.
Right, this says – Wasim? What does it say?

WASIM: Sat.

CATHERINE: No the top word where the line is [points to it].

WASIM: Name.

CATHERINE: Name. So you go there and write your name. Nice Derisha, tear my papers too. Do what you want because I don't know how your house looks; give me the address I want to come there. I want to see maybe the curtains are torn, all the bedsheets are torn, the dishes are broken. Why are you doing that? It took me time to stick it – in your book? Why are you looking at me like that? Write your name. Did you write your name? Go write your name.
[To me] Her [homework] book is in pieces I gave her a new book yesterday, brand new, and mommy said there is no cover to cover it. That's the latest.
Right, now you write your name on the first line. Here it says 'Spelling Test'. Read.

CLASS: Spelling test.

CATHERINE: Read. Steve what did I say?

STEVE: [inaudible]

CATHERINE: You are saying something else. Tell your grandma I want to see her today. Tell her I want to see her. Right, read the words for me, read. I want you to read the words Karabo because you are busy colouring. Read the words, leave the pencils and read the words for me. Sat
[Catherine reads the words and the class repeats after her. The class are told to read them by themselves. They do this badly. Catherine takes over reading each word with the class repeating it three times.]

CATHERINE: Read the first picture for me – hat

CLASS: Hat
[Mbali makes a mistake]

CATHERINE: The first picture is fat? Mbali what's the first picture?

MBALI: hat

CATHERINE: A hat. What do you do with a hat?

CLASS: You put it on your head

CATHERINE: You use it on your head. What's this? No, this is sat.

[Class reads the pictures, repeating after Catherine]

CATHERINE: Now you are going to find the word hat and here you look for the word hat and you gonna draw the line and you do it by yourself. It is a spelling test. Now start working because these marks are going in your reports, so you'd better start thinking Nosipho before you come to me. Now colour all these pictures, colour them, colour the pictures. I'm watching, I'm watching. Silas do some work. Colour. In. The. Pictures. SHHHH.

A large amount of time is used to explain what the children are supposed to do. They are made to read everything on the page including the fact that this is a 'spelling' test. The rest of the interactions are either disciplinary in nature or scaffold the test. Although the children are supposed to know these words, having done them in class and for homework, Catherine spends a substantial amount of time making the children identify the words and pictures before she tells them what to do. This is similar to the way Dawn approached the vocabulary tests for the Grade 00s, although assistance is across the board and not individual.

The interaction reveals several aspects of the ritual of writing tests: first it is essential to write one's name, otherwise one cannot be an object of knowledge. The second is reading. Children have to read to know what kind of test they are doing and follow instructions. In this case the instructions are oral and the children's actions need to demonstrate that they are listening. Mbali makes a mistake and reads one of the pictures that depicts fat, not the first picture; her public correction serves as a reminder to the rest of the class where they should be. Karabo is colouring in – the supposition is that it is not possible to colour in and listen. The children are required to colour in after they have finished. A compliant subject is one who presents neat work – there is an emphasis on presentation as well as content, but good or bad colouring has no impact on the correctness of the answers.

The reprimands Steve and Derisha receive go further than pointing out their limitations as schooled subjects; rather, a **normalizing judgement** is extended to their homes. Derisha's rough handling of her book is deemed unacceptable. She is reprimanded for not behaving responsibly with her possessions. Catherine argues that this could be a reflection of her home life. Not only is Derisha judged but her mother is too. Her mother allowed the homework book to fall to 'pieces' after less than two months of school. A 'responsible' parent would not let this happen and would ensure that the new book was covered to be protected. Steve's inattention evokes a public reprimand but he is threatened with additional external **regulation** from his grandmother if he continues to be unable to **regulate** himself.

At the end of the transcript the whole class is addressed again. They are charged to work independently and they are told what the implications of writing a test are. The act of taking the test means that the children are placed under **surveillance**, to be recorded in a network of writing which places them in a *field of documentation*. Catherine tells them there are marks involved and their performance will be recorded on their reports. The presence of this statement at the end of the transcript functions like a threat; non-conformity will mark them as different. If the threat of judgement is not strong enough another form of disciplinary power, **surveillance**, comes into play; Catherine is watching.

By the end of the Foundation Phase **surveillance** is more prominent and spelling tests take on a traditional form. The children have internalized the rules of **spatial distribution** and the hierarchical nature of **surveillance** – watching others to see they are not cheating, having books up or covering their work. Unlike the Grade 1s who sat in rows, the Grade 3s sit in groups of six. But for this test Manny sat by himself in the incarceratory space because of his behaviour. On the week of this test Thulisile was on study leave and Leslie, another teacher, filled in for her:

LESLIE: In your literacy books at the back put the date.
[Some children stand up to collect their literacy books from the shelf that runs along the left side of the classroom.]
LESLIE: That doesn't give you the right to talk.
[The class is quiet as they get their books ready and write the date. Four girls get up and stand around Leslie's table.]
LESLIE: I said put something between you.
[This sparks off another group of children who stand up to get files off the shelf to put them up between each other. This results in several conversations and an increase in the noise level.]
LESLIE: I don't remember saying open your mouth for anything. Who hasn't got ears?
[Class quietens then is silent. There is some shuffling to get ready – some of the children are looking at Leslie waiting for the next instruction. Manny scrapes his chair loudly. Megan is looking for a file – she takes her time and finally gets one.]
LESLIE: Right if you haven't got something up between you, you are going to go out – your cases, anything, that book is going to keep on falling over so use your homework book it's harder than that one.
[Manny puts up a book at 90 degrees with half of it facing the carpet and the other the group on his right. Charmaine stands up to organize a 'barricade' for her whole group so that no one can see the work on either side or in front of them.]
LESLIE: [to Manny] You really don't need to put something up – you're on your own.
[He leaves the book up.]
LESLIE: Thabo come back down to earth. Earth calling Thabo. Put something up.
[Shouts] Put something up between you! Thabo put something up in front of you!
[Someone queries the use of files.] Use anybody's file there!
[This results in another spate of children getting up. By this stage most of the children have got something up to stop the person next to them seeing their work but nothing dividing themselves from the person facing them.]
LESLIE: Take anybody's file, you are really not going to eat it you are just going to use it.
[To Manny] Are you really not happy unless you have something yourself?
[Manny has now taken the book down but he has his bag up on the right-hand side of the desk where the closest group to him is. Manny is then reprimanded by the teacher for leaving the class the previous day without being formally dismissed by her.]
That homework book – get a file…
Manny stop rocking on that chair the horse died long ago. Put your chair right and sit properly. [He scrapes his chair loudly.]
That homework book, get a file. [Leslie walks over to one group to check their arrangement.] Take that book away.
[Manny is stamping his legs under the desk making a noise.]
LESLIE: Right I catch you looking at anybody I'll give you 0. Think carefully before you write don't just write to get finished. First word…
SUSAN: Ma'am must we write … [she is ignored]
LESLIE: Anybody, any-body
[There is complete silence as the test starts. Leslie reads each word out and then repeats it. The children write the words. At the end of the test Leslie walks to the back of the class. She stops and looks at one of the boy's tests before going to her desk.]
LESLIE: Rule off. Don't take down your covers and you start your maths test.
[The maths test is on the board.]

What is evident from this transcript is the time children waste to get organized. This impacts on Leslie's gaze – she cannot see everything and spends a long time reprimanding and organizing movements. Her giving of instructions and scaffolding is minimal. All that is needed is the opening command 'In your literacy books at the back put the date' which functions as a reminder the test is about to commence, and implicitly that the classroom space needs reorganization.

What is disconcerting about this episode is the difference between the class getting ready for the test and writing it. The children's bodies looked untrained and at times aimless compared to the docile bodies who wrote the test. Writing the test is a perfect example of how the **control of activity** by individuals underpins the class working together. The class wrote in absolute silence, with a minimum of movement, confined by their partitions, keeping their heads down, only raising them to look at the teacher for the next word; there was no excessive glancing around. Why this shift? This is a typical act of **resistance**; small, unplanned, and spontaneous, a classic example of the 'go-slow'. If one or two individuals had held up the procedure they would have been reprimanded, but a whole group following instructions (albeit slowly) changes the situation. They are doing what they have been told to do. But if the principle of docility-utility is to operate, then time should be maximized. These bodies know they cannot resist the testing process outright so they find a gap created by the movement from one exercise to the next, stretching curriculum time. In this changeover there is a shift, and for a few minutes the power rests in the hands of the class. Leslie takes it back once the test begins.

Prominent in the transcript is the **resistant** subject, Manny, who pushes the boundaries of acceptable behaviour. When the class is told not to open their mouths, Manny's chair scrapes loudly. This draws Leslie's attention and he comes under close scrutiny. Leslie sees his book up to prevent copying even though he sits alone. His response is to take the book down and replace it with his school bag. The fact that Leslie asks him rhetorically 'Are you really not happy unless you have something yourself?' indicates that she has decided to leave Manny to his bag. She then remembers that he left her class without permission and is told not 'to try that stunt again'. When another child distracts her, Manny begins to rock on his chair. He is reprimanded again. He then stamps his feet loudly, which is hidden by the noise the rest of the class is making. Manny is not finished yet. Foucault has said:

> He who is subjected to a field of visibility, and who knows it, assumes responsibility for the constraints of power; he makes them play spontaneously upon himself; he inscribes in himself the power relation in which he simultaneously plays both roles; he becomes the principle of his own subjection.
>
> (1977: 202–203)

Manny disproves this. Manny is aware he is in a field of *visibility* but refuses to assume responsibility for the constraints of power. He may be subjected to an external gaze but it is not internalized. In fact Manny is subjected to two external gazes, Leslie's, and the gaze of my camera. I had spent the entire test period standing behind him filming. Despite this, the videotape shows the moment when Leslie (and her gaze) returned to her desk at the back of the class, and Manny cheats. He sits up straight with his pencil in his left hand, then bends a little into a posture that appears to look like he is going to write, swaps the pencil back into his right hand, which is poised at the bottom of the page where the last spelling words are. But, instead of writing he turns a fraction in his chair and raises his head slightly, looking left to see where Leslie is. His carefully placed school bag provides cover for cheating. He pages back in the book, turning the left-hand page over almost flat. He is on the wrong page. He turns the page back with his right hand, lifting the page on the left up. It is still not the correct page. Then, as he turns another page from the pages he is holding, he looks up at the board at the maths test. He finds the right page, has a quick look, drops the pages, leans forward, looks at the board again, and pretends to write something at the top of the page. After a few seconds he leans back and writes at the bottom of the page. In normal circumstances Manny has covered his bases: the school bag provides some cover, he is aware of his teacher's location and his peers' preoccupation, he embodies the test-taking subject, but this time perhaps there is something to be said for looking over one's shoulder.

Entering the field of documentation

The following section is a comparative analysis of three school reports: the year end Grade 0 report, the first term Grade 1 report, and the year end Grade 3 report.[2] The inclusion of reports shows a shift in the way the literate subject is constructed: the Grade 0 report reveals a preschool subject different from the primary school subject. While the format and content of the Foundation Phase reports are similar, the assessment criteria differ slightly.

Grade 0 reports

The Grade 0 report is an extensive five-page document reflecting the influence of developmental psychology. In documenting the rise of psychology Rose (1989) discusses the importance of the clinic and nursery school as sites where standards and norms were developed through the observation of large numbers of children. Developmental norms operate on a set standard based on the average ability or performance of age-specific children in executing specific tasks. These '[n]orms of posture and locomotion, of vocabulary, comprehension, and conversation, of personal habits, initiative, independence, and play could now be deployed in evaluation and diagnosis' (Rose, 1989: 111).

The Grade 0 report is divided into seven sections; the first five are indicative of these developmental norms: motor development, language skills, recognizing and naming shapes, emotional development, general development; the emergent literate subject is foregrounded in the final two sections: Letterland, and reading Dolch words. The presence of developmental psychology is evident on the report's cover page. It lists the child's and teacher's names, the child's date of birth, weight, and handedness. The date of birth indicates **ranking** since children are expected to have certain abilities at specific ages, in line with developmental norms. An element of physical development is carried in the weight category and also information about lifestyle. Of the 24 children in this class, the average Grade 0 weighs 22 kg. Charting children's weights provides evidence for determining whether children are undernourished, healthy, or obese. Being right-handed is a norm in society. Placing handedness on the front page immediately identifies a potential element of abnormality. Comprising about 10% of the population, left-handers are often marked out as having learning difficulties. In terms of literacy development, left-handers often have difficulty with handwriting. (This of course is not surprising when left-handed children are often taught by right-handed teachers who use right-handed methods to teach writing.)

The underlying tenet of the report is the notion of school-readiness. The assessment criteria in each section provide a composite of the skills needed to be considered school-ready. Mastery is rated by a tick in one of three columns provided: Yes, Sometimes, No. The first section, Motor Development, includes aspects of both gross and fine motor co-ordination. In many ways it covers the norms of posture and locomotion mentioned by Rose (1989). Insufficient control over large muscles hints at potential problems during formal schooling; clumsiness and lack of fluidity of movement can affect written work. Children are assessed as to whether they are clumsy or not, can jump up and down, walk backwards and forwards, hop, stand on one leg, play hopscotch, show rhythm by clapping. Problems with fine motor co-ordination can have serious implications when children enter school and spend much of their time writing, drawing, colouring in, and cutting out. The report assesses their ability to draw simple figures like a house, fasten buttons, draw and colour detailed pictures. Within this section the notion of balance features prominently. Children are required to demonstrate an awareness of laterality and directionality by being able to put their right hand over their left ear, knowing which side of their body is the right or left side and positioning themselves in space by walking with a beanbag on their heads. The Grade 0s are subjected to a range of activities throughout the year that require them to cross the midline. Mastery of this has an impact on writing. Lisa says:

> So I make them do exercises with their different body parts, flex their feet up and down, cross over their arms, touch the right hand to the left hip, that sort of thing, just so they can cross the midline all the time.
>
> (Interview 26 November 2002)

It is interesting that motor development is the first section – overall mastery of the body provides the foundation for mastering tasks like reading or reproducing patterns. Alongside motor development, the other sections reveal the type of literacy training and literacy practices that operate in the classroom. Children in Grade 00 and Grade 0 are not taught to read or write formally; they are supposed to be prepared for this. So, there is a greater emphasis on drawing than writing. Children are required to:

- draw a person, house, and a tree
- copy a circle, square, triangle, rectangle, and cross
- use the correct pencil grip
- colour in smaller and more detailed pictures
- draw more detailed pictures
- write their name.

Mastery of these criteria requires **control of activity**. At Grade 0 attention needs to be paid to the **body–object articulation**, which requires a mastery of the technology of writing. The control of these activities is organized incrementally – an incorrect pencil grip implies that completing detailed drawings and colouring in will be impeded because the technique is wrong and/or there is insufficient fine motor co-ordination.

Reading operates on two levels in the report – reading in preparation for print-based literacy and a more general reading of the environment. Children need to be able to:

- name and recognize the following shapes: circle, square, triangle, oval, heart, diamond, star, cross, rectangle
- tell whether something is missing from a picture
- name and recognize primary and secondary colours
- recognize their own name and at least one of their friend's names in written form
- name and recognize the letters of the alphabet
- read 30 Dolch words.

The criteria are closely linked to the drawing children do. Recognizing shapes is a way of reading the world, and builds a database literally to draw on. It also provides a foundation for letter formation. The reading of the world in this class is limited to decoding, and 'reading the word and the world' (Freire, 1972) does not operate in a Freirean sense. Reading and writing are connected but the only word children are required to read and write is their name. Children learn the letters of the alphabet in preparation for Grade 1. The Grade 0s received additional help by learning Dolch words. But they are not taught to combine them into sentences. The literate subject is also supposed to engage appropriately to the norms of the school world by 'reading' situations correctly. This behaviour requires mastery of both the skills of speaking and listening. Children need to show mastery of the medium of instruction by:

- speaking English fluently
- pronouncing words correctly
- participating in class discussions
- participating in group discussions enthusiastically
- performing confidently in the presence of others
- communicating confidently with adults
- communicating confidently with other children
- not using baby language
- formulating thoughts easily when talking about something
- not digressing from a subject when talking about it
- executing involved instructions
- executing more than one instruction.

Alongside this are expected norms of behaviour:

- concentrating for the duration of a story or language ring
- sitting still during ring time
- not crying easily.

In this class children need to conform to the identity of an English speaker by speaking fluently and not mispronouncing words. The issue of pronunciation is complicated by diversity in the class, a variety of accents, and the teacher's understanding of identity and what her notions of correctness are. Nine of the 24 children are not mother-tongue speakers of English. The rest of the children have distinctive accents. Coloured, Indian, Black, and White varieties of English with the concomitant accents are all heard in the class, although the most common variety of English spoken here is Coloured English. An examination of reports reveals that five children were marked as experiencing difficulty with pronouncing certain words. These five children spoke no English when they arrived at Southside.

The rest of the criteria deal with social interaction. The ideal subject that emerges is one who is confident, communicating with both adults and peers in a clear and logical way. There is to be no baby talk or crying. In fact in her interview Lisa states that the school-ready child

> can stand up to, for themselves, if they've got their own point of view, if they [are] independent, then they're school-ready. Even if they can't do the actual work I believe they are confident, confidence is the main thing, they're confident and they're able to do things by themselves, they'll cope in Grade 1.

(Interview 26 November 2002)

Being a 'loner' is not part of the accepted social norms; school children are socialized to conform to a particular set of social practices. These rules of engaged social interaction begin to fulfil the requirements of curriculum outcomes for which children are required to work and communicate effectively with others (DoE, 2002). The importance of following instructions is emphasized as it appears twice. This is unsurprising since schooling requires the well co-ordinated control of individuals, relying on trained, docile bodies, who are disciplined and regulated. Children have to follow multiple and complex instructions. There is a small shift in giving instructions from Grade 00 to Grade 0. In Grade 00 children are shown what to do alongside oral instructions, but in Grade 0, Lisa comments:

> If you do it for them, they'll know what to do … that is what I am trying to get away from, I don't want to have to do it, I want them to have to follow instructions.
>
> (Interview 26 November 2002)

Children who move into Grade 1 and are able to follow instructions are less likely to face punishment. This likelihood decreases further if they have disciplined their bodies and demonstrate an understanding of behavioural norms – like concentrating during Language Ring. The use of the verb 'concentrate' in the assessment criteria implies a body that is not just well behaved, a body that knows how to sit still because it is focused, but also one that comprehends the activity or story.

The final part of the report is an overall comment written by the teacher. To analyse the general comments from the reports, I listed recurring concepts and then grouped them into categories. Three categories emerged (see Table 7.1). The first related to the ability to do school work. These comments can be **ranked**. Children who performed well received 'his/her work is of a high standard'; those who had not consistently attained the standard but had shown some development, had 'strives to do her best' or 'gives of his best'; weaker children 'coped well' or had 'improved'. Only one student excelled. The second category relates to levels of interaction where the most frequent comment was 'interacts well with her peers', highlighting the communal rather than the individual. This category also reveals elements of behaviour deemed appropriate: 'is willing to assist', 'loving and caring', 'impeccable manners',

Table 7.1 Frequency of teacher comments in Grade 0 reports

Comments	Category	Frequency
Strived to do his/her best/worked to best of ability	Work	9
Work of a high standard	Work	6
Interacts well with peers/has friends	Social interaction	6
Confident	Character	6
Happy/well adjusted	Character	6
Quiet	Character	5
Positive attitude	Character	3
Sense of humour	Character	3
Willing to assist	Social interaction	2
Coped well	Work	2
Has improved	Work	2
Conscientious	Character	2
Loving and caring	Social interaction	1
Battles to concentrate	Work	1
Extremely disruptive	Social interaction	1
More effort required	Work	1
Aggressive behaviour	Social interaction	1
Aggressive manners	Social interaction	1
Excels	Work	1

compared to the inappropriate: 'aggressive behaviour' and 'extremely disruptive'. The third category refers to character traits: 'confident', 'happy/well adjusted', 'quiet', 'positive attitude', 'sense of humour'.

While Lisa's interview reveals that she considers confidence to be of great importance, her use of it in the general comments adds an element of complexity to the type of confidence valued. Of the six times it is used, it is coupled with 'quiet' three times. This may have implications in thinking about gender differences, although the limited number of times it is used does not allow for any generalizations. One girl is described as 'quiet but confident', the 'but' indicates that being quiet is a negative judgement which is balanced by the confidence. In contrast, 'quiet and confident' referring to two boys, implies the quality of confidence that is most appropriate for the boys is a quiet confidence as opposed to a loud or even arrogant confidence. Perhaps an interesting distinction is being made – in a society where women are either quiet or silenced, any sign of confidence is valued, but where men are entitled to speak and thus more likely to be confident, the way the confidence is borne is significant.

Two children are marked as refusing accepted subject positions. Lisa prefaces her comments with a statement of general development before she moves onto their behaviour:

> Jason has coped well in all areas of development. I am however still very concerned about his aggressive behaviour.
>
> Although Busi has improved in all areas of development, she is still not living up to her potential. She battles to concentrate during a language ring and she can become extremely disruptive.

Finally an interesting metaphorical pattern emerged revealing Lisa's feelings about three strong students:

> Stella is an absolute star. She has a wonderful sense of humour and was a pleasure to teach.
>
> Faizel is a shining bright light and deserves all the credit due to him. He excels in all that he does and has been a pleasure to teach.
>
> Damon has a wonderful sense of humour. He brightens my day with his positive attitude. His work is of a high standard and he has been a pleasure to teach.

While Lisa's interview indicates she values confident students, her comments show that a sense of humour, a positive attitude, and all-round excellence give rise to a sense of pleasure. This pleasure is expressed in metaphors of light, through the words 'star', 'light', and 'brightens'. This light is further increased in intensity by the adjectives 'absolute', 'shining bright'. The fact that these children are 'lights' has an affective impact; Damon's attitude effects a change in the way Lisa feels about the day.

Grade 1 and Grade 3 reports

The Grade 1 and 3 reports are less extensive than the Grade 0 report. There are slight differences in layout and ordering of content but this could be explained by alterations made from one year to the next. There is continuity in the fact that Grade 1 and Grade 0 reports contain the date of birth. This is absent from the Grade 3 report. The presence of the date of birth indicates several things: Grade 1 is the first year of school for many children. Entry into formal schooling is also entry into a new *field of documentation*. Populations are managed as children are legally required to start school the year they turn seven. An early start may indicate precocity, and a late start a child with learning difficulties, or 'negligent' parents.

The reports are divided into three sections – the first assesses academic work, which is ranked numerically. The Grade 3, 2002 report ranking criteria are as follows:

1   Outstanding
2   Good
3   Achieved
4   Partially achieved
5   Not yet achieved

This changes in the Grade 1 2003[3] report. The section is now entitled 'Progression Criteria Percentage'. The order has been switched and one criterion eliminated:

1   Not yet achieved (0–34%)
2   Partially achieved (35–39%)
3   Achieved (40–69%)
4   Outstanding/excellent achievement (70% and above)

These decisions are influenced by educational policy rather than school policies. While there have been moves to bring assessment practices in line with OBE thinking, these changes have been uneven. The inclusion of percentages is out of place when the ranking is numerical in the Foundation Phase. What is problematic is the construction of the subject who 'achieves'. There is a qualitative and quantitative difference between the student who gets 40% and the student who gets 69%. This kind of criterion can undermine the authority of the teacher. It does not show real progress, which is what parents look for – how can a Grade 1 child get a '3 Achieved' for the whole year when they could not read at the beginning of the year and can by the end? How does a teacher tell a parent that their child needs help, or needs to work harder when the report states 'Achieved'?

There are ways around this. One of the Grade 1 teachers adds a plus sign, so 3+ indicates a higher level of achievement (thus bringing back the category Good that was eliminated.)

The second section of the report **ranks** values formatively. The ranking is now alphabetical:

A   Shows *excellent* values in a variety of situations
B   Shows *good* values in a variety of situations
C   Is able to show values *competently*
D   Needs more practice to consolidate values
E   Is *not yet competent* in values. Requires intensive assistance.

The supposition here of course is that there is only one set of values. All children come to school with values, and to imply that one is 'not yet competent' is a **normative judgement**. The values that count here are the ones embodied in the curriculum and underpinned by the Constitution (DoE, 2002). But, as discussed earlier, the curriculum represents a rethinking and reformulation of the South African nation and as such the values embodied in it are an ideal and not necessarily a reality. A new truth for the way we **govern** is being put in place. This presents a practical problem as to how these values are interpreted and assessed in relation to a school population. Thus the possibility exists that the values of the school may take greater precedence than the loftier ideals held in the curriculum.

In assessing academic ability the report is divided into the three learning areas: Literacy, Numeracy, and Life Skills. I will only discuss literacy. Literacy is subdivided into three further sections: 'Oral', 'Reading', and 'Writing'. Within the Oral section the subcategory 'vocabulary used', is the only assessment criterion for both sets of reports. This is a rather limited perception of orality given that none of the other skills required for speaking is encouraged. While the child with a good vocabulary is more likely to be eloquent, it does not hold true that they are effective communicators.

Within the Writing section, Grade 1s are assessed on their sentence construction, spelling, and presentation. Spelling and sentence construction remain in Grade 3, although presentation has fallen away. 'Presentation' is a suitably vague term. Coupled with writing and the fact that the children are learning to write, it appears that presentation is a euphemism for neat handwriting. This in turn also implies a controlled spatial organization of letters and words on pages. Despite the fact that handwriting is not officially assessed in the Grade 3 report, children still have handwriting books. The presence of the categories 'spelling' and 'sentence construction', demonstrates that the Grade 3 writer is limited to writing short sentences, rather than extended pieces of writing for different purposes.

As readers, children in the Foundation Phase are required to read with expression, fluency, and comprehension. Grade 3 adds punctuation to the list. The reader in this phase is one who has mastered the art of reading aloud. The reader is not necessarily one who enjoys the task. The inclusion of punctuation is slightly puzzling. An awareness of punctuation for reading is essential. If the other three criteria are successfully negotiated then a tacit understanding of punctuation will be demonstrated. The correct use of punctuation is probably more effective within the realm of writing as a way for children to express themselves effectively.

The last section of the Grade 1 report falls under the heading 'Formative Assessment'. It assesses behaviour, participation, attitude, and homework. Level of achievement is ranked by letters of the alphabet (see above). There seems to be a mismatch between the criteria assessed and the meaning of the symbols. If a child gets a C for homework and C represents 'Is able to show values competently', what values are inherent in homework? Doing homework may foster conscientiousness, the content is value-laden, but homework in itself does not demonstrate values. In the Grade 3 reports, homework, attitude, behaviour, and participation in discussion are assessed across the three learning areas. This places the Grade 3 student under far more intensive **surveillance**. The literate subject does not only have to accede to the norms laid out orally and for reading and writing, but their behaviour, attitudes, participation, and homework are also assessed. The parameters in which the school subject can be constructed become limited. Preschool children are encouraged to develop even if they do not reach the preset norms; the Grade 1s have some space to develop and get used to the school environment. By Grade 3 this comes to an abrupt halt. All their progress is evaluated in terms of the learning areas – the subject outside the learning area does not exist. This is perhaps unsurprising and heralds the construction of the Grade 4 subject who will be locked in a mesh of discipline-specific subjects.

Turning subjects into cases: the Learner Profile

The aptly named *Learner Profile* (GDE, no date) is a prime example of how subjects become a 'case' where they are described, judged, measured, and compared against others. This blue booklet, issued by the Gauteng Education Department (GDE), is a comprehensive record that follows each child through the 10 years of compulsory schooling (Grade 0–Grade 9). This compilation of children into *cases* describes, judges, and measures their academic performance, their medical condition, their participation, their psychological well-being, and their family background and environment. Children can be compared across their schooling and against other children's records, thus classifying various elements of their being. This is also a record of the academic training children undergo; it assumes various norms and proof of interventions the school has taken to correct the 'abnormal' (Foucault, 1977).

The *Learner Profile* is also an example of the functioning of modern power that targets the population (**bio-politics of the population**). It is a confidential and legal document. Its very status as a legal document prescribes a set of behaviours for those working with it. Clearly stated on the inside cover is:

> Learner Profile GDE 461 is a legal document and pages may not be torn out or removed.
>
> Learner Profile GDE 461 must be made available by the principal of the school at which the learner was previously enrolled, ONCE THE TRANSFER CARD HAS ALSO BEEN ISSUED, to the principal of the school to which the learner moves to. It should be POSTED OR PERSONALLY AND OFFICIALLY handed to the receiving school principal and NOT given to the parents/guardian of the learner.

This document is fundamental to the work of disciplinary power that functions to **regulate** individuals and groups via administrative and bureaucratic apparatuses, thus regulating the population in order to govern life. The rationale given by the department reveals the need for uniform practices across the population. Populations cannot be monitored and governed if the record-keeping itself is flawed:

> The GDE has found it necessary to develop a Learner Profile as a standard document for maintaining cumulative records for learners. This new form of recording is based on the findings that inconsistencies presently exist among schools which use a variety of record cards for their learners. In many instances the only record of a learner's progress is the report card. These report cards often do not give detailed information about the progress of learners and thus do not lead to a better understanding of the learner. The high incidence of forged or unofficial report cards also makes the introduction of a uniform Learner Profile an imperative tool to monitor the progress of the learner through his/her school career. The new profile document will record learner's progress in line with the principles of OBE and Curriculum 2005.
>
> (Gauteng Department of Education, 2000)

The *Learner Profile* demonstrates the true power of disciplinary writing as able to situate individual subjects and groups in fields of *visibility*. The scope of knowledge garnered from the *Learner Profile* goes beyond the child whose name appears on the cover. All individuals who come into contact with or who are written into the profile are subjects of a particular kind of **governmentality** that shapes behaviour and circumscribes whole populations. Thus the individual child, and by implication, the entire population of children attending school, are recorded to be read against a set of norms. These norms will affect how the school **governs** its population. At the same time, as part of the school population teachers and the principals are also rendered *visible* by the demands of the education system. Schools have to have prescribed educational programmes in place to provide information required in the *Learner Profile*. Parents are another population group under scrutiny. Other population groups, in this case professionals like doctors, psychologists, social workers, add to rendering subjects as objects of knowledge as they themselves are entered into another *field of documentation*. The *Learner Profile* is an archive in itself, secret and official, containing folders for other documents to be collected that the individual it records is unlikely ever to see.

The inside cover of the *Learner Profile* reflects the detail required to produce such a document. While the bulk of the document produces a profile through writing, a visual profile is required by the inclusion of three photographs tracing the progress of a child at each phase of schooling (Foundation, Intermediate, and Senior Phases). The document is prescriptive in terms of how disciplinary writing is used by instructing which writing implement is to be used to complete various sections. Some sections are to be filled in using a pencil in order to keep information updated, other records require the permanence of a pen (e.g. emotional and social behaviour).

The table of contents reveals the aspects that are combined to produce a profile (see Figure 7.1). The Personal Information section is to be completed in pencil so that it can be continuously updated (p. 1.1). In fact it asks very little about the child and more about the family and its circumstances – home language, siblings, parents' occupations, contact details. The report implies that if emotional and social problems are experienced, parents will be called in; at this meeting outcomes and parental responses will be recorded. If children require some form of support, this is then documented in Section 9 and recorded. Participation in extra curricular activities for each year is followed as well as achievements (pp. 5.1–6.1). The most detailed documentation unsurprisingly charts academic development through school (pp. 10.1–10.12). Year-end school reports are collected as well as a sample of work from every learning area's portfolio annually. By the end of schooling 60 pieces of work are supposed to be compressed into this folder. Progress in each learning area every year is reported on by the appropriate teacher, and finally an overall record of whether the child passed or repeated a year and its date is filled in. Additional documentation is required if a child repeats a year. In this case teachers have to fill out the GDE 450 C form explaining why a child should be kept back (p. 9.9). Teachers no longer have the power to make this decision. The Department decides who passes and

1. Personal information
2. Physical condition/medical history
   Reports - doctor etc.
   Record of documents inserted
3. Schools attended
4. Absenteeism
5. Participation in extra-curricular activities
6. Achievements
7. Emotional and social behaviour
8. Parental involvement to support the learner
9. Report on support provided
   Evidence of areas of support
   Record of documents inserted
   Selected examples of the learner's work from the portfolios of each learning programme
   Record of documents inserted
   Summative record sheet of specific outcomes
   Record of documents inserted
   Motivation to retain a learner in the same grade in the following year GDE 450 C
   Record of documents inserted
   A learner who will receive additional support in the following grade GDE 450 B
   Record of documents inserted
10. Progress of learner - foundation phase
    Progress of learner - intermediate phase
    Progress of learner - senior phase
11. Overall progression report per grade - foundation phase
    Overall progression report per grade - intermediate phase
    Overall progression report per grade - senior phase
12. Transfer form for learner

Figure 7.1 Table of contents from the Gauteng Department of Education *Learner Profile*.

fails. It appears that the time-consuming administrative procedures and undermining of teachers' professional opinions of children's abilities are a way of ameliorating a failure rate that the Education Department perceives as too high.

A final assessment

What this chapter has tried to demonstrate is two things. In returning to Foucault's notion of **examination** as a technique of disciplinary power to frame the chapter, it provides evidence of how classroom assessment practices work to produce literate subjects. But, at the same time, I return to a point made in the introductory chapter about the importance of social context. The ways in which children are assessed, the kinds of assessments they are subjected to, the assessment criteria teachers, schools, and policy-makers use that are reflected in documentation at the expense of other criteria; and the pedagogical and regulatory practices that align or are misaligned with assessment reveal often competing or contradictory, knowledge, belief, and value systems that go far beyond the classroom. So, in thinking about **examination**, the chapter recalls other aspects of discipline like space and time, and **regulation** like **government** and **governmentality** that work to provide a more nuanced picture of the forces at play in constructing subjects.

In describing individual literacy events for testing and assessment, a particular pattern emerges around the levels of population management. The small practices children are relentlessly subjected to at school reveal the management of the subject on a small scale. This micromanagement is influenced by the **governmentality** of Departments like Education and Health, and the state itself, which oversee the larger management of populations. The level of **surveillance** children are placed under is not only intense, it is also wide-ranging, constructing them as a population group upon which particular gazes are levelled.

The construction of the literate subject is influenced by notions of the schooled subject which in turn is influenced by discourses from powerful disciplines like developmental psychology, as well as political discourses about the nation state. In examining the three levels of **examination** a picture emerges of what the (national, schooled) literate subject looks like. In rendering subjects *visible*, three levels of observation were identified as a means through which subjects are constantly seen: general observation, individual observation, and whole class testing. In the preschool it is the children's limited literacy that subjects them to general and individual observation. The ideal subject in Grade 00 is one who shows development over time. This narrows in Grade 0 and development is read in relation to norms around school-readiness. This shifts again as the Foundation Phase subject is required to show development in relation to learning areas in preparation for the new academic disciplines s/he will be subjected to in Grade 4.

The nature of **surveillance** also shifts. Assessment tasks are no longer 'fun' with supportive teachers extending individuals' abilities, they become serious *tests*. Literacy is fundamental in making subjects complicit in their own subjectification. Children identify themselves through writing their names, they read and submit to test instructions and questions and produce work that is marked not only for correctness but also for presentation. In doing so they are described, judged, measured, compared, corrected, classified, and normalized (Foucault, 1977; Rose, 1989).

Thus subjects become objects of knowledge as they are *entered into a field of documentation*. The literate subject in Grade 0 school reports requires mastery – specifically of the body. This mastery requires a **control of activity** particularly literacy implements. This literate subject is being prepared for scribehood. As a reader, the literate subject is a decoder, able to recognize patterns, letters, words. Dominant, prescriptivist language attitudes shape the schooled subject who should be a communicatively competent, fluent English speaker, skilled at social interactions, and emotionally mature. An ability to work hard, concentrate, and follow instructions reveals aspects of an ideal docile subject.

On entrance into formal schooling, literate subjects are assessed in relation to three aspects: orality, reading, and writing. As a writer, aspects of scribing persist with the emphasis on correct spelling. Although presentation (which implies mastery) is absent in Grade 3 with the assumption that the subject can write, this is in fact false. As with the Grade 00 children, Grade 3s need to demonstrate mastery before they can move on to the next level of writing implement – the pen. This is judged via their presentation of work. The reading subject is one who reads aloud, which is consistent with how reading is constructed in classroom practice. The aspects assessed do not require the subject to be engaged, find the activity pleasurable, or be critical. The reader remains a decoder.

These subjects also come under a wider level of **surveillance** as they become *cases* to be followed throughout compulsory schooling. Their health, intelligence, emotional stability, physical abilities, background, and family life all come under scrutiny. The teachers who manage the children are managed themselves. As such, all population groups come under the enormous power of disciplinary writing.

These practices raise a number of broader questions. Being caught in a regulatory web is a consequence of modern power. But how do the regulatory practices in the microcosm of the classroom reflect those in the national (and international) macrocosm? Are they aligned? If they are aligned, do the knowledge and beliefs, models of literacy, and visions of a modern citizenry reflect an **authoritarian governmentality** or **government** in which the best interests of the population are fostered? What is perpetuated in classrooms? Will mindlessly docile subjects or regulated, disciplined, critical subjects be produced? In entering children (and ourselves) into *fields of documentation* and making them *cases*, what is recoded and what is silenced? What is visible and invisible? What are the benefits and losses of visibility and invisibility for children reported in this regulatory web?

Chapter 8

Implications for literacy education

This chapter seeks to reflect on the implications this study may have in opening up spaces for us to think about classroom practice, research, and theoretical orientations to literacy education and teacher training. Many of the practices in classrooms are naturalized and thus invisible. Using the findings that emanate from the classrooms described here, this chapter considers the ways in which the invisible may be made visible and what we can learn from this.

The overall aim of this book has been to investigate what constitutes schooled and literate subjects. What kind of schooled and literate subject is produced at the end of the first phase of schooling in the South African education system? As I left the children at the end of Grade 3, these literate subjects could read, although they were no longer read to at school. Reading aloud fluently was privileged over silent reading. They had access to far more books than many children in the country. They did not have to share their readers with others. Children took readers home and replaced them with new books when they were finished. This is not the reality for many children in South Africa. They could write and were mastering a cursive script. They understood that writing must be neat. They had growing vocabularies which were underpinned by a phonics approach and the skills to spell words. But they had little space and time to read and write for pleasure in the classroom, to develop and extend their writing and reading, to write in ways that reflected their out-of-school selves and knowledge(s). Space was not created for them to imagine and create new selves and new worlds, or refigure old ones. Neither were classroom spaces opened up so that the pleasure of reading, and writing, might become fully embodied; rather they became increasingly limited. These embodiments in turn were not observable in classroom spaces. This does not mean that within these observed classrooms possibilities did not exist to produce different subjects. The space created by the Reading Corner enables the practice of lying on the floor as the Grade 00s did. It reflects the potential for developing a reading **habitus** of children who find reading pleasurable.

The chapters in this book have shown the way literacy is taught and how this works to produce a subject where meaning-making potential is not fully exploited. That said, in terms of thinking about schooled subjects within the South African context, these are functioning schools where teaching and learning happen. Time and space are organized as part of daily routines and children are, for the most part, responsive to this. Teachers and children in these schools have internalized enough rules to self-regulate so that teaching and learning take place daily. Teachers come to school and teach lessons that have been prepared. Children are given and expected to do class work and homework. What is also evident is the intensive labour teachers expend to train, manage, and control young children.

Foucault, knowledge, and practice

At the heart of this book is an interest in the human subject. In order to try and understand the forces that work on individuals to construct particular types of subjects in educational settings, this research uses a theoretical frame to examine knowledge and practice. That frame is Foucauldian theory. The central concepts I have worked with are discipline, power, the subject, time, space, regulation, and knowledge. In this work, knowledge is derived from history, policy, curriculum documents, theories of literacy, and individuals themselves. The second aspect is practice. Working with one lens to examine knowledge and enactments of practice allows theory, knowledge, and practice to illuminate each other in ways that are not possible if each is examined individually. This combination of theory, knowledge, and practice has enabled several insights.

For example, Foucault's emphasis on the body has been extremely useful. When he makes the connection that power is targeted at the body, and that power carries a set of practices that are internalized, it provides a way of identifying naturalized practices. It is practically impossible to analyse the **habitus** we have as adults and to unpack its palimpsestic layers written into our bodies over years. While we may be able to identify key moments and events that have produced who we are, there are other parts of ourselves to which we cannot attribute an origin. They are just there. So, to go back to the beginning, to examine how young bodies starting their institutional lives are trained and become schooled, is useful. Being in schools as a researcher allows one to see the institutional forces at work and the shaping practices that become internalized and then invisible.

Foucault provides a detailed set of tools with which to see how this process happens. His work makes training visible. In focusing on how bodies are trained to become literate, binaries are challenged. Literacy is not a set of skills or social practices. Literacy is not just about bodily mastery or cognitive processes. It is both. The practical examples presented in the data show the need for thinking about both. The examples allow us to do this thinking when we analyse what is present and absent in the training children undergo. Travis, the writing subject discussed in Chapter 6, needed the bodily training of the earlier grades to manipulate implements to draw and write. Mastery of various cognitive processes allows him to put the correct combinations of letters and words together to make them meaningful. This needed to become habitual to achieve a level of fluency. Without these skills and cognitive processes he cannot use literacy to articulate who he is as an individual. But the skills model that predominates in his school does not open enough space for him to express this individuality in writing.

In providing a number of techniques of disciplinary power Foucault gives us tools for examining practice. But his work goes beyond just identification. His theory of power necessitates that we do not simply identify techniques to show the workings of power on bodies, and the subsequent internalization and self-regulation of practices and beliefs. The theory of power, because it includes a space for discourses which hold particular views of the world, allows us to see how tools are used in contexts and the frequency with which they are used. These are not the same in each classroom, let alone all contexts. The fact that they are not the same means there will be different outcomes in relation to the subjects produced. This is apparent with regard to the issue of self-regulation over time. What emerges in analysing the data is that there is not a clear developmental trajectory. Children do not become increasingly self-regulated in increments. The process is far messier because of the complexity of real human interactions. There is no need to account for why there are exceptions to the developmental stages of regulation. Rather, there are degrees of regulation and resistance as children remain within the institution of the school. The ways in which teachers order space and time have an impact on levels of regulation. The consistency with which children are punished, rewarded, or reprimanded affects regulation. Teachers' dissemination of disciplinary knowledge engages or disengages children, which in turn affects their levels of self-regulation. Children's growing understandings of how the institution of the school functions, and who they are becoming as subjects within it, affect how far they will push back. And, competing discourses and ways of being at home may also be in conflict with newer ways of being at school. Although these children are young, the ways of being they have already learnt in the home are durable. The ways in which home and school practices align affect who subjects are, how they regulate themselves, and who they become.

In using the tools provided by Foucault to examine practice, the importance of space and time come to the fore as powerful analytical concepts. The operation of time and space in producing subjects are naturalized for teachers and thus remain unquestioned and invisible. Working with space and time provides an entry point to examine the ways in which pedagogical practices are manifested. In doing so, the operation of time and space are made familiar again and open to interrogation. Such an analysis may include the ways in which space is organized, how children are distributed in time and space, how time is ordered, how time is controlled, the movement of children and resources in space, the movement of children and resources across time, as well as the interrelatedness of time and space in classroom operations.

The practices presented in Southside and Acacia's classrooms highlight the importance of space and time in regulating and managing children. The bodily training required to become literate happens in particular configurations of space and time. What emerge are pictures of children struggling in the spatial confines of a desk to master writing so that the pencil becomes a well-managed bodily prosthesis. To control the movements of a pencil on the space of a page requires time: time scheduled into a timetable, regular enough for a routine to develop so internalization happens; time to think about what to do next to work out which way the letter 's' goes; time to be a writer. Space and time function at the level of the real and the symbolic. Literacy training happens in real time and space. Within the space and time of literacy training, boys can explore themselves in the symbolic realm and Travis can be a musician-soccer player. They can read books that require a suspension of disbelief. Girls can be storytellers and story-makers in Reading Corners. The external constructions of time and space as well as their symbolic manifestations are both internalized in the process of making subjects.

Teachers, knowledge, and practice

In linking content knowledge with the body in time and space, this book provides educators with a different way of thinking about pedagogy and its effects. The presentation of real classroom literacy practices invites comparison and reflection.

Using the tools Foucault provides for thinking about training enables one to focus attention on the presences and absences in everyday classroom management and regulation. Because many of these techniques are invisible, and experienced teachers use them intuitively, we do not always see them. Making them explicit is a way of directing attention to how they work and the ensuing consequences. This is far more helpful than thinking about the consequences of practice in a broad, undefined sense. When practices and techniques are often invisible, paying attention to the body gives us a focal point at which to direct our gaze. What the bodies do, where they go, and how they react provide a way of working backwards. So, in focusing on the body and its actions, that is, on embodied actions, we can interrogate practice. We can identify which disciplinary technique or techniques were engaged and evaluate the efficacy of them. And we can also work in the other direction – applying a particular disciplinary technique can be analysed in relation to children's responses and actions.

But, the techniques are not meant to be used in a list-like, reductionist way. This provides no insight into how disciplinary knowledge affects the utilization of techniques. For example, organizing children together in space and teaching them through morning ring times and group work, and using communal resources in the preschool, presuppose that learning happens in a particular way. Sitting at desks in silent rows with individually owned resources presents another understanding of learning. Disciplinary techniques are filtered through our understandings of disciplinary knowledge and vice versa.

The relationship between knowledge and practice and the outcome of producing particular subjects require us to think carefully about the way in which knowledge itself is constructed. It is not enough to know what educational policies and curricula require of teachers. Policies construct subjects. In taking up these constructions and embedding them in daily practice, teachers produce subjects. There needs to be an explicit awareness of the ways in which policy constructs subjects and the implications on schools and societies if such subjects are in fact produced. While these visions of the 'ideal subjects' require critical examination, critical examination is not necessarily a critique. Requiring citizens to be productive and responsible in South Africa so they can contribute to the functioning of society is positive. But, we do need to be critical of how we take up these constructions and enact them in practice.

This requires an awareness of competing discourses. There are different conceptualizations of literacy and these conceptualizations necessitate different pedagogical approaches. Teachers should be able to identify dominant discourses and see how competing discourses manifest themselves in their schools. Some discourses could be in tension with each other and dilute good practice. For example, at the height of the conflict between the genre and process approaches to teaching writing, choosing one over the other could have diluted the benefits for students. Since it is now acknowledged that both approaches offer good learning opportunities, both can productively be brought together to teach writing. In the same way Wolf (2007) comments that proponents of Whole Language underestimate the benefit of phonics instruction and Whole Language has benefits for young readers beyond pure phonics instruction.[1]

Practice should be carefully interrogated in relation to our own naturalized assumptions. We need to consider what we understand literacy to be, what we believe it is for, what we use it for, and what the value of being literate is in our communities and the world. Then we need to consider how our understandings of literacy play themselves out in practice. This requires some careful thinking. What are our understandings of literacy and their concomitant practices in the outside world that do not enter the classroom? When are we like the teachers in Gains (2010) and Janks' (2010) examples, who work with their own children at home to talk about and design texts, but do not do this in their classrooms? When and why are our enactments of practice located firmly in the confines of the school and for what purpose? When do our understandings of literacy cross the boundaries of the school so that they can be productively used by children in the world?

This brings me to the relationship between space, time, and pedagogy. This work has drawn attention to how space and time are fundamental in the planning and teaching of literacy lessons. It provides a different way of interrogating practice. One of my colleagues argues that if we cannot see what is present, because it has become naturalized and invisible, then we have little insight into why and how something works (or does not work). If we can only see what is present we are unable to see what is possible.[2] What is present in teaching is not just the content disseminated or the methods used to disseminate content. Space and time are also present. The use of space and time affect how effective teaching is. The institutional organization of space and time also enable or reduce our ability to teach effectively. A seven-day timetable saves time for teachers in higher grades but it can negatively affect young children's learning. Using time and space as lenses to examine practice provides a reimagining of the possible. An example of this comes from a short written piece by a master's student in my department's postgraduate programme. He made a comment about practice when reflecting on his teaching in high school in a township. He argued that overcrowded classes and limited resources force teachers to use the chalk and talk method. It was not possible to provide every student with their own worksheet. Overcrowded classrooms are not ideal for teaching, and neither is a paucity of resources. While these are certainly constraints they do not necessitate the permanent use of a teacher-centred method. Space and time were invisible to this student when thinking about his practice.

But, in bringing space, time, and practice together, the possibility for reimagining teaching emerges. If he reorganizes his teaching space and the distribution of his students within this space, then small groups of students could work with the limited number of worksheets available. The worksheets could be reused because students could write answers in their exercise books. Small groups of students might be sent outside the classroom to escape its overcrowded confines. But they could still be close enough to be seen by the teacher. He might have to divide time so that half the class worked with him in the classroom while the others worked with the limited resources and then the groups swapped. Rethinking the use of space and time provides a way of opening up pedagogical possibilities.

Foucault, academic knowledge, and research

Using Foucauldian theory to structure this research allows a theoretical gaze to be placed on the data presented. It also provides a means through which disciplinary knowledge and its instantiations can be interrogated along with an examination of enactments of practice. This is a useful way of structuring research so that theory, knowledge, and practice can talk back to each other.

This research provides an additional piece of evidence for the argument that Foucault's work is not so abstract that it cannot be used as a structuring principle for research. And it can be easily applied to generate insightful readings within educational contexts. This happens primarily in two ways in this book. The first is that in using the tools that Foucault gives us to work with we have greater insight into what constitutes disciplinary knowledge in the field of literacy education. The ways in which literacy is enacted in the classroom allow us to see the manifestations of a particular kind of disciplinary knowledge in the South African context. Foucault's work is as powerful in allowing us to unpack the processes of learning that 4-year-old children undergo as it is in examining the grand narrative of apartheid education. There is enough coherence in his work, despite some criticism to the opposite effect (Fraser, 1981; Philp, 1983), that the larger political, social, economic, and state moves can be seen to shape small daily practices in a classroom of 4-year-old children. The consequences of governing the entire population in a country, of governing population groups like schoolchildren, the ways in which we are named, distributed, organized, the rights we are given and the responsibilities we are expected to take on, play themselves out in small classrooms where teachers teach children to be, know, value, and act in particular ways.

When the spatial and the temporal are beginning to emerge as interests in educational research (Leander & Sheehy, 2004), Foucault's conceptualization of space and time is a powerful means through which to analyse the workings of educational institutions. Applying space and time from a Foucauldian perspective in this book is an important element in considering what constitutes subjects. Space and time provide a way of extrapolating the implications of the workings of educational institutions because of Foucault's insistence that power produces subjects.

A Foucauldian framework also provides a means of analysis that the New Literacy Studies does not provide. I am not arguing that the two are incompatible though. A social practices approach has informed this research and enabled a number of insights. It is useful in identifying manifestations of an autonomous approach to literacy, the micro-ethnographic perspective allows thick descriptions of practice to show what children 'do' with literacy. But it is a theory of literacy with its own particular gaze that is used to analyse literacy. If Southside Primary's approach to literacy was located in a social practices paradigm then using the same analytical lens is potentially more like looking into a mirror than using a tool to provide new insights. Understanding literacy as it is practised in communities is one thing for such an approach, using it as a tool to evaluate itself is limiting. Foucauldian theory is unencumbered by views about what literacy is or should be, and provides a different way of examining literacy practices. The concepts of space and time deepen analyses about what literacy means to people and how literacy is practised in different spaces and times. As such, it opens space for analysing how particular enactments of literacy may become embodied in particular spaces but not in others and why this may happen. Space and time offer more concrete ways of transforming pedagogical practice because they help to point out practices that are naturalized. This is in contrast to the lack of direct pedagogical explication in the social practices approach.

In addition to this, from a multimodal perspective, space and time are modes which operate in classrooms. Work from this perspective is more likely to include space as a mode than time. The role of space is often underplayed as other modes are foregrounded and the interrelationship between time and space has not received the attention it deserves. In considering space and time as having a disciplinary function and not just as modes in which meaning-making can take place, the role of power is present. The operation of modes in the classroom is not neutral. They are implicated in a mesh of power relationships. Space and time work to manage, regulate, and produce particular kinds of subjects because they are embedded in knowledge/power constructions.

This discussion has dealt predominantly with literate subjectivities. But, the literate subject is only one part of people's subjectivities. This raises the question of how the utilization of time and space work to produce other kinds of subjects. How are these subjects constituted in educational spaces across time? That is, what happens when these children reach high school? What is the relationship between architecture and the construction of subjects? What impact does being schooled in a building in the inner city have, compared to a large suburban school? How are children constituted outside the classroom (for example on the sports field)? How are they constituted outside the school, in home and community spaces, and later at work in a profession as, say, a social worker, teacher, or lawyer?

As is evident from these questions, a Foucauldian lens allows us to work across space and time, tracing continuities and change. In enabling this movement the ways in which subjects can be constructed do not become fixed. Rather, as we grow and develop and move into new spaces and learning experiences, who we are will shift and change. We will take on elements embedded in bodies of knowledge and practice that will become part of our **habitus**, and exposure to other bodies of knowledge which we choose not to invest in will leave us relatively unchanged.

Foucault's work also asks us to consider what constitutes different areas of disciplinary knowledge. This book focuses on early literacy by working through enactments of practice. But literacy in the political South is not the same as in the political North. How is literacy as a body of knowledge different across countries and continents? Alongside this a comparison is needed of the ways in which bodies of knowledge construct subjects. How does a body of knowledge construct a subject with an historical gaze as opposed to a literary, mathematical, or scientific gaze? Further investigation is needed into the specific techniques that are central to training subjects in particular disciplinary areas.

Knowledge, practice, and teacher training

Teacher trainers lie at the intersection between academic knowledge and knowledge produced by research, and the ways this informs teaching practice. Decisions made by teacher trainers about the training of new teachers and the retraining of in-service teachers matter a great deal. In this intersection it is important not only that student teachers are enabled to reflect upon their understandings of literacy but that we, as teacher trainers, reflect upon our own.

Standing, as we do, between knowledge and practice, our understandings of the former impact on the latter. This requires serious reflection on our position as trainers. We need to think about the ways in which we are complicit in entrenching particular discourses and the knowledge, values, and beliefs embedded within them. We need to ask questions about what we actually do in our teaching spaces. Although we may believe we locate ourselves within a particular perspective it can be undercut by the way in which we manage learning. Requiring our students to learn, listen, and respond in particular ways does not always align with what we actually expect them to do. In the same way that teachers cannot expect children to analyse narrative structures if they only read instructions on worksheets, we cannot expect to see child-centred discovery-oriented lessons if our own classes are teacher-centred.

Sometimes the discourses we claim merely cover us like the clothes we wear. The real person and their body of beliefs lie underneath. These stronger and more deeply entrenched knowledge and belief systems have not been transformed by what we think we do. They can be read through our bodies. In South Africa many teachers and teacher trainers claim to be doing OBE but in fact practices remain fundamentally unchanged.

This brings to mind our student teachers who have been introduced to a variety of methodological practices to encourage classroom interaction. But when they enter the classroom they teach the way they have been taught. The new ways of 'doing' have not replaced the old ways of being and knowing. This is unsurprising. For many students, their school experience is characterized by teacher-centred lessons. A child-centred lesson is an abstract concept. There is not enough deep knowledge of the approaches and methods that can be applied in a classroom for them to draw on. The beliefs and knowledge about practice student teachers are introduced to have not been internalized or worked with exhaustively. The principle of *exhaustive use* does not include the word exhaustive for nothing. This is made more challenging when government policy changes and requires teachers to take on new approaches. After considering the performance of Grade 12s in their final examination and the poor literacy and numeracy results from a number of national and international assessments, OBE will be overhauled by the government. There are signs that there will be a greater focus on teaching from textbooks and Foundation Phase teachers teaching from scripted lessons. Young teachers who have just begun their teaching careers will be caught between two systems. Experienced teachers are unlikely to substantially alter their practice. In periods of educational and curricular change certain practices will remain entrenched and work against what the government hopes to achieve.

Thinking about our own embodied practices in relation to literacy and the knowledge we are required to disseminate gives insight into student struggles. This relationship may also partly explain why the teachers who make alphabet books (Janks, 2010) and talk about texts at home with their children (Gains, 2010) do not do this in their classrooms. These are new practices which are in the process of being internalized – by the teachers and their children. These practices were not part of the formation of their literate **habitus** when they were children. That they are taken up speaks to a recognition of the potential and value of talking about and designing texts. That they are located in the home says something about the home as the space in which learning first occurs.

As educators we require greater insight into the ways in which literacy practices are affected by teachers' understanding of literacy; and how the literacy training our students undergo during their schooling entrenches a view of literacy. We need to make present for our students these naturalized assumptions about literacy. This requires that students reflect on their own experiences and compare them with examples of practice from real classrooms. In dealing with what literacy education is, students need access to bodies of knowledge as well as manifestations of practice. Classroom practices should be read in relation to the particular discourse(s) on literacy that circulate. That requires asking what literacy can be in the range of discourses that circulate in the field. It means being able to identify which discourses are enacted in practice. The implications for subject constructions can also be considered.

One of the challenges facing teacher education in South Africa is that many teachers do not have sufficient knowledge about the discipline in which they teach. The same is true of many students who enter university to train as teachers. If students do not understand what it is to be located in a discipline, what counts as knowledge in the discipline, what knowledge is valued, how it is used, what it is used for, and what makes it different from other disciplines, then they cannot teach effectively.

Providing access to bodies of knowledge alongside techniques utilized for training children is important. An examination of disciplinary power can be a productive way of critically examining practice. Knowing which techniques and procedures to draw on and which ones work more effectively in schools, across schooling, and within disciplines is powerful. Getting students to experiment and try these techniques out in localized contexts is more so. South African student teachers have varied experiences of disciplinary power. Some have been educated in highly functioning schools and others in schools where discipline has broken down. Bringing these two sets of experiences together is a useful way of unpacking what is present in functioning schools and what is absent in dysfunctional schools as well as what lies between. It is important that disciplinary practices are not reduced to a list but are integral to disciplinary knowledge. This helps us evaluate how the absence of particular techniques, or the overuse of techniques, impacts on literacy teaching and student knowledge. If we have a principled way of examining practice we go beyond 'tips for teachers' that don't take disciplinary knowledge or power seriously.

Foregrounding the use of time and space as integral to classroom regulation and management is a way of moving beyond lists of 'teacher tips'. As concepts, space and time bring ways to explore and examine lesson planning, organization, and the management of children and resources. This knowledge can be made explicit. Although time and space are abstract concepts, they can be worked with practically. Micro-teaching with peers or enactments of exercises or problems help to build experience when student teachers move into the classroom.

Brave new world

One aspect that this book has not raised in relation to schooling and literacy education is the impact digital technologies have on the construction of schooled and literate subjects. As is evident from the data presented here, working with new technologies is not part of teachers' pedagogical practice. In many schools basic computer literacy is hampered by a lack of access to electricity, safe spaces to house technology, and the financial and human resources to use them effectively. In other parts of the world the presence of computers (and mobile phones) and access to sophisticated software packages and the internet are naturalized in- and out-of-school practices for teachers and children.

For schools where technology is a norm and the virtual interactive worlds produce multiple selves, the ability of the spatial and temporal as analytic frames to work at the level of the real and the symbolic offers exciting opportunities to understand how the literate subjectivities of teachers and children are being embodied.

These new technologies have transformed the way in which we operate in space and time. These changes require investigation. Time and distance are truncated as communication becomes instant. The sharing of information instantaneously can take place simultaneously in multiple modes as we read, talk, and see each other. We can do this one-on-one or with a new community of linked individuals. Time and technology allow for multiple acts of communication. We can send a text message to a friend at the same time we talk to another on Skype. Certain acts that could only take place in particular physical spaces have now moved beyond them: access to a wireless connection means we can work at home, in airports, on trains, planes, and automobiles, in hotels, or in front of the television. As more people provide information about their lives on-line, the boundaries between private and public spaces begin to blur. Who we are as subjects becomes more complex as our access to knowledge increases, and the practices of being on-line become more sophisticated.

The move away from physical spaces into virtual spaces presents new challenges to thinking about education and literacy. Semantic constructions like virtual reality, augmented reality, cyberspace, and hypertext reflect an openness and new ways of being in space and time. Hypertext challenges spatial knowledge and embodied practices gained from learning to read and write print-based texts. Cyberspace presents a move into uncharted territory for many teachers. Augmented reality overlays information we have access to in real spaces and virtual realities enable identity work in real and symbolic spaces simultaneously. The openness of platforms we have access to requires that we ask new questions about **regulation** and **surveillance**. They also ask for a re-examination and application of the concept of modern power. Which aspects of modern power that Foucault identified as emerging in the seventeenth and eighteenth centuries remain, which have morphed into something else, which are defunct, and what needs to come into being so that we can explain the ways in which subjects are (re)producing themselves? It is time for Foucault's toolbox to move into cyberspace.

Notes

2 Schooling and space

1 The Witwatersrand refers in this case to the greater Johannesburg metropolitan area that runs 280 km along the length of the gold reef.
2 This sum (in South African rand) is roughly equivalent to US$480 or £305.
3 Racial classification used by the apartheid government to denote people of mixed race.
4 During the period of observation this space was not opened up.

3 Space and time

1 Apartheid education was influenced heavily by what was referred to as Christian National Education. While religious diversity is supposed to be foregrounded in state schools thus lessening the dominance of Christianity, the power of Christianity which is practised by many people remains in many schools.
2 The children are also required to pray before they eat their lunch each day.
3 The perceptual playground is a special playground built for the Foundation Phase children, with jungle gyms and climbing equipment to help build co-ordination.
4 Dolch words, named after the originator, are the 220 most common words used in English. They are often pronouns, adjectives, adverbs, prepositions, conjunctions, and verbs that do not follow decoding rules and need to be learnt as sight words.
5 This piece of information was proffered by an experienced Grade 1 teacher at another primary school who revealed that the frequency of writing and numeracy tasks earlier in the day was not confined to Southside Primary but also operated at her school.
6 When children enter Grade 4 the number of learning areas increases to languages, human and social sciences, natural sciences, numeracy, arts and culture, life orientation, economic and management sciences.

4 Managing and regulating bodies

1 The other issues were: the Pass Laws, the Group Areas Act, the Native Resettlement Act, the Suppression of Communism Act, and anti-trade union measures (Christie, 1999: 229).
2 In order to analyse such events, a transcript of the verbal interaction was made from the videotape. Then the videotaped incident was broken down into a frame-by-frame sequence. Where the frames did not match up to events or gestures relevant to the transcript, the intermediate frames were examined. Relevant frames were then selected to represent patterns of bodily interactions, instances of compliance or resistance, that demonstrate the disciplinary techniques integral to such events in the form of photo stories.
3 Unfortunately it did not seem that the English children learnt African languages in this context as most of the switching was done into English by the children speaking African languages to accommodate them.
4 *Skyf* is Afrikaans for move.
5 The irony is that there is no monolithic 'White' South African English accent.

5 Reading bodies

1 This, of course, is not to say that old models are necessarily 'bad' and new ones 'good'. Both are can be used highly successfully but they have their flaws.

2 Barton (1994: 141) makes the distinction between 'books for children, books to read to children and books for children to learn to read'.

6 Writing bodies

1 The inability to cross the midline is often reflected in children's handwriting where they begin writing with a level of control but on reaching the mid-point of the page (or sometimes the right-hand page) the writing deteriorates. Physical exercises where children use the left hand to pick something up on the right side of the body, or touch the left ear with the right hand help to improve co-ordination. See Lisa's comments on crossing the midline in relation to assessment in Chapter 7.
2 It is important to note that the children did not write in the fieldnotes every day. I was also aware that this interaction was unsanctioned and could provide a distraction to the other children and teacher. I have also been asked if their interest had to do with the fact that they were seen as important enough to be written about. This may be partially true but the joy at drawing/writing in the fieldnotes often overtook discussions about what the fieldnotes actually said.
3 In South Africa handwriting can sometimes be a means through which race and class can be identified. This group handwriting is not unusual as Thornton (2001) points out in her investigation of the types of handwriting taken on by classes in colonial America. From a South African point of view it links back starkly to the connection made earlier by Clark and Ivanic (1997) that the insistence on a style of handwriting can have a homogenizing effect by creating docile citizens. They argue that it is a political imperative that is not admitted. I would argue that during apartheid South Africa it was admitted. Many Africans who had been subjected to schooling in the era of Bantu education emerged with a distinctive style of handwriting, one that identified a particular subject. This does appear to be changing as a general observation of university students' assignments and exam scripts indicate. This is possibly also because of the greater access to private and well-resourced former White schools where the approach to teaching handwriting may be different. It may now be a marker of class rather than race as children educated at township or rural schools retain this style of writing.

7 Assessing bodies

1 This is in fact not a spelling test. It seems to be a reading test. Spelling tests require children to produce the correct spellings of words, usually in writing, but this test requires the children to decode the text which requires letter and sound recognition, the skills required for reading.
2 I do not have the Grade 00 reports as I only collected reports handed out during my period of observation.
3 These years are not chronological because I observed the Grade 3s and Grade 0s in 2002 and the Grade 1s in 2003.

8 Implications for literacy education

1 Whole language is a philosophy that focuses on reading for meaning in context above decoding and spelling, the focus of a phonics-based approach. It gained in popularity in the 1970s.
2 I need to thank Lynne Slonimsky for bringing my attention to what our gazes will allow us to see and (re)imagine.

References

Andrews, G., & Chen, S. (2006). The production of tyrannical space. *Children's Geographies, 4*(2), 239–250.

Anning, A. (1999). Learning to draw and drawing to learn. *Journal of Art and Design, 18*(2), 163–172.

Bakhtin, M. (1986). *Speech genres and other late essays.* Austin: University of Texas Press.

Barton, D. (1994). *Literacy: An introduction to the ecology of written language.* Malden, MA: Blackwell Publishing.

Barton, D., & Hamilton, M. (1998). *Local literacies.* London: Routledge.

Barton, D., & Hamilton, M. (2000). Literacy practices. In D. Barton, M. Hamilton, & R. Ivanic (Eds.), *Situated Literacies* (pp. 7–15). London: Routledge.

Bindman, G. (Ed.), (1988). *South Africa, human rights and the rule of law.* International Commission of Jurists. London and New York: Pinter Publishers.

Bourdieu, P. (1977). *Outline of a theory of cultural practice.* Cambridge: Cambridge University Press.

Bourdieu, P. (1992). *Language and symbolic power.* Oxford: Polity Press.

Calkins, L. (1986). *The art of teaching writing.* Portsmouth, NH: Heinemann.

Cannella, D. (1997). *Deconstructing early childhood education: Social justice and revolution.* New York: Peter Lang.

Carson-Dellosa Publishers. Rules for Good Listening Chartlet. CO 6068.

Christie, F., & Rothery, J. (1989). Genres and writing: a response to Michael Rosen. *English in Australia, 90,* 2–12.

Christie, P. (1991). *The right to learn: The struggle for education in South Africa* (2nd edition). Johannesburg: Ravan Press.

Christie, P. (1998). Schools as (dis)organisations: The 'breakdown of the culture of learning and teaching' in South African schools. *Cambridge Journal of Education, 28*(3), 283–300.

Christie, P. (1999). OBE and unfolding policy trajectories: Lessons to be learned. In J. Jansen & P. Christie (Eds.), *Changing curriculum: Studies in outcomes-based education in South Africa* (pp. 248–279). Kenwyn, South Africa: Juta.

Christie, P. (2001). Improving school quality in South Africa: A study of schools that have succeeded against the odds. *Journal of Education, 26,* 40–65.

City of Johannesburg (2009). Official website of the city of Johannesburg. http:www.joburg.org.za. (accessed 3 June 2009).

Clark, R., & Ivanic, R. (1997). *The politics of writing.* London: Routledge.

Clay, M. (1975). *What did I write?* Auckland, NZ: Heinemann.

Collins, D., & Coleman, T. (2008). Social geographies of education: Looking within, and beyond, school boundaries. *Geography Compass, 2*(1), 281–299.

Comber, B., & Simpson, A. (2001). *Negotiating critical literacies in classrooms.* Mahwah, NJ: Lawrence Erlbaum and Associates.

Comber, B., Thomson, P., & Wells, M. (2001). Critical literacy finds a 'place': Writing and social action in a neighbourhood school. *Elementary School Journal, 101*(4): 451–464.

Davenport, T. (1991). *South Africa: A modern history* (4th edition). London: Macmillan.

De Klerk, V. (2002). Language issues in our schools: Whose voice counts? Part 1: The parents speak. *Perspectives in Education, 20*(1), 1–14.

Dean, M. (1999). *Governmentality: Power and rule in modern society.* London: Sage.

Dixon, K. (2004). Literacy: Diverse spaces, diverse bodies. *English in Australia, 132*, 50–55.

Dixon, K., & Dornbrack, J. (2010). 'They said we were the Impossibles': How a detention system in an ex-Model C school works to create racial and gender divides. *Journal of Education, 48*: 37–54.

Dixon, K., Place, J., & Kholowa, F. (2008). In(sites): Examining early literacy practices at home and school in rural Malawi and South Africa. *Southern African Review of Education, 14*(3), 5–22.

DoE (1997a). *Language in education policy.* www.polity.org.za/govdocs/policy/edulangpolicy.html (accessed 6 July 2008).

DoE (1997b). *National qualifications framework document.* Pretoria: Department of Education.

DoE (2002). *National curriculum statement grades R–9 policy: Languages.* Pretoria: Department of Education.

Doke, C. (1990). *Textbook of Zulu grammar.* Cape Town: Maskew Miller Longman.

Dornbrack, J. (2008). *Reflection as a tool for managing difference in a post-apartheid high school* (Unpublished PhD thesis). University of the Witwatersrand, Johannesburg.

Dreyfuss, H., & Rabinow, P. (1982). *Michel Foucault: Beyond structuralism and hermeneutics.* New York: Harvester Wheatsheaf.

Dyson, A. H. (1993). *Negotiating a permeable curriculum: On literacy, diversity and the interplay of children's and teacher's worlds.* NTCE Concept Paper 9. Salem, MA: National Council of Teachers of English.

Dyson, A. H. (1994). Confronting the split between 'the child' and 'children': Towards new curricular visions of the child writer. *English Education, 26*(1), 12–28.

Dyson, A. H. (1995). The courage to write: Child meaning making in a contested world. *Language Arts, 72*(5), 324–333.

Dyson, A. H. (1997). *Writing superheroes: Contemporary childhood, popular culture and classroom literacy.* New York and London: Teachers College Press.

Dyson, A. H. (2003). *The brothers and sisters learn to write: Popular literacies in childhood and school cultures.* New York and London: Teachers College Press.

Foucault, M. (1977). *Discipline and punish: The birth of the prison* (A. Sheridan, Trans.). London: Penguin Books.

Foucault, M. (1978). *The history of sexuality: Vol. 1. The will to knowledge* (A. Sheridan, Trans.). London: Penguin Books.

Foucault, M. (1980). *Power/knowledge: Selected interviews and other writings 1972–1977* (C. Gordan, Trans. and Ed.). New York: Harvester Wheatsheaf.

Foucault, M. (2000a). Different spaces. In D. Faubion (Ed.), *Essential works of Foucault 1954–1984: Vol. 2* (pp. 175–186). London: Penguin Books.

Foucault, M. (2000b). Self writing. In P. Rabinow (Ed.), *Essential works of Foucault 1954–1984: Ethics subjectivity and truth: Vol. 1* (pp. 207–222). London: Penguin Books.

Foucault, M. (2000c). On the genealogy of ethics. In P. Rabinow (Ed.), *Essential works of Foucault 1954–1984: Ethics subjectivity and truth: Vol. 1* (pp. 253–277). London: Penguin Books.

Foucault, M. (2002). Space, knowledge and power. In D. Faubion (Ed.), *Essential Works of Foucault 1954–1984: Vol. 3* (pp. 349–364). London: Penguin Books.

Fraser, N. (1981). Foucault on modern power: Empirical insights and normative confusions. *Praxis International, 1*(13), 272–287.

Freebody, P., & Luke, A. (1997). The social practices of reading. In S. Muspratt, A. Luke, & P. Freebody (Eds.), *Constructing critical literacies* (pp. 1–18). St Leonard's, NSW: Allen and Unwin.

Freire, P. (1972). *Pedagogy of the oppressed.* Harmondsworth, UK: Penguin.

Gains, P. (2010). *Learning about literacy: Teachers' conceptualizations of literacy and enactments of early literacy pedagogies in South African classrooms* (Unpublished PhD thesis). University of the Witwatersrand, Johannesburg.

Gallagher, M. (2008). 'Power is not an evil': rethinking power in participatory methods. *Children's Geographies, 6*(2): 137–150.

Gauteng Department of Education (n.d.) *Learner Profiles.* Johannesburg.

Gauteng Department of Education (2000). GDE Circular 5/2000 www.education.gpg.gov.za/legislation/circulars/circulars.htm (accessed 6 March 2007).

Gee, J. (2003). *What video games have to teach us about learning and literacy.* New York: Palgrave Macmillan.

Goodman, Y. (2001). The development of initial literacy. In E. Cushman, E. Kingten, B. Kroll, & M. Rose (Eds.), *Literacy: A critical sourcebook* (pp. 316–324). Boston: Bedford/St Martin's.

Gore, J. (1995). On the continuity of power relations in pedagogy. *International Studies in Sociology of Education, 5*(2), 165–188.

Graham, S., & Harris, K. (1997). Self-regulation and writing: Where do we go from here? *Contemporary Educational Psychology, 22*, 102–114.

Graham, S., & Harris, K. (2000). The role of self-regulation and transcription skills in writing and writing development. *Educational Psychologist, 35*(1), 3–12.

Grant, G., & Flinn, T. (1992). *Watershed town: the history of Johannesburg city.*

Graves, D. (1982). *Writing: Teachers and children at work.* Portsmouth, NH: Heinemann Educational Books.

Gregory, E., & Williams, A. (2000). *City literacies: Learning to read across generations and cultures.* London and New York: Routledge.

Grundlach, R., McLane, J., Stott, F., & McNamee, G. (1985). The social foundations of children's early writing development. In M. Farr (Ed.), *Children's early writing development.* Norwood, NJ: Ablex Publishing Co.

Hadi-Tabassum, S. (2006). *Language space and power.* Clevedon: Multilingual Matters.

Hamilton, M. (2000). Expanding the new literacy studies: Using photographs to explore literacy as a social practice. In D. Barton, M. Hamilton, & R. Ivanic (Eds.), *Situated literacies* (pp. 16–34). London: Routledge.

Heath, S. (1983). *Ways with words.* Cambridge: Cambridge University Press.

Holloway, S., & Valentine, G. (2000). Children's geographies and the new social studies of childhood. In S. Holloway & G. Valentine (Eds.), *Children's geographies: Playing, living, learning* (pp. 1–23). London and New York: Routledge.

Hunter, I. (1994). *Rethinking the school: Subjectivity, bureaucracy criticism.* Sydney: Allen and Unwin.

Hutton, P. (1988). Foucault, Freud and the technologies of the self. In L. Martin, H. Gutman, & P. Hutton (Eds.), *Technologies of the self: A seminar with Michel Foucault* (pp. 121–144). Amherst, MA: University of Massachusetts Press.

Hyland, K. (2003). *Second language writing.* Cambridge: Cambridge University Press.

Jackson, F. (2000). Ways of understanding the reading process: Implications for teaching. In M. Inglis, C. Thomson, & A. Macdonald (Eds.), *Language and learning in teaching (LILT)* (pp. 155–168). Pietermaritzburg: University of Natal Press.

Janks, H. (2010). *Literacy and power.* New York: Routledge.

Jenks, C. (2001). The pacing and timing of children's bodies. In G. Dahlberg & K. Hultqvist (Eds.), *Governing the child in the new millennium* (pp. 68–84). New York: RoutledgeFalmer.

Johnston, P., & Rogers, R. (2001). Early literacy development: The case for informed assessment. In S. Neuman, & D. Dickinson (Eds.), *Handbook of early literacy research: Vol. 1* (pp. 377–389). New York: The Guilford Press.

Jones, A. (2000). Surveillance and student handwriting: Tracing the body. In O' Farrell, D. Meadmore, E. McWilliam, & C. Symes (Eds.), *Taught bodies* (pp. 151–164). New York: Peter Lang.

Jones, M., & Cunningham, C. (1999). The expanding worlds of middle childhood. In E. K. Teather (Ed.), *Embodied geographies: spaces, bodies and rites of passage* (pp. 27–42). London and New York: Routledge.

Kamler, B. (2001). *Relocating the personal: A critical writing pedagogy.* Albany, NY: State University of New York Press.

Kamwangamalu, N. (2003). Globalisation of English, and language maintenance and shift in South Africa. *International Journal of the Sociology of Language, 164*, 65–81.

Kane-Berman, J. (1993). *Political violence in South Africa.* Johannesburg: South African Institute of Race Relations.

Karolia, I. (2010a, 3 February). Teachers go on the rampage at Tshwane College. *Eye Witness News.* http://ewn.co.za/articleprog.aspx?id=31670 (accessed 5 February 2010).

Karolia, I. (2010b, 3 February). Lecturers turn themselves in after vandalism. *Eye Witness News.* http://ewn.co.za/articleprog.aspx?id=31710 (accessed 5 February 2010).

Kendrick, M., & McKay, R. (2004). Drawings as an alternative way of understanding young children's constructions of literacy. *Journal of Early Childhood Literacy, 4*(1), 109–128.

Kress, G. (1997). *Before writing: Rethinking the paths to literacy.* London: Routledge.

Leander, K., & Sheehy, M. (2004). *Spatializing literacy research and practice.* New York: Peter Lang.

Lefebvre, H. (1991). *The production of space*. Cambridge MA: Blackwell.

Levin, I., Both-De Vries, A., Aram, D., & Bus, A. (2005). Writing starts with own name writing: From scribbling to conventional spelling in Israeli and Dutch children. *Applied Psycholinguistics, 26*(3), 463–477.

Luke, A. (1996). Genres of power? Literacy education and the production of capital. In R. Hassan & G. Williams (Eds.), *Literacy in Society* (pp. 308–321). London: Longman.

Mail and Guardian Online (2006, 19 July). School violence: Blame placed on education system. www.mg.co.za/article/2006–07–19-school-violence-blame-placed-on-education-system (accessed 23 January 2010).

Mail and Guardian Online (2007, 31 May). Do something about school violence, principal pleads. www.mg.co.za/article/2007–05–31-do-something-about-school-violence-principal-pleads (accessed 23 January 2010).

May, J., & Thrift, N. (2001). *Timespace: Geographies of temporality*. London: Routledge.

Maybin, J. (1993). Teaching writing: Process or genre? In S. Brindley (Ed.), *Teaching English* (pp. 166–173). London: Routledge.

Maynak, P. (2004). Literacy instruction, disciplinary practice and diverse learners: A case study. *Journal of Early Childhood Literacy, 4*(1), 129–149.

McKinney, C. (2007). 'If I speak English does it make me less black anyway?' Race and English in South African desegregated schools. *English Academy Review, 24*(2), 6–24.

Mda, T. (2004). Multilingualism and education. In L. Chisholm (Ed.), *Changing class: Educational and social change in post-apartheid South Africa* (pp. 177–194). Cape Town: HSRC Press; London and New York: Zed Books.

Molnar, B., Gortmaker, S., Bull, F., & Buka, S. (2004). Unsafe to play? Neighborhood disorder and lack of safety predict reduced physical activity among urban children and adolescents. *American Journal of Health Promotion, 18*(5), 378–386.

Morrow, W. (2007). *Learning to teach in South Africa*. Cape Town: HSRC Press.

Newman, M., Woodcock, A., & Dunham, P. (2006). 'Playtime in the borderlands': Children's representations of school, gender, and bullying through photographs and interviews. *Children's Geographies, 4*(3), 289–302.

News24.com. (2008, 26 August). School violence due to social ills. www.news24.com/Content/SouthAfrica/News/1059/545c191460c24d20883d36214a1af796/26–08–2008–01–20/School_violence_due_to_social_ills (accessed 23 January 2010).

Ormerod, F., & Ivanic, R. (2000). Texts in practices: Interpreting the physical characteristics of children's project work. In D. Barton, M. Hamilton, & R. Ivanic (Eds.), *Situated literacies* (pp. 91–107). London: Routledge.

Parker, T. (2003). Recognising and managing low muscle tone: A physiotherapist's perspective. In *Department of Education and College of Education at Wits in-service teacher training manual for the Foundation Phase Module 1*. Johannesburg: University of the Witwatersrand.

Parnell, S., & Phiri, G. (1991). Johannesburg. In A. Lemon (Ed.), *Homes apart: South Africa's segregated cities*. Cape Town: David Philip Publishers.

Percy-Smith, B., & Matthews, H. (2001). Tyrannical spaces: Young people, bullying and urban neighbourhoods. *Local Environment, 6*(1), 49–63.

Philp, M. (1983). Foucault on power: A problem in radical translation? *Political Theory, 11*(1), 29–52.

Prinsloo, J. (2002). *Possibilities for critical literacy: An exploration of schooled literacies in the province of Kwa-Zulu Natal* (Unpublished PhD thesis). University of the Witwatersrand, Johannesburg.

Review Committee Report on Curriculum 2005 (2000, 31 May). *South African curriculum for the twenty-first century*. http://education/pwv.gov.za/Policies%20and%Reports/2000_Reports/2005. (accessed 18 September 2003).

Riley, J., & Reely, D. (2005). Developing young children's thinking through learning to write argument. *Journal of Early Childhood Literacy, 5*(1), 29–52.

Rose, N. (1989). *Governing the soul: The shaping of the private self*. London and New York: Routledge.

Salinger, T. (2001). Assessing the literacy of young children: The case for multiple forms of evidence. In S. Neuman, & D. Dickinson (Eds.), *Handbook of early literacy research: Vol. 1* (pp. 390–418). New York: The Guilford Press.

Smart, B. (2002). *Michel Foucault* (revised edition). London: Routledge.

Smith, F. (1982). *Writing and the writer.* London: Heinemann Educational Books.

Smith, F. (1988). *Joining the literacy club: Further essays into education.* Portsmouth, NH: Heinemann.

Snow, C., & Ninio, A. (1986). The contracts of literacy: What children learn from learning to read books. In W. Teale & E. Sulzby (Eds.), *Emergent literacy: Writing and reading* (pp. 116–132). Norwood, NJ: Ablex.

Soja, E. (1980). The Socio-spatial dialectic. *Annals of the Association of American geographers.* 70(2): 207–225.

Soja, E. (2000). *Postmetropolis.* Malden, MA: Blackwell.

South African Institute of Race Relations (2008, 5 February). South African schools most dangerous in the world – only 23% of pupils safe. www.sairr.org.za/press-office/archive/south-african-schools-most-dangerous-in-the-world-2013-only-23-of-pupils-safe.html (accessed 23 January 2010).

Stein, P., & Prinsloo, M. (2004). What's inside the box? Children's early encounters with literacy in South African classrooms. *Perspectives in Education, 22*(2), 67–84.

Street, B. (1993). *Cross-cultural approaches to literacy.* Cambridge: Cambridge University Press.

Street, B. (2001a). *Literacy and development: Ethnographic perspectives.* London: Routledge.

Street, B. (2001b). The new literacy studies. In E. Cushman, E. Kingten, B. Kroll, & M. Rose (Eds.), *Literacy: A critical sourcebook* (pp. 430–442). Boston: Bedford/St Martin's.

Taljaard, S. & Bosch, P. (1988). *Handbook of IsiZulu.* Pretoria: J. L. van Schaik.

Thornton, T. (2001). The lost world of colonial handwriting. In E. Cushman, E. Kingten, B. Kroll, & M. Rose (Eds.), *Literacy: A critical sourcebook* (pp. 52–69). Boston: Bedford/St Martin's.

Toohey, K. (2000). *Learning English at school: Identity, social relations and classroom practice.* Clevedon: Multilingual Matters.

White, R. & Arndt, V. (1991). *Process writing.* Harlow: Longman.

Van Zyl, D. (1986). *The discovery of wealth.* Cape Town: Don Nelson.

Vasquez, V. (2004). *Negotiating critical literacies with young children.* Mahwah, NJ: Lawrence Erlbaum and Associates.

Veitch, J., Salmon, J., & Ball. K. (2007). Children's perceptions of the use of public open spaces for active free-play. *Children's Geographies, 5*(4), 409–422.

Vygotsky, L. (1962). *Thought and language* (E. Hanfmann & G. Vakar, Trans.). Cambridge, MA: MIT Press.

Vygotsky, L. (2004). Imagination and creativity in childhood. *Journal of Russian and East European Psychology, 42*(1), 7–97.

Walkerdine, V. (1997). *Daddy's girl: Young girls and popular culture.* Cambridge, MA: Harvard University Press.

Walkerdine, V. (2001). Safety and danger: Childhood, sexuality and space at the end of the new millennium. In K. Hultqvist, & K. Dahlberg (Eds.), *Governing the child in the new millennium* (pp. 15–34). New York: RoutledgeFalmer.

Whitehead, M. (1990). *Language and literacy in the early years.* London: Paul Chapman.

Wolf, M. (2007). *Proust and the squid: The story and science of the reading brain.* New York: HarperCollins.

Wolf, M., Barzillai, M., Gottwald, S., Miller, L., Spencer, K., Norton, S., Lovett, M., & Morris, R. (2009). The RAVE-O intervention: Connecting neuroscience to the classroom. *Mind Brain and Education, 3*(2), 84–93.

Wray, D., & Medwell, J. (1991). *Literacy and language in the primary years.* London: Routledge.

Wray, D., Medwell, J., Poulson, L., & Fox, R. (2002). *Teaching literacy effectively in the primary school.* London: Routledge/Falmer.

Yang, H., & Noel, A. (2006). The developmental characteristics of four- and five-year-old preschoolers' drawing: An analysis of scribbles, placement patterns, emergent writing, and name writing in archived spontaneous drawing samples. *Journal of Early Childhood Literacy, 6*(2), 145–162.

Index

Note: Page numbers in **bold** denote figures.